ENERGY UNBOUND

Line drawings and photographs, with a few exceptions, by the author.

The cover design is taken from a pottery decoration by Maureen Reed, 1944. See page 188.

Kenneth Barnes was in charge of the Science department at Bedales School from 1930. With only a few hundred pounds, but ably partnered by his wife Frances, he left Bedales in 1940 to found another co-educational boarding school at Wennington, near the border between Lancashire and Yorkshire. It was to be an egalitarian school that would take children from a complete cross-section of society. What seemed an inauspicious moment— when the war was opening with terrible violence — proved the best possible time to develop the qualities he sought.

He claims that independent education can avoid being divisive, and he urges that while we move towards greater social justice we must at the same time, especially in education, encourage intrepidity and safeguard freedom for responsible innovation.

As an author, Kenneth Barnes is best known for *He and She* (Penguin) which reflects his pioneer work in sex education and has been selling steadily for 22 years.

He has travelled widely, mainly in the service of the Society of Friends, taking the opportunity to visit schools and universities in most of the African countries, in Australasia and North America. He has been involved in BBC radio and television discussions since 1948. He was professionally trained in physical science and psychology but is also a keen amateur artist and craftsman.

He has a doctor daughter, a son who is a university lecturer in education, seven grandchildren and one great-grandson.

By the same author:

Sex, Friendship and Marriage
He and She
The Creative Imagination
Making Judgements and Decisions
The Involved Man
A Vast Bundle of Opportunities
Has Science Exploded God?

ENERGY UNBOUND

THE STORY OF WENNINGTON SCHOOL

Kenneth C. Barnes
Founder and Headmaster 1940–68

WILLIAM SESSIONS LIMITED
YORK, ENGLAND
1980

First published in 1980
ISBN 0 900657 51 0

Printed and Published by William Sessions Limited
The Ebor Press, York, England
in Times New Roman

Contents

Illustrations

Foreword

The first script, compiled from copious records, was too long for publication. The difficulty of abbreviation will explain any awkward discontinuities that may remain. That script was read by former pupils and colleagues, and other friends. I am deeply grateful for their suggestions and I have followed their advice where possible. The most authoritative advice was to reshape the whole script to make it more coherent; that was too daunting and would have involved long delay.

Some asked to what kind of reader was it addressed, and what was the book intended to be: an autobiography, a philosophy, a treatise on educational psychology and methodology? The answer is all these things and more. It should appeal specially to any who undertake an educational enterprise or the creation of a community with total personal commitment. In such a venture, every single day brings an oscillation between the severely practical and the deeply reflective, between attention to persons and preoccupation with things, between the understanding of others and the examination of oneself. Nothing is ever final, but I hope that the loose ends easily discoverable in the book will prove growing points for the reader.

An explanation is required about the words 'my wife'. Mostly, the reference is to Frances, co-founder and tireless fellow-worker. She died shortly after our retirement. I married again, hence the reference to my present wife Eleanor; she had been Head Girl of the school seventeen years earlier.

In order to avoid a parochial atmosphere, it was my general intention to avoid using names, but a few crept in and it seemed pointless to try to eliminate them. These few names are not an indication of relative importance and I must say thank you, as warmly as the printed word will allow, to all those un-named men and women who took an eager part in the 'continuous creation' of the school, to the boys and girls, now far into adulthood, who became our friends, to the people who spared time from their demanding work to become governors of the school, to the parents who dared to trust us, and to the auditor and solicitor for their wisdom and personal concern.

1. Frances Barnes

2. Kenneth Barnes

1940 — the founders as they were then —

3. — and where it all began: Wennington Hall, Lancashire

CHAPTER I

Beginning

IT WAS THE LATE SUMMER of 1940 and the Battle of Britain had begun. I was nearing the end of a complicated journey from Hampshire to North Lancashire and in a late night train that would take me from Leeds to Skipton. The compartments were lit by thc dimmest of blue lamps. The long-funnelled old tank engine was chuffing away and I was drifting into sleep, when I was brought sharply awake by three whumps. Bombs falling somewhere. 'Perhaps Keighley', someone said. I looked out of the window but for a while there was only darkness. Then in an instant the area round the train was lit up by a score of intense white points of light, smoking incendiary bombs.

The train came jerkily to a stop. My compartment was behind the engine, and I watched the driver climb down onto the line, look along his train, then up to the sky. He raised his closed fist. His broad Yorkshire pronunciation gave an impressive vehemence to the expletives that poured out of his mouth.

The train was undamaged and after the driver had climbed back into his cab we trundled on to Skipton. There we, the few passengers, stood silently in an underground passage until the 'all clear' came through. I was hoping to get to Wennington, a junction on the Carnforth and Heysham line, and it was already very late. There seemed to be no train to cover the remaining thirty miles. Asking round I discovered that the Heysham boat train was due to stop at Skipton at some hour during the night and I went to the stationmaster to explain my problem. Well, it was war-time and he was kind. He obtained special permission for the train to be stopped at Wennington.

In the darkness of Wennington station I walked up to the guard's van and extracted the ancient bicycle to which was strapped the little luggage I had apart from my rucksack. It was not far to Wennington Hall, and I had visited it before. My feeble bike lamp lit up grotesquely the two eagle-headed gryphons on their pedestals at the gateway, and I pushed up the drive towards the battlements dimly visible against the sky. The huge oak door creaked as I pushed it. I knew enough of the geography of the house to find my way, with the help of my lamp (I daren't switch any lights on), to the room where I expected my wife would be sleeping. It was two o'clock in the morning, and she got a shock as her slowly waking thought struggled to perceive what was coming into the blackness of the room. She thought it was my ghost, for I was two days late and she had begun to think of me as a blackened corpse in the London blitz.

I had persuaded her to start from Petersfield in advance, leaving to me the last bits of clearing up. She and her recently widowed sister had set off on a circuitous route to avoid London, she carrying our beloved cat in one basket and her sister her new-born son in another. They too had met some bombing, in full daylight at Banbury, where a plane made an attempt on the aluminium works.

This drama marked for us the beginning of our school. It was trivial compared with the drama and tragedy that other people were passing through in heavily bombed areas, but it serves now to emphasize the oddity of starting a new school when the war was opening with intense violence, and the surprising appearance of an opportunity we had long hoped for, at a time when it was least likely to offer itself. I had been for ten years in charge of the science department at Bedales, a school I enjoyed and appreciated enormously yet which stirred us to try something a little different. Throughout the thirties my wife, Frances, and I had been much concerned with practical politics as well as education. We had been caught up in various activities designed to mitigate the evil effects of unemployment; constructive ventures that enabled the men and their families to provide for themselves, finding them land and workshops and taking groups of boys and girls to work with them. With many others in this kind of work, we had become critical of an economic and social order that not only permitted this to happen but inevitably treated men and women as things to be disposed of when they were no longer a source of profit.

We became involved in the refugee problem, in the complicated issues of the Spanish Civil War, and alarmed by the challenge of a fascist movement in Britain able to capture the imagination and feelings of too many ordinary people.

With all this in mind we had begun to want to carry 'progressive' education further, to make it more relevant to the total social and political situation, to take independent education away from its exclusive association with the well-to-do.

We dreamed of creating a new boarding school that would be a classless society. In 1936 we printed our manifesto: *A Proposal for a New*

School. From the perspective of forty years I can read it again with fascination, but mixed feelings, aware of real achievement yet recognizing how political hopes, always to some extent frustrated, expose such a venture to cynics.

In that manifesto we referred to

> . . . some point at which might be laid, without violent upheaval, the foundations of a changed and just society within the scope of the common people . . . .

and the belief that

> . . . the change to a new and just society will come only by the will of the significant and producing masses of mankind whose inheritance in the world's wealth is now largely withheld.

The copy of this manifesto that I am scanning must have been lent to someone in recent years, for it has a scribbled note of mine on it: 'Written in 1936; a little out of date, alas!' Out of date, yes, where some problems of the thirties are concerned, but right up to date in the diagnosis of the basic ills of what we have now come to call the consumer society. For it goes on to refer to the way in which advancing mechanization has degraded the worker to a machine minder and – to use that modern existentialist term – alienated man from himself. The injury to the spirit of the unemployed men we tried to help, an injury that often stood in the way even of their attempts to help each other, made us ask what could be done to save society through its children, what could be done to develop resilience, originality, constructive insight so that a new generation would know better what to do.

Our *Proposal* looked at the state schools and the independent schools. The secondary schools were too much used as a ladder to climb from the working class into the professional or property owning class. The ultimate intentions of the progressive independent boarding schools seemed frustrated by class divisions:

> They are aiming at a development of character which, if circumstances allowed the process to be completed, would be instrumental in social change. But elements in their very nature prevent the completion of the development of the necessary sensitiveness, courage and vision. These schools are dependent on fees and must cater for the middle and upper classes. And they usually are isolated from any real working community. However much may be achieved in personal relationships and advanced social *thinking,* social action in later life often remains determined,

especially in a crisis, by class interests and the fear of loss of property and privilege.

Some opponents of independent schools hope to abolish them by making it illegal to charge fees. It might seem that our forty-year-old statement provides as strong an argument against the independent progressive schools as against the Public Schools which are the main object of the attack. But thought about education-in-community carries the argument beyond the deceptive state-versus-private conflict. All generalizations about what a *category* of schools does are of only temporary significance; we must pass beyond them to the more complex problem of the relation of a child to the community in which he grows up; otherwise all our changes will end with the same disillusionment.

How could we provide a similar education for children from all income levels? What kind of a school community would get rid of the consciousness of class, so that all its former pupils, whatever their origins, would be ready to accept the consequences of social justice?

This aim could not be achieved through political indoctrination; it would be an attack on a child's integrity to persuade him to accept a political doctrine at an age when he could not use his own informed judgement. And we were very conscious, during that era, which, like our own now, was one in which political ideas were proliferating wildly and often superimposed on the most primitive of urges, of the need to go much deeper than ideas or ideals in the search for integrity of thought-and-action. We reminded ourselves that politics was for persons, not persons for politics.

To start our school we needed money, but we had not the self-confidence that fund-raisers need. We thought perhaps £10,000 would be enough, but we had no idea whom to approach. With painful hesitation we wrote to a few wealthy socialists, only to be turned down, courteously but firmly. So little progress did we make, and so ominously did the threat of war appear over the horizon, that we gave up hope. After all, Bedales was a very good school to work in, full of opportunities for friendship and enterprising projects; it was not too disappointing a thought – that I might settle down there.

But at the time when the project had dropped out of our minds, the way suddenly opened. Quakers had established a temporary evacuation school at Yealand, near Carnforth, to accommodate children from Manchester and other cities, to get them away from danger or to set their parents free for whatever additional duties the war had placed on them. It was quickly proving not only a good educational experiment but an interesting venture in community living. Soon after this a letter appeared in the Quaker weekly, *The Friend*, offering another building for a similar purpose. Wennington Hall was an imposing manor house further inland, nearly into Yorkshire, and it had been purchased by the Grey Court Fellowship – an offshoot of the Holiday Fellowship – for a guest house. It was fully equipped for living but the Fellowship saw little prospect of its being used during the war. I applied at once and was called north to discuss our plans with its representatives Samuel Maltby and Arthur Leonard. Almost before I could draw my second breath, we were offered the use of the building.

The rent was to be nominal, a pound a year. We were to pay for depreciation of fabrics and furniture, but there was no need for any payment at all to begin with. Frances and I had about £200 in our bank account and though it was smaller than the £10,000 we had wanted, it was enough to give us confidence. The world was in turmoil, the bombs had begun to fall; anything was possible. As the retired Head of Bedales, J. H. Badley said to me when he warmly encouraged me to get on with it, there was an invasion in prospect and the Germans might soon be swarming over the South Downs. Only action mattered.

The way had opened in a form that was totally unexpected. What was impossible in the caution and reluctance of peace had become possible in the shake-up of war. What threatened people's lives had also awakened their imaginations. It was not going to be a school to fit our theories; it was not going to be near an industrial area but far from any. We were not going to depend on an extensive and integrated scheme such as a sociologist might envisage, but only on our own resources and the goodwill the war had stirred up.

This happened in mid-August and we intended to open as early in September as possible. We set to work packing our goods to the accompaniment of thumps and rattles as occasional bombers attacked the military camp a few miles away. I could not resist the temptation to run outside now and then to watch a dogfight overhead and the sight of German pilots baling out. There was a terrifying moment when with our two children we shot under the dining-room table as a burning bomber roared down over our house to plunge into woods beyond. In quieter intervals we took turns in hammering away at our typewriter, preparing advertisements and a preliminary prospectus. Facing the need for travelling and the increasing disruption of communications – and still the danger of invasion – we prepared elaborate labels with detailed instructions to hang round our children's necks lest they should become separated from us. And every now and then I had to race up to the school to put my papers in order and leave the laboratories ready for someone else to take over my work. This was all crammed into a fortnight.

We sent our children to stay for a few weeks in the Yealand school, then set about the final stages of clearing up before starting out on our separate journeys through a railway system that had ceased to operate any foreseeable timetable.

Many other people had replied to the advertisement of the Grey Court Fellowship and some of these provided the nucleus of our staff. Some were conscientious objectors who had been dismissed from their posts in publicly maintained institutions, and were very capable. A married couple, both with first-class degrees and equally good teaching ability, were able to cover between them all that we needed to offer in mathematics, biology and geography. There was an experienced historian, his wife a junior teacher, and a term later an art teacher, ejected from a city college of art, began what eventually proved to be a most significant development of graphic art and pottery. We soon had among us the captain of a Trinity House lightship; he had been deprived of his post because he had refused to have a gun installed on his ship. He must have been trained on sailing ships, for his ability to climb up vertically proved very useful when it came to blacking out the enormously high window over the stairs of our building. His wife was a musician, and she began the musical education of the school. These were the people who joined us in the first months; others came as the school expanded.

Children came in response to advertisements placed in the newspapers of northern cities that were being bombed. The need was great. Some children had been evacuated to areas where education was difficult to provide. Some remaining in towns were proving difficult to control, running out into the streets to watch the fireworks the Germans provided. In many instances both parents were involved full-time in work and needed to be relieved of the care of their children.

We took children for whatever their parents could afford to pay. The minimum payment was 12s. 6d. a week, the amount the government paid as an evacuation allowance. The maximum actually paid (no one offered to pay more) was £100 a year. We were able to offer reductions because we, the staff, were prepared to do without the usual teachers' salaries. During the first term none of us received any payment at all, indeed we paid for our keep at the rate of 25s. 0d. a week for every adult. During the second term we paid nothing and received nothing, while during the third term we were all of us paid, from the common funds, 5s. 0d. a week. There were children's allowances, and insurance premiums were cared for. The payment of 5s. 0d. was adhered to for several terms and eventually rose, by stages, to two pounds. It remained at this level for some years; and the payment was the same for everyone, headmaster or kitchen helper.

History repeats itself in what people try, usually thinking they are the first to venture in a particular direction. When living near Philadelphia in 1970 we heard a good deal about experimental communes, where people lived in financial equality, trying to share all the work. It was said that there were at least a hundred communes in the neighbourhood of that city but that, if their experience followed the usual pattern, all but a few would fold up within three years; further that most would come to an end because their members could not agree as to who should do the cooking and who should clean the loos. Community ventures were much in our minds during the thirties, as they are today and they were somewhat glamorized by the experiments of people like D. H. Lawrence and Middleton Murry. It seems now that the only experiments of this kind that will survive are those that have a purpose beyond themselves, an intention to contribute something to society.

Wennington staff lived in financial equality for eight years until, as will be told, Burnham Scale Salaries had to be adopted.

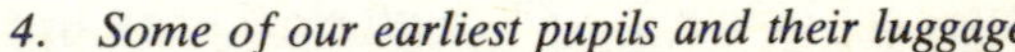

4. Some of our earliest pupils and their luggage

CHAPTER II

My Partner and Myself

EDUCATION IS CONCERNED WITH PEOPLE and what they do, with their impulses and feelings as well as their conscious intentions. The effect of their work is more the result of their essential quality as persons, of what they have become as a result of experience than of educational ideas.

Soon we were aware in our school community of each person as an individual who had to be encountered as a unique product of his relationships. Each brought with him his own past.

I had my own history and background. My father, a municipal clerk, was the son of a Wiltshire labourer who had migrated to London to become a mechanic in a flour mill; but about him I know little. My mother came from a line of Scottish crofters; her father a McInnes from the island of Luing, one of the many Scottish boys from poor families who found their way to universities. He is said to have walked to the university each morning with William Thompson, later Lord Kelvin, but seems to have been as eccentric as Thompson was rational. It is amusing to think of him arguing for a flat earth, with an approaching apocalyptic end, against one who was destined to become a famous physicist. He was an able scholar in Greek and Hebrew but turned away from university appointments because he thought them worldly. His schizophrenic behaviour made my mother leave the family at the age of nineteen and run away from Glasgow to London. There she found a husband who was as intelligent as her father and equally uninterested in making money, but in other respects as sane and practical as her father was odd.

So there was nothing in my inheritance to incline me towards a divisive middle class boarding school tradition. I grew up in Battersea, one of the most left-wing boroughs in London. From my earliest thinking days I was aware of politics all round me. But my father, though always tending to move leftward, wanted more than political theory as a guide to life. He discovered the Society of Friends and became a Quaker when I was three. He was an experimenter and all his life a searcher. With no more formal education than that of the elementary school, he tried everything adventurous, including economics, Marxism, philosophy and psychology. With his Quakerism and Christianity to give a core of stability, everything ephemeral fell away as its inadequacy was revealed. So I grew up with a conscious need to draw all things together, to perceive contradictions and inconsistencies and try to resolve them. I could not be content with the kind of religion that denied my science, nor a Christianity that could not be the inspiration of politics. I was taught always to be practical, testing ideas by their capacity for use and being ready to train my hands to any kind of craft.

I left my elementary school, a good one, at the age of eleven to go into a highly respected grammar school, an ancient foundation that largely filled up with London County Council scholarship boys, of whom I was one. It had a small minority of fee payers. It was to a marked extent the kind of school that produced snobs, offering the escape I have already referred to – the escape from the working class into the lower-middle. You were called a swank by your old elementary associates as soon as you got into it and you rarely talked to them again.

This was during the 1914-18 war. There soon arose in my mind a sharp conflict between the attitudes of my family and those the school attempted to develop in its boys. The two things the Head was plugging the whole time, especially in his exhortations during morning assembly, were the Officers' Training Corps and the school's aspiration to Public School status. The school was not at that time represented, as were some other day schools, on the Headmasters' Conference, but unlike the ordinary secondary schools it had an Officers' Training Corps instead of a Cadet Corps. The difference lay in the fact that the O.T.C. prepared boys for a direct commission and that the boys' uniform was half-way between that of a ranker and that of an officer, with a highly polished leather belt instead of a webbing belt, and plus-fourish trousers.

The difference in status was emphasized ponderously and *ad nauseam,* and we were exhorted to think of ourselves as superior to the pupils of other schools. We played rugger while they played soccer, and we strove to make our fixtures with schools of definite Public School status. It was *de rigueur* for rugger teams to wear bowler hats when travelling to other schools, and I think back incredulously to the sight of fifteen pimply louts crowding into railway carriages in bowlers. This gave me almost my only occasion for wearing such headgear – the only other being my appearance at fancy dress dances much later in life as the spitten image of Charlie Chaplin.

1920, with the war over, saw me in the Science Sixth, with a small group of revolutionaries. We were a friendly form and even those who were not in revolt retained their good feelings; they never turned on us, but those in other groups did. Those of us who were watching international events were disillusioned about the war, and we resented the continued propaganda for O.T.C. recruits. There came a day when our property in the Science Sixth was raided and destroyed, after the O.T.C. had been given a pep talk that hinted at subversive elements in the school.

That school was not wholly bad, and some of its staff were fine people. After that raid I was given a quiet word of encouragement to hold my ground – from the senior teacher who was Captain of the O.T.C.! Most important of all, for a while earlier in the school I was taught by George Lyward, himself an old boy of the school. It was the beginning of a life-long friendship and probably that experience was the first to open my eyes to the possibility of friendship and freedom between teacher and pupil. His therapeutic work at Finchden with difficult boys, over the thirty years that preceded his death, is well known.

My next lesson in how not to educate was at the college of London University to which I went for my science degree. It was a college that prided itself in getting the highest number of first class honours degrees in Chemistry; indeed a little more than half my year took firsts. This was at too great a cost. To many of the students it was slave-driving, under threat of demotion to pass course. To them, work became a burden when it ought to have been a joy. Our lecturers knew little about teaching method and their knowledge of the relation of science to education was minimal, however great their knowledge of chemistry. There was little appeal to the imagination, and I remember only one of our teachers who seemed real as a person. There was no stimulus to think about the philosophy and methodology of science.

Emerging from that three years' work was like emerging from a long tunnel. There were other reasons for the gloom of that period. My father died as one of the victims of the post-war influenza plague. In the middle of my course, the Government cut down sharply on grants to students and I nearly had to leave. There was little money available; I reduced my expenditure on meals to seven pence a day and tried walking the four miles to college and home again instead of taking the train – until I found that the wear on leather cost more than it saved. Even more significant was the quickly growing recognition that I was not nearly as bright a student as my school teachers expected me to be; there were many in our year more competent in their studies and for me there was to be no quick way, just unremitting hard work. This was an important lesson for an intending teacher. Without this I might never have understood my pupils' difficulties. Finally, I made no friendships with girl students.

My next experience was a surprise; I was offered a place, at no cost, at the Quaker International College, Woodbrooke, which had a small group of education students and where I could prepare for a post-graduate diploma under the aegis of the Cambridge Syndicate. Now life began to open up quickly. It was, and still is, a small college for both sexes and all ages. In it friendships were possible between men and women that were exciting and enriching without there being any pressure to hot them up. The education tutor, Victor Murray, was an original and lively person to have as an adviser and friend. He was alive to everything worthwhile that was happening in education; his mind was with the practising teacher and his opportunities, rather than with education as an academic subject. Had I been in a university department I would have been sitting in a row in front of a lecturer; but here I was day after day with Victor at a table, involved in a dialogue of continuing interest. He seemed to know every unusual kind of headmaster, and one of them was William Hamilton Fyfe, the Head of Christ's Hospital. The result of this was that I went off for a term's teaching in the science department at Christ's Hospital instead of the scattered bits of teaching that so many students had to suffer.

So here I was in 1925, after my dislike of the Public Schools and all that they represented, teaching in one of them. The headmaster had the warm support of many young men on the staff and he was thought of as a socialist, though I remember that when he invited me to dinner thirty years later, after he had retired from being president of a Canadian university, it was at the National Liberal Club. Further, here was a school that had really kept the charitable quality that so many of the Public Schools had begun with but not maintained. The school owned immensely valuable property in the City; and it took most of its pupils free. I had nearly qualified for it myself in the London County Council scholarship examination. Those who didn't come to it free were nominated by representatives in various parts of the country. They were supposed to need help, and at that time the fees could not be higher than £50 a year. It was a standing joke in the Common Room to refer to the number of poverty-stricken parents who could afford Rolls-Royces, but in fairness I should say that I did not observe these vehicles.

So there was enough that was unique in that school to enable me to settle down and enjoy what it had to offer. The young men seemed none of them conditioned by class or tradition; they were all good to know, enterprising in their personal outlook and their teaching. The science department was the birthplace of the heuristic method of science teaching: the research method, find-out-for-yourself. Barnes Wallis, of dam-buster fame, had been a boy there.

I could not have had a better start. The method had its contradictions;

it was well planned and there were sheets of directions for the teacher to follow. Clearly the pupils, though following an experimental method, were expected to find out what we wanted them to find out. Though there were loose ends left for discussion, there was not much room for surprise. But this was perhaps just the degree of security a young teacher needed. It is interesting that after more than thirty years, the science department at Christ's Hospital became one of the roots of the more imaginative Nuffield Science Projects.

For a boarding school, Christ's Hospital seemed enormous – 820 boys – and it was an impressive experience to watch them being marched in separate cohorts to the dining hall, converging on the central square to the rhythm of a brass band, in their charity-school tunics with their yellow-stockinged legs. The size had its disadvantages. I slept in a junior housemaster's room and it had a hatch-way that opened on a dormitory in which beds seemed to stretch endlessly into the distance like something seen between two mirrors. But the size made possible a standard of educational equipment that was, for the period, marvellous. The two art teachers befriended me and I spent much time with them. I owe to them a vision of what art could mean in school life and the stimulus that re-awakened in me the desire to paint, from which I had turned away when I became fascinated by chemistry. I improved my water-colour technique and learnt to do pottery, woodcuts and lithography.

Yes, it was a good place in which to begin my teaching career, and with this experience there began also the desire to get beyond the impulse, already mentioned, to criticize institutions *in categories*, and the desire to find out in every instance what is really happening to people and between people. My first permanent appointment was in sharp contrast. It was in a country grammar school in a town hidebound by the narrowest religious and political tradition. I taught chemistry, physics, biology, geography and, though I can hardly believe it now, singing. This last activity was restricted to sea shanties, for I knew nothing else. The noise caused many a wrinkled brow outside in the high street. The most useful thing I did was to organize a science club, meeting after hours. I begged a few pounds to buy a simple lathe and a few other tools; and with these we made our own club apparatus.

The local lads, known as the 'brickies', were always at war with the boarders. The school staff were at war, or rather involved in a conflict expressed in mumbled obscenities, with a different section of the community. The atmosphere in that town was so repressive that it drove the two more emotional members of the staff into the Communist Party. They celebrated their final repudiation of the place and their impending departure, by marching into the crowded public bar of the local pub, ordering double whiskies and drinking to the damnation of God and the British Empire.

About this time I found a wife, Frances; so I must turn to the story of my partner. She, too, came from humble origins. Her parents never had a home of their own and by the time she had reached independence the family had moved twenty-six times. Her father was a Lancashire man and her mother Ulster Irish. He was a navvy missioner, a lay preacher and social worker who went with the navvy encampments wherever their contracts took them. The projects were always in the North, tunnelling for railways, building dams and reservoirs in Derbyshire. He was an unassuming little man, but he must have had great courage, for he often had to interferc in family quarrels to cope with drunkenness and stop big Irish navvies from beating their wives. He had to find help in sickness, debt and other emergencies, to advise illiterate men on their legal rights and the social services there were for them. My wife's family always had to live near or among these people.

These were not good conditions for the education of a daughter, and somehow help was obtained to send Frances to a small boarding school run by two ladies in Hathersage. A school run by two ladies is a description that should be sufficient to make it an object of ridicule; but ridicule would have been undeserved. They must have had character, and their relationships with girls were stimulating and challenging. One incident stood out in Frances' memory as specially significant. There was a day when the senior of the two ladies found a whole loaf stuffed into the pan of a loo; it was impossible to extract without the help of a plumber. Casual enquiries led to no admissions. So the girls were lined up, all of them, and the headmistress went steadily along the line, peering into each face and asking: 'Did you put the loaf in the lavatory?' No, no, no, came the replies. Until she reached Frances, who had been in torment until nearly the last moment, a torment of indecision. 'Did you put the loaf in the lavatory?' 'Yes, Miss ——, I did'. She stood there, expecting expulsion or at least a scathing indictment. But no such words came. Instead: 'Girls, here is one of you who knows how to speak the truth. The incident is closed'.

It sounds a bit stilted and schoolmarmy, doesn't it? But it did much for Frances. She had been a somewhat naughty girl at home and often in trouble with her low-Church moralistic parents. She had been terribly shamed on one occasion when she had been found treating all the children in her village school to sweets, of which she had a huge bag. A severe interrogation revealed that she had stolen the money. *Stolen* it, from her own money box! It can be imagined that to be offered trust by her headmistress and not a hint of punishment, meant much to a girl troubled with guilt – guilt about more than a loaf in the loo.

The other lady was, as it happened, a Quaker; and she was a specialist in physical education. She gave those girls clear information about human anatomy, physiology and sex – and this was before 1910. Frances had been well trained in the use of her legs before she reached her teens, for she had had to walk four miles to a village school, and back over moorland roads, in winter covered with snow. It was indeed the dangers associated with this that had made her parents reluctantly think of a boarding school. At Hathersage the girls walked as many as twenty miles on a Saturday or Sunday, accompanied by their physical education lady, and they learnt a lot of botany as they went. These walks became an experience of deep enjoyment to Frances.

By some kind of deal that involved part-time domestic work, Frances got herself into an Oxford teachers' training college, Cherwell Hall. No longer in existence, it was the personal venture of a redoubtable character, Katherine Dodd, formerly an education lecturer and Herbartian theorist at Manchester.

Cherwell Hall gave her a stimulating experience, but the years immediately following seem to have been clouded for her. She held off a series of importunate suitors, including a cathedral canon, an actor and a 'MacHeath', and she drifted into preparatory school work. Then she discovered the Society of Friends and with it a new direction. We met one Sunday in Brighton Friends' Meeting House in the autumn of 1925. In a Quaker Meeting the group sits down in silence, each person trying to reach a contemplative state in which new insights can appear. Then someone who feels he has something of value to contribute may stand and speak. In 1925 I was young, somewhat in revolt against the old and traditional. I was certainly trying hard to derive ideas freshly from my own experience and to find my own words. I must have been in good form that morning, during the five minutes in which I stood. Frances, who could see only the back of my head, nearly jumped off her seat. After the meeting she came straight up to me and put a direct question: 'Did you mean what you said; and would you act on it?' That was the beginning of an interesting, stimulating friendship.

She was then working in a small South coast town packed with preparatory schools preparing boys for Public Schools. I found it odd that a fellow Quaker should be teaching in a school to which, it seemed, half the navy's admirals and the army's generals sent their sons. But there was another side to it. Her headmaster had an unconscious genius. He was sent down, or took himself down, from Cambridge before he could take his degree. He gaily bought the school from its previous owner and he made it hum. He had an inborn ability for dealing with boys between seven and thirteen. He could romp with them without ever losing the control he needed at other times, and without having any theories about it he practised a creative form of education. He bought a derelict Sussex barn and a lorry. Whenever he felt inclined he cancelled classes and took a crowd of boys in the lorry to the barn, which they proceeded to dismantle carefully, without damaging the bricks and roofing. In the course of time they transported all the bits to the school, where they set about building a library and a chapel. This man had received no training in any craft but I had opportunities to inspect his work, and though it was rough in places, there was an intuitive rightness about it.

He was endearingly unscrupulous. In the garden of a house in another part of the town he spotted a long stone that he was sure would be just right for the mantelpiece of his library. At dead of night he took some members of his staff round to the house in his open car and together they lifted that large stone: literally stole it.

Many of the bad things of preparatory education remained, however. Most of the boys left home for boarding school and the rugger field too early. Their fathers had gone at seven, and what was good for them was good for their sons. Frances, the only woman on the teaching staff, had to try to reassure the tearful mothers and later to comfort little boys weeping on the stairs. She was critical of team games coming too soon so she became a scoutmaster; she ignored the conventional aspect of scouting and made very good use of its educational opportunities.

It was inevitable that her unorthodox views should be discovered. Some of the generals and admirals and other parents got together and asked for her dismissal. She was charged with being a pacifist, a Quaker, a socialist and a Bolshevist. The Head came to her very apologetically; he valued all she had done and said he would have to appoint at least two people to cover her work. But he had no choice, she would have to go. She took this, as she took all subsequent crises, with resilience, almost gaiety; but it led to an unexpected development. We tried to face the prospect of her having to move to a distant part of the country in search of a new job, with the consequent diminution of the friendship. It occurred to us simultaneously that this problem could be solved by marriage. The decision was made thoughtfully by exchange of letters, and the appropriate emotions – the feelings that usually precede a decision to get married – erupted into consciousness when next we met. Our most lavish wedding present came from her headmaster.

CHAPTER III

Bedales – A New Experience

THE NEXT MOVE was to a northern industrial city, where I taught for a while in a large grammar school. In some ways this was a grim experience, certainly a grimy one, for smoke control was not then very far advanced and a wash was necessary after marking every pile of exercise books. It was after the industrial slump had hit Britain and many of the workers were unemployed. To help their families some of the boys were up at six in the morning doing milk and paper rounds. Generally speaking it was a cram school. Every bit of work had to be marked and all marks were added up at the end of the week. In each form the boys with the highest total and the lowest were sent to the head for appropriate treatment, which might involve beating. The cunningly developed techniques of some of the elementary schools enabled them to get boys of only moderate intelligence through the eleven-plus examination, and these soon showed their inability to cope with a grammar school curriculum. They congregated in the D-stream, which too easily became known as the Dustbin, and they were difficult to manage.

I do not look back to this experience as an empty one however. Again I started a Science Club and with some difficulty got the use of the well-equipped workshop, otherwise used for only formal exercises. One of the boys who came to that club eventually became a Fellow of the Royal Society and a Vice-Chancellor. He has verified for me that four other boys of that period achieved the same scientific distinction. If this great achievement is attributable to anything beyond the boys' ability, it is not to the school, but to one person – a quiet unassuming chemistry teacher who did not even aspire to become head of the department but had a wonderful ability to make his subject live, who knew how to communicate, how to develop a searching attitude. This is one more evidence for the belief that if we are to realise the full possibilities in education, we must pay attention to relationships rather than systems.

The amount of grumbling and cynicism among the staff was appalling. It began with the lunch-time food and spread to everything else, the headmaster, the boys, the education authority and, with extreme hostility, the Director of Education. It could be argued that I should have stayed in that school and fought my way through the difficulties. But I was looking for opportunities that were more inclusive. I had one specially significant experience there. The Head assumed that because I was a Quaker I was qualified to give Religious Instruction; so he threw the Sixth-Form R.I. at me and said I could do what I liked with it. I started by asking questions, leading eventually to : 'What are you really interested in outside school?' There were meaning looks across the room and sniggers behind hands. A reply came, followed by guffaws: 'Girls!' This was the beginning of a widely ramifying discussion that developed throughout the year, and the beginning of my adventures in sex-education. It was a revelation of the need for a personal education in values, and it made the thought of a boarding school more attractive.

The post of senior science master at Bedales became vacant. I applied, and on the day of interview I was able to sit about and talk in the staff common room. I had not been in a co-educational boarding school before and I found among those men and women a normality and relaxation previously unknown to me in schools. I was later to discover that there were tensions, but they were the tensions inseparable from ordinary life in community, not the tensions of frustration and hostility. My interview with J. H. Badley lasted an hour and was all about education, contrasting sharply with the five minutes of formal questioning I had suffered when encountering committees.

In relation to the story of Wennington, the ten years' experience at Bedales was important, because as we have seen, what one does creatively in education is a product, not so much of intellectual sorting out, as of what becomes built into one's personality as a result of what one goes through – in every dimension.

Bedales began in 1893 and became co-educational in 1900. By 1930, when I arrived, it had become well established, and carefully kept records showed that its results were most impressive. Not only had its former pupils made the grade academically, but they had retained their liveliness, with a high degree of originality and intrepidity, shown over a broad spectrum of adult activity. Its impact on education in general seemed to be developing through these observable results rather than by an appeal to progressivism.

John Badley was not a propagandist. He had written a straightforward book describing the school's life but did not subsequently seek any publicity for himself or his views. He had detached himself from the Public School image experienced as a boy at Rugby, and at Cambridge he moved steadily, but never noisily, through stages of enlightenment, thoughtfully pondering each new experience and deciding what to do next. When he joined the Abbotsholme staff, he valued the escape from the tyranny of games and the substitution of constructive outdoor work for the community. When he founded Bedales it was as a boys' school, but because he recognized this as a limitation it became co-educational. So for him a school had to be open to the future and had to grow as it recognized hindrances and opportunities. He was not a vehement rebel, nor was he an idealist replacing one pattern of ideas by another. He sought development by wisdom and insight. So Bedales was essentially practical; it grew by what was seen to work, and by response to need. To me it seemed essentially a place of opportunity, where things could happen.

The Chief, as we always called him, was austere, abstemious and usually restrained. He always wore a grey flannel suit, plimsolls and a loosely-knotted red tie. To some extent he was a product of Edward Carpenter socialism, a socialism that was not so much directed at an overthrow of capitalism as a personal attempt to hold back the destructive influences of industrialism and set the creative spirit free. He kept a *pied-à-terre* at Grasmere, where his sisters always lived, and we sometimes thought of him as another bearded Wordsworth, striding over the fells, stick in hand, against a backdrop of turbulent skies.

His reserve was painful to some, though, surprisingly, many of his pupils got to know him well. Women were shy of him and many men found him difficult to approach. He had no small talk whatever and in an interview in his study silences would fall during which he seemed to be withdrawn, reflectively tapping his knee. But he got on well with Quakers like my wife and myself, perhaps because we were used to silent meetings.

He was an intellectual in the good sense – a first-class classical scholar and one who knew the Bible from end to end, with all the scholarly critical approach to it. He was a philosopher, but when he wrote on philosophical themes, his long sentences defeated the ordinary reader. When I try to assess his greatness, which is enigmatic, I think he must at least have had a genius for giving other people the opportunities they needed.

The first and lasting impression of Bedales was of ebullience, the fearlessness that made this possible, and the energy that was released. A man coming into co-education for the first time could not help looking specially at the girls. They did not fit the conventional picture of schoolgirls; they looked well cared for and were physically vigorous, combined a self-confident poise with open friendliness. Indeed it was quickly possible to establish with both the girls and the boys a friendship that transcended the us-and-them relationship of pupils and teachers. You could maintain the necessary discipline within the classroom and safely discard your authority outside it, dropping into a dialogue in which, though you were older and in some ways wiser, there was a sense of equality.

In the thirties there was not only Summerhill, but there were several other schools among the progressives that were seeking for 'freedom' and loosening the compulsions and obligations imposed on children in the past. Their theory was that a child should grow up freely and become himself instead of growing into a pattern established by authority; that he was inherently good and only needed to unfold in his own way in order to fulfil his potential; that therefore he should be allowed as far as possible to make his own choices and should participate largely in the community decisions that affected his daily life.

What Bedales demonstrated was that a real freedom of development was possible within a recognizable structure of classwork and community obligations. The word 'recognizable' implies that a teacher from an ordinary school could see in Bedales a structure that was not too unfamiliar, one that he could begin to understand, not a set of conditions on which he had no foothold. He could then be all the more effectively challenged by those qualities that were unusual. It is difficult to estimate the influence that a particular pioneer school has had on education in general, but my guess is that the influence of Bedales is the most widespread, and that this is because its procedure could be transferred to a more traditional school without a total dissolution of structure. What it asked for was a transformation of the spirit and intention of education.

The freedom that was, as I saw it, consistent with obligations, was the freedom that is conferred on the partners in a relationship when fear is removed – the freedom that is discovered in friendship and marriage at their best. We all need to achieve it; and in some measure we do, in spite of living in a society in which there are inescapable disciplines and obligations, severe necessities that cannot be ignored. The removal of fear implies the removal of anxiety, guilt, hostility, individualism, all the conditions that box up children – or adults – within themselves. That this was happening in the boys and girls could be seen in their faces, the way they looked at you, the interest and acceptance they showed. It established relationships of mutual trust. The removal of fear also set the mind free to explore, gave a child confidence in the ideas that came to him. The evidence of its achievement was in the high degree of originality, already mentioned, in the careers of the people educated at Bedales.

Bedales is now said to be a highly selective school. But I arrived in 1930 when the economic depression was rapidly deepening. Some parents lost their incomes overnight and children left – or stayed on, we suspected, through the Chief dipping into what was left of the inherited fortune with which he established the school. New pupils were admitted irrespective of intelligence or previous achievements. Among them were some who, as we put it, had done the grand tour of the progressive schools and been sent to Bedales in the hope that it would finally achieve what the others had not. We found that these tended to have huge gaps in basic skills and knowledge, gaps that it was too late to fill. Too great a freedom of choice had let them down. Moreover, there was sometimes a listlessness that we suspected was due to their having been treated, not as persons for whom teachers had a direct responsibility, but as the material of undisciplined experiment.

So at Bedales there were many things that a pupil had to do. He had to go to classes and follow a curriculum in which there was a balance of subjects. He had to take a good deal of physical exercise. Everyone had to join in the outdoor work twice a week, in farm or gardens, in constructional or repair work. If he disliked games he could escape by doing extra outdoor work. He had to attend morning and evening assemblies, form meetings and the Sunday evening 'Jaw'. The latter was a service of a simple religious nature in which a twenty minute talk was given by a visitor or by one of the more articulate members of staff. (Quakers have a reputation for combining silence with a capacity of talking, so I was caught the moment I arrived and gave thirty talks in ten years.)

To some apostles of freedom, compulsion to attend a service, however simple, might seem the worst form of coercion. But the attitude to the Jaw was remarkably good. The defections were rare. This was consistent with a strong resistance to institutional religion. There was an occasion when rumour threatened an address from a bishop in gaiters. The idea was not well received. But there was a good response to what can be called secular Christianity, whether it was an avowed attempt to relate the gospels to ordinary life and politics or a talk about conduct and ethics in which neither Christianity nor religion were mentioned. If the speaker did well, he would be likely to be a centre of discussion afterwards or during the week. We found little impulse among pupils or former pupils to urge that the Jaw should be abolished or made voluntary.

The school must have had a considerable influence on the progress of co-education. By the thirties it had definite prestige in this respect, and if you were head of a department you had a good chance of being appointed to the headship of a state school in an area where co-education was favoured. In 1930 *residential* co-education was still something to raise eyebrows, even though there were several respected Quaker schools not far behind Bedales in their practice of it. It was assumed that unmentionable things happened if boys and girls not only studied but lived under the same roof. Thirty years later boys' Public Schools began to consider the possibility of admitting girls to their Sixth Forms, and now

Cambridge and Oxford mens' colleges are becoming co-educational. The major factor in this development is probably the new attitude, developing in society as a whole, towards equality, the rights of women and their contribution to human need. But it is likely that Bedales provided much of the insight and confidence with which co-education ultimately spread.

Co-education as it first developed in Bedales from 1900 onwards seems to have been a little odd. There was no experience to guide it and it may have been bewildering to the first girls. But by 1930 sexuality was well understood and accepted and 'couples' were not frowned upon. But sex education was not carried beyond anatomical and physiological information in any planned way. Soon, however, the Chief recognized my interest in this, and asked me to go ahead with whatever course I thought fit, also to take some responsibility for keeping in touch with couples – not to exercise any kind of authority over them, but to encourage them to be open and to recognize that what was happening between them was happening in a community. So I began on a Sixth-Form course that extended the usual facts of sexual anatomy and intercourse to cover also pregnancy, embryology and birth in considerable detail. I had specially in mind the need to give boys, as potential fathers, much more knowledge of these matters than men are usually expected to have. This led further into a discussion of personal relationships in their wholeness, of what needs to be thought about in preparation for marriage, parenthood, family planning and the upbringing of children.

When we recognize that even in the seventies sex education is still deplorably inadequate and all too few teachers are willing – or few qualified – to undertake the more personal preparation for sexual relationships and marriage, it can perhaps be claimed that what we did at Bedales was pioneer work. Much of the material of the course was written by my wife and myself and published by Allen & Unwin under the title *Sex, Friendship and Marriage* in 1936. In the time-table the course was euphemistically called Social Biology, crudely but kindly referred to by the boys and girls as Social Bilge.

As time went on it became evident that this kind of education was, much of it, needed at an earlier stage; so by the end of the decade I was having regular discussions with groups round about 13 and 14, supplementing the anatomical and physiological information given earlier.

CHAPTER IV

Finding a Philosophy

Why do we need a philosophy of education? Once in a discussion I said to A. S. Neill, after he had spoken in a characteristic way: 'What you've said is pure Rousseau' (I had in mind Rousseau's *Émile*). Neill retorted, 'Who's Rousseau?' He probably knew perfectly well, but he was having a kick at educational philosophy. He tended to associate a subject of study with the way it was taught at its worst.

We do need a philosophy, one that helps us to see what we are doing in relation to the total situation, that impels us to reflect on our impulses and ask questions of ourselves as to the origin of our aims. It is not good enough to rebel against restrictive tradition and to claim that in so doing we are necessarily putting ourselves on the side of the child and giving him what he needs. An awareness of the nature of dialectic process should make us aware that the rebel is always in danger of taking over some of the characteristics of the system he rebels against. We need to get beyond the conflict of thesis-and-antithesis.

We need a philosophy that helps us to look afresh at the total environment, at society and its effects on human beings, helps us to see what we are doing in an historical perspective. Without a philosophy and a sense of history we are in danger of repeating the mistakes of the past and becoming, in spite of our idealism, the victims of an everlastingly swinging pendulum.

In recent years the philosopher who has most severely criticized all established education in its whole setting is Ivan Illich, sociologist and Jesuit. His *Deschooling Society* characterized organized education in the developed countries as manipulative.

His writing is directed against the power of the state and the large corporations that increasingly associate themselves with political power. Under their power, however much veiled, the schools become the instruments of the consumer society. Education is thus *manipulative.* It cannot be otherwise, whether it is in the service of capitalist, socialist or communist organizations. He looks therefore to the deschooling of society. Since organization is necessarily manipulative, the new education must be the peer-matched grouping of children round adults who are not teachers in the usual sense but creators who can draw children into their enjoyment of the work they do. This will be a convivial association, a sharing of life, a communication of joy and significance in activity.

What is new in Illich's writing is his examination of societies and the education they cannot avoid establishing. He usefully surprises us by the contrast of the words *manipulative* and *convivial,* but in this he is bringing again to our notice a conflict in educational direction that has been in and out of our minds for half a century. It should be pointed out in passing that in the use of *conviviality* to describe creative personal relationship he was anticipated by Michael Polanyi, who, twenty years earlier, put a chapter on it in his *Personal Knowledge.*

The idea of deschooling is apt to polarize attitudes. Very many teachers see it as idealistic and hopelessly unpractical, and they are right when they say that to take the educational system to pieces would be to invite disaster, for the number of children who would spontaneously come to centres of creativity would be small. On the other hand some teachers clutch at the idea eagerly, in all too many instances because they have a chip on the shoulder, a resentment about society and a desire to throw over its restraints simply because they are restrained. Paranoia, of which this is an example, is an increasingly dangerous mental disorder in our present society, showing itself in ever more violent forms, so that, for instance, socialism, from being a sensitive and constructive response to human need, becomes an excuse for hi-jacking and murder.

It is to be hoped that in between these polarized attitudes there will be many educators who will show 'negative capability'; they will allow themselves to be permanently disturbed by Illich's analysis of what is happening and therefore uncertain of the value of their own work, and without projecting their resentment into the situation, will look for points where development can begin. These may be points where the breakdown of existing organization makes the need clear, and something has to be done. Illich may be right when he says that breakdown will inevitably come, from increasing instability.

The early nineteen-thirties were a period when the sense of breakdown was all around us, first from economic recession and unemployment, later from the rise of fascism and the threat of war. The B.B.C. put on a series of fourteen broadcasts in 1930 and 1932 by the philosopher, John Macmurray, who was then at University College, London. They were printed in the *Listener* and later published as a book: *Freedom in the Modern World.* There was, for my wife and myself, an early opportunity to meet John Macmurray, and from this grew a close friendship that lasted until his death in 1976.

I have provided a survey of his philosophy in an earlier book *A Vast Bundle of Opportunities,* (Allen & Unwin) 1975, but in the present context must at least say something about this first work of his and its impact on educational thought. He was concerned with the whole human predicament, and, as a philosopher asking for attention from the ordinary man, he stood in sharp contrast to the rest of professional philosophers. These were being swept into the tide of logical empiricism that derived its impetus from the earlier Wittgenstein and what was known as the Vienna Circle of the twenties. As Kolakowski (1972) puts it, this kind of philosophy rejects as unworthy of attention, or meaningless, problems that cannot be formulated in accordance with logical principles; it tends to narrow down all philosophy to the philosophy of science. It disregards matters of value and conduct and in its most extreme form becomes the escapist's design for living; it exempts us from the duty of speaking up in life's most important conflicts, encases us in a kind of armour of indifference.

This tide of philosophical fashion has ebbed somewhat in the last forty years, but John Macmurray's work still remains outside the attention of most academic philosophers. This is not surprising, because it is the very academicism of the departments of philosophy that his work implicitly attacks. His philosophy is for living, not mainly for thinking about thinking.

The impact of his work on education and religion has been great. Many of our most enterprising religious writers confess to having been profoundly affected by him and I think it can be fairly said that he, more than anyone else, is responsible for the growth, largely beginning in the thirties, of attention to the quality of personal relationships in education. The primary importance of personal relationships, first in family and then in school, was implied in the work of the depth psychologists and in schools like Summerhill, Dartington, Bedales, but in John Macmurray we found a philosopher showing us what we were doing in the whole pattern of living activity, saying that here was the primary focus to which everything else converged, from which every intention radiated.

He could be said also to run parallel to the empiricists in one respect. In the religious field he directed attention away from 'beliefs' of which no one knew the meaning, to the central religious experience which everyone could know and in some measure understand: friendship and the consciousness of a community.

'Freedom' was very much talked about among teachers in the many progressive schools of the thirties and we needed something to make our thought more disciplined, less directed by the mild paranoia that tends to blame outward circumstances for the limitations we inwardly suffer. I must try to put the message of *Freedom in the Modern World* briefly.

Freedom, John Macmurray says, is simply the ability to do what we want to do; it is the absence of restraint upon spontaneity of action. To act spontaneously is to act from oneself, from within outwards, so that the action expresses the agent and has its source wholly and simply in the agent. We thus live in terms of our own nature. The nature of human beings is different from the nature of inanimate objects and from that of animals; we express our nature in *spontaneous objectivity*. It is our nature to apprehend and enjoy a world that is outside ourselves, to live in communion with a world that is independent of us. We are completely ourselves when we live in the full knowledge of what is not ourselves. This is *rational* living – whether it concerns thinking or feeling or simply doing.

Associated with this is a discussion of reality. This word in itself is difficult to define; we can more easily approach it by considering what is obviously *unreal*. If we think we can drive a car endlessly without providing oil, there will eventually be a breakdown and further travel will be impossible, for it is in the nature of a car to use oil. John Macmurray gives a more complex instance. A man may be everlastingly suspicious, believing that all others are trying to do him down. He misinterprets even acts of kindness. In the end all relationship is poisoned and friendship becomes impossible. He has been thinking something to be real that is not real.

The fulfilment of our human nature is in friendship. The word friendship is more useful than love, because the latter carries so many distortions and overtones. We cannot begin to achieve any humanity at all without a responsive relationship with another human being – in the first place the mother – and the full achievement of our humanity is found in a continuous development of relationship with others. This is freedom at its highest level, spontaneous. Anyone who knows the difference between the guarded statements that might pass between an employer and his employed and the ease with which we can drop into a conversation with one we love and trust, will know what this freedom is. And it is spontaneous objectivity, for the ease of action or conversation depends on knowing the other person fully and objectively and therefore being unafraid of him. Further, the mutuality of the relationship implies that in discovering the truth and reality of the other person we discover our own true nature. Knowledge of the other and knowledge of self are one in friendship. This is too brief. The whole of *Freedom in the Modern World* should be read, and also *Reason and Emotion;* but they may have to be searched for in libraries.

There were several occasions when John Macmurray said to us: 'Discipline is the key to freedom'. He said it with a sort of reluctance, perhaps because he knew the unhappy construction that might be put on it by a conventional use of the word discipline. But it was a significant statement. Some of the advocates of 'freedom' for children were rejecting all discipline in the mistaken thought that the child has only to unfold. Others were thinking of the development of self-discipline as a condition that the child could naturally achieve. Yet others were thinking of self-discipline in a way that was really tied to the old obedience concept – a fierce imposition on yourself of rules that would achieve more effectively what authoritarian discipline set out to impose.

To us, what John Macmurray was urging was a sensitive adjustment of our inner life and our actions to the objective nature of the world and other people. It was not an effort to make other people fit into a pattern of behaviour or morality that we thought good, nor a willingness to discipline ourselves to another person's pattern. It could be better compared to the discipline of science. This is not a submissive discipline; it is a study of how things really work and it confers on us a freedom – one that has opened up incredibly in recent years – to do what we want with material things.

So the discipline he refers to can perhaps be expressed in the words: What are *you* really like, what is *my* real nature, what do we really want to do and how can we work together? That takes us back to the definition of freedom as the ability to do *what we want to do* and leaves us with that most difficult question : how do we discover what we really want to do?

Readers will fear that if everyone does what he wants to do there will be conflict and chaos. But we have already seen that to recognize the nature and needs of other people is a large part of the objective discipline we must accept if we are to be free. We cannot have freedom if what we want to do is in unresolvable conflict with what other people want to do. Living in community necessarily assumes that our essential nature is expressed in that kind of living; we were made for living in community.

Adults can deceive themselves to the extent of asserting that other things are more important than friendship; money, power, success, football or research. But if you watch children, who express their basic needs more openly than do adults, you will see that the worst possible fate is to be friendless. It is not only Christianity that puts love (in its objective sense) in the middle of the picture. Every civilisation that has survival value assumes this, even if it seems not to admit it. Nazism overtly denied it and was therefore self-destructive.

So the nurture of friendship is the aim of all community life and the central aim of true education. It makes possible the highest degree of spontaneity, trust and intrepidity.

The education of the whole person is necessarily concerned with morality and values. Towards the end of those talks recorded in his first book, John Macmurray linked his thoughts about this to the three kinds of freedom. A stone falls *freely* when it is not hindered, but its 'freedom' is strictly within the 'laws' of nature; it cannot do otherwise. This is mechanical freedom. A plant or animal can vary in its behaviour as it adapts itself to its environment and the variation is directed towards the survival and evolution of the species. Its freedom is organic. Sharply distinguished from either of these, human freedom is personal freedom, it is expressed in mutal responsiveness between people who are each attuned to the other's reality and needs.

A morality that depends on the idea of obedience to moral law offers no more freedom than that of a stone, it is sub-human, a mechanical morality. An organic morality may seem more attractive; it focuses on service and duty so that the group will survive as do animal species. Roman civilisation was based on precisely this, expressed in the Stoic philosophy of Cicero and Seneca; and those who watched *I Claudius,* or read the books, will have seen how a most effective organization, maintaining a highly developed sense of duty and service, coincided with gross insensitiveness and obscene brutality. The Nazi and Fascist regimes were similarly based on this organic morality.

The Christian might try to reply that what was wrong was the kind of service and its direction, but that is not valid. Remember that Jesus said : *henceforth . . . not servants but friends.* The care for the other person that a follower of Jesus rightly seeks is not developed by making service the object of attention; it is the spontaneous by-product of a personal relationship that is enjoyed; it comes then, not because we 'ought', but by the 'grace of God', which is a theological term for loving spontaneity. It has to be recognized that through its association with Roman power the Christian church took over its Stoicism and thus inverted the message of the Gospels. In our own time, it is only slowly releasing itself from an organic philosophy and morality.

We have to recognize that laws are necessary; without them we could not move towards freedom. But the laws of the state are not moral laws; they are an expression of practical necessity, though they may be instituted by people with a moral sensitivity. We are always in some difficulty when using the term morality, for the *morals* of a people strictly means its established forms of behaviour, often stated in rules and regulations. But now we more often mean by morality what it is good and constructive to do in a given situation, what will truly meet needs.

John Macmurray was strongly convinced that a philosophy really concerned with living could be expressed in simple language capable of being understood by people with no training in philosophy. What I have briefly recalled had a great impact because of this. Perhaps readers will recognize what a sorting out of thoughts its clarity and simplicity made possible to those of us who were right in the middle of the turbulence of those days, and how it began to clear the way for action.

Several other books followed quickly from his pen. *Reason and Emotion,* developed his concept of rationality, seeing it not as merely intellectual or logical, but as an adjustment to what is real outside ourselves. So we could speak not only of rational thinking, such as that used by the scientist, but of rational feeling. This is not feeling that is intellectually dominated, but simply feeling that is appropriate to what is real. It is rational to be afraid of burglars in a district infested with criminals, but not rational to be afraid of snakes under the bed, or of ghosts.

Along with this goes the need for education of the emotions, an education in which emotions are encouraged to develop and test themselves against reality; this is even more important than rational thinking, for all thinking has behind it feeling, whether it is recognized or not. We need an education in (not just *about*) the arts and poetry, and even more the conduct of school life in which children understand and develop their feelings about each other and life as they meet it.

Rational thought and feeling meet in rational action, and John Macmurray dissociated himself from the strongly entrenched tradition in school and university education that assumes that man's primary experience is of thinking. Descartes' statement *I think, therefore I am* is not logical, but if it is taken as an expression of an attitude it should be replaced by 'I act, therefore I am'. Both in the life of an individual and the development of the whole race, action comes first. It is when we act impulsively and meet difficulty that we stop to think. By reflection on the problem we overcome frustration in action. So thought arises from action and it serves to improve action.

This constitutes an attack on the idea that if you have learnt a subject in school or taken a degree at a university you are necessarily superior to one who has not. The test question is has this affected the way you live, has it made you a more effective agent in your relation with others and the world? Or, if not yourself, has your thinking enabled others to be more effective agents?

This centrality of action is related to a refutation of the dualism that has long infected our culture, our education and religion. We cannot avoid the polarity with which we think of human beings: mind-and-matter, body-and-spirit. This does not make us dualists. We become dualists when we think we can separate the poles and give each an independent existence, imagining separate worlds of body and spirit each with their own 'laws'. This often ends up with a spurious monism (spurious because it begins with the assertion of a dualism) in which we become materialists who think that thoughts and feelings are the *mere* accompaniments of physiological changes, or spirit-ists who think that the experience of the material world is evanescent and will ultimately give way to an eternal and purely spiritual world. For John Macmurray, a purely spiritual world is a purely imaginary one.

The only way to live is the way we in fact have to live, accepting that body and spirit are the inseparable sides of one coin and that coin is our experience as persons.

The educational implications of this should be obvious, but it may not be realized that it goes further, into an attack on idealism, and not merely an attack on philosophic idealism. John Macmurray was, in the deepest sense, a Christian, though he did not associate himself with any group until after retirement he became a Quaker. He saw idealism as the enemy of religion, the disease that has robbed it of its life and made it largely irrelevant to our problems. To understand this we have only to think of the way in which Christians have persistently turned their attention away from their relations with their neighbours and attached their emotions to ideals, in a way that justified mutual destruction.

The challenge cannot be evaded by saying that it will be all right if we only have the right ideals. The world is full of good ideals and our progress towards them is desperately slow. John Macmurray did not decry the use of the imagination in finding a way forward. Its proper use is to discover what is possible in the actual circumstances that are presented. Along with ineffective idealism the world shows a dismal poverty of *imagination in action.*

A good example for teachers is this. Perhaps you disapprove, as I do, of examinations, so you imagine and campaign for an education that is without examinations. What is the result when you face the fact that examinations remain throughout your teaching life? Probably that you go on teaching in the same old way and blame the examinations. What is needed, here and now, is the imagination that penetrates the facts you cannot wish away, and that may enable you to release the child from the crippling effect that the examinations would otherwise have.

This is all too short and inadequate an account of John Macmurray's philosophy. It is unfortunate that most of his books are no longer in print (though possibly obtainable from libraries). For those able to deal with a more professional presentation, there are the Gifford Lectures, still in print: *The Self as Agent* and *Persons in Relation,* published by Faber and Faber.

Ironically, it was the coming of war that cleared the way for a greater fulfilment at Wennington School of such a philosophy in education. Mortal danger dispelled the lesser objectives that clouded our vision. People mattered just as beloved persons whose simple survival was the overruling desire. So parents thrust their children upon us, trusted us to care for them and went back into the bombed cities. Sometimes, during our busily occupied day, we took too much for granted our relatively safe position in the country. We were reminded poignantly of the truth, after dark, when we saw the children crowding to the windows of their dormitories, watching the sky whitening over distant Liverpool and Manchester as the incendiary bombs began to fall. We were too far from these cities to hear the high explosive that followed, but the silent flickering was awesome. Most of the parents were somewhere in the middle of it.

5. John Macmurray, inspirer of the School's educational philosophy and Chairman of the Governors up to 1967

CHAPTER V

The Growth of a Community

WE RETURN TO THE EARLY DAYS of the school, but keeping in mind what has been said in the two previous chapters. We were not starting from a mood of revolt, but from a good experience that we wanted to develop and extend. We were not seeking a new ideal but were concerned with the quality of relationships, and we wanted to be ready to deal constructively with whatever emerged, however unforeseen. We had to work within our own limitations, the limitations of those who worked with us and of the environment offered to us.

The building was an advertising asset; parents would say when visiting the school for the first time: 'What a lovely place you've got here!' They were impressed by its appearance of romantic antiquity. In fact it was not more than a hundred years old, a good specimen of what is sometimes called Scots Baronial Gothic. The main building was surmounted by a squat Norman tower, battlemented all round and with a smaller bell-tower poking up from it. Beyond a courtyard stretching out to the west, there was a big postern gate with another Norman tower above it. The windows were mullioned and the fretted stonework required the most odd shapes of glass; we were lucky that there were so few breakages while we occupied the building.

The building had cellars that could be described as dungeons and there were two spiral staircases with bowmen's slits at intervals. It was exciting for the children, and they subsequently remembered it with affection, but it was not convenient for a school: draughty corridors, big open galleries, innumerable nooks and crannies for the collection of dirt, and an ancient central heating system, greedy for fuel and only slowly oozing heat through huge cast-iron pipes. But there were many rooms, and one well-fitted for my study. It had two doors, one opening into the entrance hall and the other into a back passage. I liked wearing informal clothing, shorts and an open neck shirt, for my time-table was unpredictable and I alternated between desk work and hastily undertaken manual jobs, often dirty. But I did not, at this stage, feel it wise to confront new parents with this unheadmasterly image. My windows gave a view of the drive, and when I spotted what looked like parents I dived into the back passage, where I kept a pair of trousers and a tie.

The setting in the countryside was magnificent. Wennington village is on the river Wenning, a salmon and trout river that runs through Austwick and Clapham to join the Lune above Lancaster. Its source is behind Ingleborough, towards which our eyes were drawn every day, looking in forbidding weather like a crouching lion and in winter like a sliced wedding cake. Beyond it lay Whernside and Penyghent. In this remote area, with moors stretching for miles between us and the towns, there were few attractions for bombers, and parents thinking of safety were impressed by the fact that the walls of the building were in most places three feet thick.

The atmosphere of those early days can be captured by reading through the bulletins circulated nearly every term to interested people outside the school. In these the depressions, the rising of hope, the mistakes and successes, are all recorded. This was the beginning of a habit, continued into the more established period of the school's history, in which annual reports were research documents and attempts at assessment rather than morale boosters. Children came quickly enough: 25 by the end of the first term, 40 by the end of the second and 50 by the end of the year. Many came for a negligible fee and our policy of pay-what-you-can allowed us, as I see more clearly in retrospect, to be diddled by a few parents who could well have afforded the maximum fee.

Our pupils came from varied backgrounds; there was no common understanding from which we could start, no common social experience except that of the disturbance of war. We had to start from scratch. We thought we could do without a uniform, but then found that many of the children had no idea of the appropriate attire for a particular activity. Girls would turn out to dig the garden in high-heels or paper-thin shoes, and few knew what clothes were suitable for mountain tops. Either we had to inspect each child before a particular activity or we had to have a uniform, so that we could say: 'When you meet me at 2.30, all of you must have on your . . .' It could be argued that the first alternative was the most educative, accompanied by a shopping expedition and a personal discussion on suitability, but there simply wasn't time when we were already working sixteen hours a day.

It might have been expected that all children, whatever their background, would respond to humane treatment. I am sure that is true – in the long run, sometimes the very long run. However, one boy thought I could not be a proper headmaster because I did not use the cane. He did not respond to my friendly overtures; he set out to be beaten, and when he had plainly failed, he left.

There were many other examples among the children of an initial failure to understand what we offered in a way of life. It might have been expected that in the obvious dangers and scarcities of war-time the need for all hands to do whatever was urgent would be understood. But many of these children had only seen potatoes on sale in shops and peas in tins. They could accept as a biological statement that land had to be dug for potatoes to grow; but the force behind the spade has to come from the heart, not the head, and the heart had yet to feel the connection between digging in the autumn and dinner next year.

There was, however, a sense in which we had the war on our side. The difficulties of getting food from suppliers in a district in which we were newcomers, and the possibility of supplementing our rations by our own efforts, began the process of 'education for community'. We got to know the local farmers, who were small farmers living close to the soil and working intensely hard. The grocers in Bentham, where we shopped, were old-fashioned grocers who knew all their customers, and they began to know us and care about us. A group having in it so many conscientious objectors might have had a hard time elsewhere; but in this area Quakerism was deeply rooted and respected. Our neighbours could see that ours was a hard-working community, a bit odd but nevertheless accepting the discipline of necessity in a time of national austerity and danger.

The problems set by the staff were different and more serious. Children may seem full of reluctances, but they are adaptable; even when you think you have failed with them, suddenly they change with astonishing rapidity. Adults are less adaptable, and the more idealistic they are the more severe the problem. Idealists can work together happily on committees to decide what the world ought to be like or what statesmen ought to do; but put them all in one house to live together and share the routine duties and you will meet plenty of trouble.

On the back of one of my bulletin copies I made a pencilled list of the staff who had worked in the school during the first two and a half years, with comments about them. Not more than a quarter proved able to work together without destructive disagreement. What was it that held that quarter together? Here it is necessary to make a distinction between idealism and commitment. Sometimes it is not necessary to make the distinction, but too often idealism is the desire to realize a pattern which appeals to the intellect, to the conscience or to moralistic judgement. It can be self-centred in that it makes the idealist feel good, feel right, feel that he is really meeting the problems of society. Commitment, in the sense used to make the distinction, is a willingness to *respond to need,* however it may appear, however disturbing it may be to any preconceived ideas we may have. It is a readiness to respond to other people, to engage with them in an exploration that may be self-revealing and disturbing, prompting a frequent reassessment, not only of what is outside ourselves but also of the kind of beings we imagine ourselves to be.

Those who were committed in this way were largely pragmatic; they had to think their way through crisis after crisis, devising techniques in a way never required before. They had to help children grief-stricken at being separated from parents returning to dangerous areas, others for a while shattered in spirit by the collapse of a house round them as a result of a bomb, and perhaps by a death as well. Some were refugees from Nazi Germany and had lost the whole of their families to the gas-chamber. These personal needs, as well as the practical problems of the household and classroom, had to be met creatively, and that means not according to a pattern of what is 'right', but in a way that leads to growth.

Many of the staff were pacifist – some of them Quakers – and that is why they joined us. Some were the salt of the earth, people whose pacifism arose from the kind of commitment described above. Others showed that idealist pacifism can cover a hyper-critical attitude to others; a moralistic self-righteousness too quick to point out when the other person has fallen short. This emerged painfully when the person criticized was the one who had to act and take responsibility for a decision. I remember being morally criticized by a young man for 'not acting in a spirit of love' when I sent a boy away. The boy had never accepted my authority or my responsibility for him, and he showed this by defiant behaviour. This I might have coped with patiently, but his defiance in general matters made me convinced that he could not be trusted in his relationship with a girl. Some time after he had gone, some boys and girls in his group told me that he had been sent away only just in time to prevent what they feared would be a deplorable situation.

Love must indeed be the fundamental urge that moves us, the guiding light, but you cannot squeeze love into a moral pattern. It has to work within the complications of real life. Educational ideas and projects are often in the same category as ideals; they can be strongly held as what *ought* to be done. In the first year some of the staff felt strongly that we had an opportunity to start self-government in the school and ought to begin straight away. I was doubtful, having in mind the lack of common experience and background among the children. What we call democracy in our political life is something we have worked towards through a long history; it is not 'natural'. However, we gave it a trial: a school parliament in which the problems of the community were discussed and rules made.

The experiment failed, and because it was the imposing of an adult idea on an unprepared group of children who hardly knew each other. They used the forum to air their views, to express criticism and hostility; and they made decisions that were not put into action, either because they forgot them or because the defeated minority at once set out to make the decisions of the majority unworkable. There came a day when it was necessary to say to the school: 'Look, you've used this simply to express discontent, to create sides, to get at odds with each other. It hasn't made you any happier. I'm going to put an end to it for the time being. I'm going to declare myself a benevolent dictator until a more wholesome form of self-government become possible and begins to grow'.

Men and women, and boys and girls, develop creative and well-founded forms of co-operation better when they are responding to necessity than when they try to realize an ideal that they think to be desirable. It might be said that all our longings for something better are a response to necessity in some form or other. Our imagination is stirred by a need and leaps ahead, sometimes very far ahead, of our experience; it needs a discipline, and the sharper the necessity the more effective the discipline.

Children are often saved from having to face the demands of reality because they are protected by parents, teachers or institutions. But at Wennington children could not help but be aware of the almost overwhelming load of work the staff were carrying, and as the community grew they were caught into a general awareness of very practical needs. We made no secret of our financial problems. I have described how we managed for a while on our savings and paid for our keep. There were moments when we thought we should not survive; one came in the middle of the first term. There was no money to pay for anything. My wife and I had an almost sleepless night wondering what to do. But in the morning I opened a letter from Geraldine Cadbury who, with her husband, Barrow Cadbury, had taken an interest in our work for the unemployed in the thirties. The envelope contained a cheque for £200, and the letter was brief, to this effect: 'I don't know quite what it is you two are doing, but if you are doing it, it must be good'. Although two hundred pounds would be represented by a much larger sum today, the fact that such a sum saved us does show how we were making do by human effort and ingenuity rather than by money.

A year later this paragraph appeared in one of the bulletins:

> Finance is not yet the greatest of our problems; we have always managed somehow. But we are realising now that our first year was helped out by donations and the savings of staff, amounting in all to about £500. In this second year we have nothing but our

> income from fees. An increase in the number of older children has made unavoidable further expenditure on equipment. Alarmed by rising prices we have laid in stocks of food and other materials, and we ought to go on with this process. It is distressing to put off the purchase of a tool or other apparatus that we know we must buy eventually, and watch the price rising while we delay. But what are we to do? We have about enough money in the bank for a fortnight's expenditure, and it will be six weeks before more fees come in. Our largest purchase this term has been of laundry equipment – about £125. (December 1941.)

I do not remember how we bridged that financial gap, but I do remember vividly the emergency that arose when the washing machine broke down. It was an ordinary machine of the old type, a tub with an agitator and a wringer; and the electric motor had burnt out. As a teacher I had been showing boys how to make small motors in laboratory and workshop but I had never faced the rewiring of an A.C. induction motor. However, I stripped the stator of its running and starting coils, measured the gauge of wire in both and sent an urgent order to the London Electric Wire Company. To my surprise, in spite of the difficulties of war-time, the wire was posted by return. I spent a day winding the large number of coils on formers and stayed up all night slotting them into the stator. After the motor was reassembled there was an anxious period while I connected up and pressed the switch – followed by moments of pure joy when the motor hummed away.

Two days later, on a Saturday evening, a desperate group of women came to me. The washing machine was out of action again, really broken this time! The gear case was split in two. For a moment I felt blank, defeated and angry. I sat down for a quarter of an hour and thought; and the answer came. A couple of iron plates and the borrowing of a set of Whitworth taps and dies solved the problem in time for Monday morning. It is worth thinking about this incident from the educational point of view. It was a moment of triumph. I walked about on lighter feet for a while and seemingly endless worries fell into a more tolerable perspective. Just because a motor whirred away at the touch of a switch! How can we make sure that every child has his triumphant moments? It's not a matter of conceit, hardly even of pride; it is the sheer enjoyment of resourcefulness.

We had a few adults, perhaps six or eight, who were committed to seeing us through at least till the war should end. For the rest we had to accept the help of people coming for brief periods. Some were devoted friends tearing themselves away from their proper jobs to give us a term or two. Some were the flotsam washed up on to our shore by the tide of war. Some were longing for community as the answer to their own personal problems.

It was difficult to keep domestic and kitchen jobs filled. My wife's main educational interest was in the teaching of English but she was torn away from it time after time by the departure of a cook or a matron; often she tried to do more than one full-time job and got desperately tired at a time in life when most women expect to ease up. We were presented with exasperating situations when we had to choose between having yet another gap in the staff and tolerating someone who was not fit to remain in the job.

One couple came, she to be matron, he to teach. A few weeks later it was revealed that she was pregnant; I had not suspected this when she was interviewed for the job. Further, she had been warned against the danger of miscarriage and, therefore, expected to spend a lot of time in bed. It can be imagined that I was more than a little angry when I heard this. An interesting development was presented when the women staff heard of my anger. They looked at *me* with accusing eyes and prepared to stand on guard lest I should express my feelings to the bed-ridden patient. All quite simple and primitive; she was pregnant, therefore she was right and I was wrong. This couple didn't stay long.

There were some desperately sad cases. A Jewish refugee woman came to do domestic work; she had lost her parents and all her relatives to Hitler's gas-chambers. She tried hard to meet our needs. But one day I saw a long wet trail across the big gallery to the door of her room; she had presumably been mopping a floor and had walked away from the job trailing the mop behind her, to collapse in her room. She passed on, hopeless, and we had no idea where she went or what happened to her.

Occasionally we were joined by someone really superb. A Quaker couple came – people from farming stock – he to be a financial secretary, she to be the cook. And what a cook she was! In spite of war-time rationing she produced meals equal to any that a careful mother would produce in peace time. Good food contributes more than any other material thing to the happiness of a community, and surely she made us happy. Her husband was a wizard too; he could make hens lay eggs when no-one else could.

When, alas, this marvellous cook left us, she was succeeded by a German woman who was not Jewish herself, but had married a Jew and, therefore, become a refugee. She was tall, distinguished-looking in a Prussian way, with long grey hair that reached to her waist when loose. She had the oddest ideas of food-reform. The ideal diet was stewed nettles, carrot juice and linseed. She claimed she herself lived on this; she never ate with the rest of us and we had more or less what we wanted. Stewed nettles appeared once – never again.

She insisted that the milk should be poured into shallow pans so that the cream could settle. She wanted to skim it off for making sauces! At this time we had a brilliant young English graduate straight from Cambridge who had been exempted for work in schools. He divided his time between teaching and kitchen work. He wrote poetry, and he read poetry better than anyone else I know. Although an avowed atheist, he could raise our spirits in times of despair by his superb reading of Gerard Manley Hopkins' *The Leaden Echo and the Golden Echo*. He was a most lovable person and, in what he gave to the community, always buoyant. Our German cook invariably used every saucepan and every other kitchen utensil when she prepared meals; and she burnt many of the saucepans. I have a vivid memory of the kitchen after a midday meal, of Stephen capering round in the lady's presence, waving a saucepan and crying, 'burnt again!' And she would say in her German accent, as she surveyed the huge pile of things to be cleaned, 'Oh Stephen, I am so sorry for you. Now I go to my room'.

As cooks go, she went. Which of us tired of the other, I do not remember, but her departure was shortly after the occasion of an outdoor play, performed by the boys and girls, to which we had invited local people. Perhaps our cook had been an important person in her own country; anyway, when the critical moment arrived, she was all dressed up, graciously welcoming the vicar on the lawn, while Frances, my overworked wife who was the producer of the play, was discovering that no preparations had been made for tea-and-cakes in the interval. It had been taken for granted that *she* would attend to this!

It certainly seems that the number of men who exasperated us was smaller than that of the women. Perhaps it is true that men accept a communal existence more easily than do women, though I think women contribute more in sheer devotion and labour. I can remember men who were judgemental and opinionated but not so many oddities. There was, of course, the intelligent and high-principled teacher who was seen to be taking two meat rissoles at lunch when the rations permitted only one, and who, when challenged, maintained that since his wife was unwell and not eating her lunch he could claim her rissole as well as his own.

How significant is all this information about the oddities of particular people in an account of an educational venture? The difficulties and idiosyncracies were intensified by war-time circumstances, but basically they constituted part of the truth about human nature. They made a tremendous demand on our resources and understanding and they brought to the surface forms of awareness and intuition that are not normally demanded in institutional education. If we thought of education in community as a nourishment of the whole personality then we had to be prepared to accept, and meet constructively, all that is in humanity – so very much more than we are normally willing to meet in the classroom.

We did get terribly exhausted at times, but not more than millions of men and women in Britain who were working in difficult and dangerous conditions. If I ever felt a trace of self-pity I could remind myself that my mother, a widow, well on in the sixties, was insisting on remaining in London while the bombs removed houses from street after street, living alone and travelling every day through broken glass and rubble to an office in the centre where she worked on the allocation of ration books. (She lived to be 97 and looked back on that as being the most adventurous period of her life.)

However pacifist we may be, if we forget for a moment the carnage and ruthlessness of war, we have to recognize that total war – war that involves a total demand on the civilian population as well as on the services – is the only experience that draws on all our resources as a national community and shows us that we can summon up from the depths much more energy than we ever dreamed possible. Not only could we not have started our school without capital in peace time, but we could not have bred into the school at the outset the qualities which became so much a part of its character.

When members of staff left, often we could not immediately replace them. Every one of the bulletins, circulated to our friends, contained an appeal for help. Can you find us a cook, a matron, a handicraft teacher . . . ? Often we had to share the extra work among us. But even when we felt overburdened, there were great compensations. A clear memory is that of craft teaching, the bubbling enthusiasm of the juniors waiting outside the workshop and the race to the benches as the door flew open. There was just as much enthusiasm for this among the girls as among the boys.

Science teaching without orthodox apparatus was not an insuperable problem. Even at Bedales, with a well-equipped laboratory, we made a point of using everyday objects and constructing apparatus of our own design. Some of the first few physics lessons at Wennington made use simply of bicycle pumps, from which you can learn a great deal, especially if you include the reversal of the leather washer after you have used it normally. The most important consideration is not that the teacher should have lavish equipment, but that there should be an imaginative and exploratory dialogue between him and his pupils. There will be more to say about this later on, in relation to the Nuffield Science Project.

If we had trouble with difficult and unreliable staff we had also reason for the deepest appreciation of the qualities in others – the committed ones. For instance, the two who covered the geography, maths and biology. They looked solid and they were solid. You could throw any problems at them and they stood firm, turning their minds towards the solution they were sure could be found. They were superbly competent as teachers, giving the children the confidence that they were in good hands. The man soon became my tireless deputy and once he was found in a typical pose at the beginning of term, in the kitchen at 2 a.m., with the timetable spread out on the huge working surface, absorbed in juggling and not in the least harassed. Only once was he upset. Listening to my description of the insertion of a cannula into my vein to withdraw a pint of blood he – tough rugger player that he was – fell in a dead faint. Otherwise he was imperturbable. One day I rounded a corner in a corridor and found him confronted by a vehement Irish girl. She was repeating over and over again a word that would have taken the hair off the heads of her previous teachers. She had been at a repressive convent school, had become unmanageable and therefore had been transferred to Wennington. My colleague registered no shock; he smiled sweetly at her and she rushed away. I don't think she used the word again.

Among the teachers who were able to give us only one term there was a woman who had become exhausted by the difficulties of school work in Southampton, subjected to intensive bombing. She came to Wennington for a rest! She was a tremendous tonic to our spirits. She taught English and produced *A Midsummer Night's Dream* before returning to endure more blitzes. She could not resist visiting us for a week during the following term and when the children heard she was coming there was a spontaneous whoop of joy.

Some of our most useful staff could not help letting us down – inadvertently, by way of nature. We took several young married couples who had come from very difficult war-disturbed areas. At Wennington they perhaps had only one room into which to cram their furniture. They got five shillings a week each and their food, and any insurance premiums paid for them. It was not much by outside standards, but they were safe – no longer threatened. Then the inevitable happened. I would be halted in mid-flight along the hall by a dewy-looking young woman wanting to have a private word with me. As I closed the study door, I would say: 'You needn't tell me what it's all about. When is the baby due?' This happened so often that we began to say that the motto of our community was

Liberty, Equality, Maternity. Usually the mothers were not out of action for long. In a residential school it is not difficult to find moments to feed a baby in the course of a teaching day and there are plenty of eager girls – even a boy or two – to wheel out a pram.

Encouraging too was the help we had from young people from other schools:

> A dozen sixth formers from Bootham, The Mount and Sidcot schools came to help with practical jobs, making black-out screens, doors and tables, painting and distempering, clearing land drains, cementing, putting up racks. They appreciated what we are trying to do in our school and the friendship they felt to exist. We are so aware of our deficiencies and of the problems still awaiting solution that we do not often realise how much we have already achieved. These young people helped us, perhaps more than any others have done, to realise how much we have accomplished in the first year. There was much discussion, and there were many dances in the evenings. Later some of my own old Bedales pupils came, now undergraduates at Cambridge, to do similar work; and they provided us with several musical evenings.

One young man came straight from Bedales at the age of 17 to teach craft work. He was not yet liable for military service and was a born teacher, endlessly resourceful in every emergency. After his national service (he was a conscientious objector assigned to agricultural work) he returned to Wennington to give many years of enterprising and tireless work.

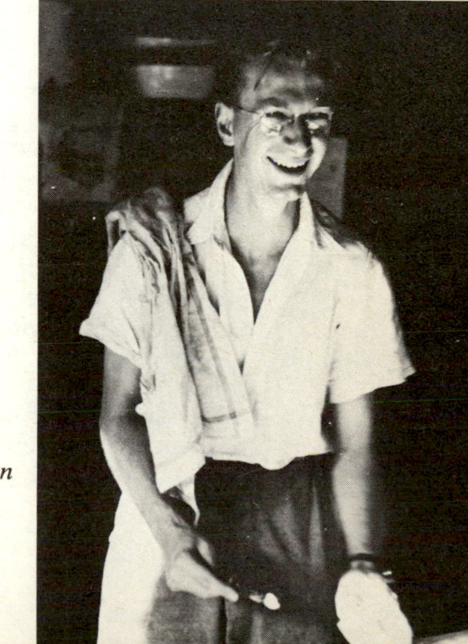

6. Stephen

CHAPTER VI

Myth, Music and Pigs

It has been shown that the experiment in formal self-government failed. Soon, however, the boys and girls were moving towards a surprising manifestation of responsibility.

(December 1941)

> Not only do children now accept without complaint or criticism their share of the daily chores, but they find other things that need to be done, and take charge without waiting for the staff to suggest it. Some boys of 12 and 13 have realised that washing up after a meal for 70 should be a matter for system, especially as regards stacking. They exercise a benevolent tyranny over staff and fellow pupils, even when they are not themselves on duty, in order to see that the system is well-established.
>
> Girls are helping in the sewing room, ironing and mending often in their own free time and of their own initiative. They distribute clean clothes and sheets at week-ends. The older girls (15-16) supervise the junior school siesta, look after lost property, see to the washing of hands before meals and do many other duties, all without the prestige of being called prefects.
>
> The older boys are responsible for workshop cleaning, boiler stoking, supervising of shoe-cleaning and drying, and many outside jobs. There is obvious enjoyment in the way the boys and girls carry out these tasks. Thus in one of the major aims of the school we are succeeding; what was once a matter of hope is now a fact. The awareness that all the staff do their share, and the absence of any social distinctions, is the key to this development. The significance felt is different from a feeling of importance; it gives them a sense of belonging, in function and as persons.

(November 1942)

> The scullery, now under the control of boys and girls, has reached a standard of order higher than it ever reached under staff control. Woe betide those who leave a sink dirty, or even wet! A group of

> four is responsible for this surprising success. It is almost a mania with them but we are persuading them to train others to the same standard to widen the responsibility. Members of this self-appointed group are often seen inspecting sink, plates and cutlery after others have washed up.

This is the way for responsibility to emerge, first in particular areas, so that roots can be put down before generalizations become conscious. But this is not an argument for letting children find things out *by themselves*. The idea that children have 'got it in them' and simply have to be given freedom for it to 'come out' is an idea that blinds the adult to his responsibilities. These children were in constant reciprocity with hard-working adults (and some lazy and irresponsible adults!). These conditions provoked insight through a 'dialogue' that was no less effective for being almost unconscious. It was in the junior school that a spontaneous development of self-government first appeared:

(December 1941)

> On their own, the Juniors have organised a Council, appointing the most capable member as Chairman. He has handled the meeting with demands for brevity and keeping to the point that would be an object lesson to Mayors and Town Councillors. They have organised their own library, working out a system of tickets and penalties for leaving books about. They solemnly discuss the making of faces by one member, pinching and petty bullying by another, and they extract from the erring boy or girl promises of amendment.

Among those of secondary age, forms of authority were emerging with hesitation. By this time the whole group was meeting as a Council to take part with the staff in working out the development of the school.

(November 1942)

> The school council has been much busier. We, the staff, had been forced into the position of policemen, our main job to see that reasonable rules were kept and the school organisation made to work. It was not the job we ought most to be doing, which was to know each pupil and to help him to make the best of his life. If the boys and girls relieved us of policing we could do more constructive work. The Council has since held frequent meetings and is dealing with dormitory discipline and order at meals. No-one questioned the desirability of discipline, quietness, regular bed-times, although there was freedom to do so. The staff absented themselves from the first meetings in order to make free discussion

possible; it might have been hindered by our mere presence. Later they returned. The staff have been asked not to make suggestions or present the Council with solutions; their function is to help clarify each problem and clear the way for boys and girls to reach a solution of their own. We need the patience to let them make mistakes and discover the inadequacy of some of their proposals.

But the pupils have not yet fully accepted the need for authority among themselves. Democracy at present means general consent, spontaneously arrived at. Putting this into action they find they can keep the dormitory quiet after lights out by general consent for a week, but not for a fortnight. They are now trying the experiment of vesting authority in one person, whose job is to remind them of their group decisions and to call upon them to eject noisy offenders to a lone couch elsewhere. This provides political experience, an understanding of the function of authority in democracy. Will they ever go so far as to institute any general authority, such as a prefect system?

Whenever they thought of having one of their own number in authority, fears of favouritism and unfairness were expressed. When asked if they could think of one person whom they would accept, nearly all the girls said yes, but not one of the boys.

When the school opened in 1940, we took children of any age. One little girl of three came to us the day after her house had been bombed and she had been found under the staircase, the only part of the house not collapsed. It was surprising how little shock she was suffering from. Eventually we had to stop taking children of nursery age but retained in our junior school the 7–11 range that Frances was interested in. This group showed great spontaneity and this was evident in their reaction to myth. Frances had always been fascinated by the great myths and legends and we thought these to be essential nourishment for children. The word *myth* has, however, become debased – to mean any untruth popularised for political or other purposes. On the contrary it properly means a truth about the deep currents in human nature, expressed in the behaviour of legendary or archetypal figures, in stories that could be 'felt in your bones' and handed on from generation to generation. A recent and fascinating treatment is to be found in Rosemary Haughton's *Tales from Eternity*.

The use of the term nourishment is deliberate; it has to be frequently pointed out that the word education is derived from *educāre* not *educĕre*. It means not drawing out but giving mental food: experience to be assimilated at all levels of the mind or psyche. Children are all the time assimilating some kind of myth. It may be superficial myth of the mechanical imagination such as *Dr. Who, The Daleks,* or *Superman,* but the ancient myths contain the truth about all that is in us. Impetuously we started our juniors on Homer:

(December 1941)

> The Juniors are the most interesting part of the school. There has not been time for their education to become confused by bad schooling and we do not meet the deep personal problems often apparent in older children. They have little self-consciousness or feeling of inferiority.
>
> With them we can begin at the beginning, and can achieve a unity of work and play. This has been shown in the way they have lived their literature: the story of the Iliad. They have taken every opportunity to continue the battle of the Greeks and Trojans over our terrace wall, with dustbin lids and wooden armorial shields found in the cellars. Patroclus and Hector have died a hundred times outside the walls of Wennington Hall. There is discipline in this play, of their own making, and it has somehow melted away the irritation and feuds that existed among them before this began. Petty bullying has disappeared. The Trojan War, with its savagery and merciless revengefulness, sublimates their own spite into poetic justice. They have found an outlet, understood by the whole group, for the primitive emotions that surge in the breasts of the under-tens. They discuss the conflict and their minds leap ahead of the games they are playing without any prompting from staff. They criticise and judge their own primitive behaviour, seen as it were in the mirror of Achilles, and get ready to repudiate it and pass on to the next stage of their development.

With those juniors the usual resistance to the Bible was overcome by its association with the rest of ancient literature and the search for underlying meanings. Bible stories were dramatized, not to convey conventionally accepted meanings, but to encourage the children to explore the meaning through imagination. The Eden story was staged outdoors and local people invited. The juniors were fearless and spontaneous, and there was no difficulty in getting Adam and Eve to appear naked in the Garden. At the guilty moment Eve pointed with well-acted astonishment at Adam's little penis and cried: 'Oh! You're *rude!*' Both then dashed into the darkness of laurel bushes and re-appeared with rhubarb leaves tied over their middles.

Many of the men and women who were juniors in the early years of the School remember with special gratitute what they received from my wife's sister, Ruth, who also was a teacher trained for work with young children. While others of the junior school staff came and went, she remained for many years the one continuing and completely dependable adult, giving her whole time to their part of the School, and concerned with basic skills. She had the kind of competence as a teacher that combined security with liberation; the children knew they were being lovingly *well-taught,* and thus they felt safe with her. She gave them direction, something to aim at by which they could judge their achievement; but at the same time they were not restricted, their creative impulses were being stimulated and their feelings expressed.

A young woman teacher who came for only a few terms started off a period of intense artistic activity among the Juniors. They produced paintings of an imaginative and symbolic quality that astonished, and puzzled, the teacher who had set them going. There was another time when puppetry and stage design took over.

(April 1943)

> The Junior School undertook a fine puppet project last term. The Robin Hood ballads provided the literary basis. To adults these seem a little dull but for children they have a fascination; some of the boys and girls listening to a recent broadcast – the death of Robin – were moved to tears, one or two being heartbroken! Every one made at least one puppet: made of clay and baked, a shell of papier mache being made from this. The results were most interesting, bearing out in nearly every case Leonardo's observation that the artist tends to create images in his own likeness. The resemblance to their creators was comic in some instances. The dresses were scraps of velvet, the stage was fitted with electric foots, battens and floods, and good backcloths were produced in art classes. The scenario for the end-of-term show was entirely by the children, and in the last scene they somehow managed to arrange that all the characters should appear on the stage at once. The crowd of children jammed into the box below stage level was fantastic.

It was in the first term of 1941 that our artist and his wife joined us. Louis Jones was versatile. He could strip a car down to its components and put it together again. His old B.S.A. three wheeler became for several years our only means of fetching-and-carrying. He had been a lecturer to the decorative trade in the Birmingham College of Art. He had not taught children before but his love of a broad canvas took him into the right approach, and soon large sheets of newsprint paper were covered by imaginative and eagerly executed work. We had a small commercial pottery near us, at Burton in Lonsdale, and I had with me a heavy potter's wheel I had made myself. Our art master went for a day once a week to the commercial pottery to gain experience and soon we were building our own kiln.

This had to have a long horizontal flue leading to the muffle, adaptable to the partial use of wood, of which we had plenty, as well as coal. It was impressive when completed and the first opening of it was one of the most exciting experiences. We were prepared for a high proportion of cracked pots and ruined glazes – but what our delighted eyes took in was a 90% success.

(June 1943)

> Pottery goes ahead with great enthusiasm. We built a kiln to Rural Industries Bureau design, during the Xmas holidays; two boys staying behind to help. It is about seven feet high and ten feet long, made with throw-out bricks obtained for the cost of cartage. It holds about a hundred pots at a firing. We have been making red biscuit earthenware (from black clay) for firing in this kiln, instead of the stoneware that was previously made for firing in the Burton kilns. We are going back to stoneware now, but it will be more difficult to get up to the extra two hundred degrees needed in our own kiln. Some of the children are becoming competent throwers, making bowls, vases and jugs eight or nine inches wide and high, and able to turn in the neck of a bottle.

Perhaps purists would have insisted that we should continue to accept the discipline of a kick-wheel. But Louis wanted his pupils to be free to give all their attention to the control of clay. He geared an old bicycle to the spindle; one child pedalled while the other threw a pot. After 1945 we installed power-driven commercial wheels.

At first music was less well provided than the arts. The wife of our sea-captain was our first music teacher; she gave us a good start but did not stay long. Nor did successors. Nevertheless there was a strong awakening of interest in music, right through the community. I wonder why? Did the war sensitize us? I remember the mid-day concerts in the National Gallery in bombed London, and the occasion when I listened to a quartet, entirely Jewish, giving us all that was in them to give, while within a few hundreds of miles their fellows were being exterminated in conditions of unspeakable obscenity.

Our first school musical 'experience' was a parallel to this. At Bedales

I had been teaching a German Jewish boy coming from a family distinguished in art and philosophy. One day he disappeared; the police had snatched him, he was over sixteen and they interned him. Later he was stupidly packed off to Canada. His father was also interned, and when liberated from the camp on the Isle of Man, joined our staff as a language teacher. In the camp he, Kurt Cassirer, joined with Paul Hamburger and Alfred Schweitzer (a physiologist of whom more will be said later) to occupy themselves in making music.

All three met again to play to us. It was an unforgettable occasion, almost unbelievable in its quality. Paul Hamburger of course played the piano, Kurt Cassirer the violin and Alfred Schweitzer the violin or viola. For me the Bach Double Concerto is forever tied to the memory of that performance. All the fifty children were present and it seemed wise to tell the juniors that they need not come back after the interval. Not one of them wanted to go. They insisted on staying, from the teenagers right down to the five-year olds, for the whole two-and-a-half hours, listening with rapt faces.

That was the beginning of a long association with all three. Paul Hamburger began to come frequently and toyed with the idea of joining the staff, not only to teach Music, but also Mathematics. He was at that time, just after release from internment, working in a factory canning peas. Later he began to bring with him the soprano Esther Salaman, whom I knew as a former Bedales girl.

I have shown how some subjects were well taken care of by committed staff, such as Geography, Biology and Mathematics, and this remained true for the five years the School was at Wennington Hall. What we lacked in conventional laboratory accommodation we made up for by using the marvellous countryside. Few biologists and geographers are provided with an environmental laboratory so full of material. In quiet periods the Wenning was a crystal clear river and from the bridge we could look down to watch for the trout, flickering almost invisible against the stones. We could see the salmon leaping at Bentham, and when we went down to bathe in the meanders of the Lune we could see enormous but wary salmon in the pools, elderly beasts whose cunning time after time saved them from fishermen and poachers (the cleverest of whom, it was rumoured, was at one time the local Irish R.C. priest).

Two boys, one of them my son, got a blacksmith to make them a vicious-looking gaff-hook, with the intention of hooking an unwary salmon out of the water, but this bit of field biology was unsuccessful. The other boy was successful at tickling trout. Caught one day in restricted waters by the local squire he undermined the latter's anger by his charm of manner. The squire was caught into a discussion of the private life of the trout and the boy returned home to cook his catch.

Ingleborough, Penyghent, Whernside and Dentdale provided entrancing country. Sometimes we abandoned school work, made a heap of sandwiches and set off walking (it was only six miles to Ingleborough). There was a spice of fear in those excursions, for it is limestone country, with pot-holes and underground streams. A favourite objective was Gaping Gill.

When one is responsible for a crowd of boys and girls it is a nightmare, a great black hole plunging vertically into the earth, with the waters of the beck roaring into it and no protection round it. Moreover it is not a shaft drilled into the ground like a coal mine, with sharp edges at the top. That would have enabled our fascinated brats to wriggle towards the edge until they could look down in reasonable safety. But the opening of Gaping Gill funnels out, to a slope. Imagine watching twenty children inching down over that curve, the wet grass and the slimy stone, in the hope of being able to look right down into the blackness!

We had to develop versatility in subject teaching. After the second year we lost two experienced teachers – of History and French. But a young Quaker couple had come to live in the district and the woman was an English graduate of Cambridge who could also deal with French. So she took over the French and the senior English and my wife and I, with no paper qualifications at all, shared the History between us.

Frances at least had a love of history to start from, centring in the point where mythology, religion, cultural habits and national conduct meet. She could start from Jerusalem and Troy, the Nile and the Aegean. As for me, way back in 1919 History was the one subject in which I failed School Certificate – deliberately because I was so bored. It was not until I met Marxism that a real interest came to me; then at last – though I never became in any committed sense a Marxist – I saw there could be a coherent pattern in what had been just one-thing-after-another. The understanding of a dialectical process was a revelation.

Further, I had become interested in the history of science and moved through that into an attempt to look at history generally. So the three older groups were launched into the history of the 17th, 18th and 19th centuries, starting from the scientist's point of view and being concerned mainly with progress in science and invention, basic political movements, social conditions and legislation.

We had children with widely varying intelligence and equally varying previous education. We could not select from them reasonably uniform groups. So we planned a Dalton system in which there was less group teaching and an increased amount of assignment work which the boys and girls had to get through in private study. They had to organize their private study to give adequate time to weak subjects. Bright children could plunge ahead with what interested them. I had seen this system at work in Bryanston and was impressed. We reported:

> Attitude to work is definitely better. Many of them say their effort is better because they know what they have to get through in a month and they have to plan their time accordingly. It is always a joy to me, when I am detained and late for class to find everyone quietly at work instead of ragging. This alone is a big argument for a Dalton system. We have extended the assignment system to cover not merely class work but the whole of school life.
>
> We want no child to miss any essential training in, for instance, practical adaptation to life. No boy or girl should be incapable of dealing with an electrical emergency in a house, a worn tap washer or a stopped waste pipe. Nor should he be unaware of the nature of local farming or industries. All such things we have grouped in lists on a large chart, with such headings as: Farming, Nature, Dormitory routine and Hygiene, Bicycle maintenance and repair, Housecraft, Home repairs, Exploration, Games, Gardening and outdoor work. These provide a guide to the knowledge each should be gaining in everyday life, partly in school work, largely in free time. Each reports on a monthly report card what he has done under each heading. This is, as will be recognized, partly a development of Scouting technique. Many things are getting done now that would otherwise be neglected, or left to the staff. Certain children now have a sense of personal achievement in things that matter. Whenever possible, electrical faults and other breakdowns in the house are left to be dealt with as soon as possible by a boy or girl who wants to complete a stage in this work. Each outdoor work group has to complete an assignment in certain specified activities during the term (including indoor work such as the preparation of vegetables and washing-up).

This experiment went on for a sufficiently long time to add a lasting discipline to many of the pupils' working habits, but eventually it partially broke down and ordinary class teaching increased.

Another determined attempt was made after the transfer to Wetherby, for similar reasons. It lasted for a while and again had to be partially replaced. A residue remained in that assignments continued to be set, rather than 'prep' work, that need not be done on a particular day but had to be completed in the course of a fortnight or month. Again we could say that it developed self-discipline in study. Our pupils going on to universities reported that they were more favourably prepared for university life with its heavy responsibility for self-direction. They were not liable to first-year failure as were students from more orthodox schools.

The scheme was devised with the awareness of the wide variation in ability in our classes, to let the able children go ahead while the less able, instead of struggling along behind always out of breath, could go at a pace that allowed consolidation of knowledge. In fact the highly intelligent benefited greatly; the scheme was a joy to many of them; but those of moderate ability slipped through our fingers; repeatedly they failed to fill in their assignment records. Such children needed a tighter system, to be at a certain place at a certain time, so that the teacher saw their faces and knew he had to do something for them as well as for his more able pupils.

Bryanston's success must have owed something to the fact that it was a highly selective school in the matter of intelligence. Wennington, though mainly for children of 'grammar school ability' never wanted to close its doors to children who had not that ability but needed the encouraging and therapeutic experience of a caring community. So we had to discover a workable compromise. Compromises need not be failures; the factor of primary importance is in the teacher's intentions, his degree of concern and the quality of relationship with his boys and girls. What Wennington retained was the encouragement of enterprise; while disappointment had to be faced in one project surprising opportunities were opening out in another.

My teaching of physics and chemistry left me with dissatisfaction; I could not give enough time to preparation, without enough apparatus I relapsed too often into chalk-and-talk. However, as in other subjects, where one could relate science to the environment it came vigorously alive. Necessity supported us; we had to grow food. For the expertise of the 'green thumb' we had an excellent gardener who cycled in from Low Bentham. Kelbie Tomlinson was a delight. He was more community-orientated than most of the self-conscious seekers who joined us; he was utterly dependable in his job and in his feelings. He was, not of his own desire, but because he lived out, paid a statutory wage, more than any of the rest of us. The big walled garden was his concern and in that we planted cordon apples and soft fruit that would bring a quick return. We ploughed up other land for potatoes, brassicas, peas, beans and roots. We had soil analyses done, found serious deficiences and rectified them. When we had a large area under a particular crop we divided it up on the Roman square system, used varying treatment and found significant differences. But there was always a tantalising vision of a greater scientific treatment than was really possible.

The following extract merits two explanatory comments. So long as the bombing of cities continued we could not close the School during the holidays; many of the children had to be looked after and provided with interest and occupation. Some of us got no more than a week or two of release in a year; so we often had to cope with exhaustion. The reference to spring flowers, however, records an experience of exhilaration we did not expect when we took over the building. As the first winter receded, acres of grass and stony soil threw up the green spears of tens of thousands of spring flowers – so many that getting Marks & Spencer to sell all they could take seemed to make no difference:

> The Easter holiday has been the best we have experienced here. All the children went away this time, leaving us free to give all our energy to constructional and land work. To speed up the growth of early vegetables we purchased twenty pounds' worth of glass and made 250 large cloches. We have expanded the kitchen garden from one acre to three. The coming of spring, and all this activity, made a great difference to our spirits. (These were low towards the end of term.) The first spadeful of earth turned over and the first seed sown meant more this year than ever before as a joy and an affirmation of faith. To add to our enjoyment this holiday, the spring flowers have appeared in their tens of thousands all over the grounds. We send about two thousand of every kind of daffodil, narcissus and jonquil into Lancaster every other day.
>
> The work in the garden has been so interesting and the planning of crops, fertilisers, etc. so absorbing that I want to put it all under scientific control – like a miniature Rothamsted. But the work involved, the technique of the analyses necessary, would not allow me to be a headmaster as well. However, we make it as scientific as possible, and we shall make agriculture a project during the coming term. We were encouraged by the enthusiasm in an entirely unplanned and spontaneous science class – the sort that a teacher pulls off once in a blue moon – that began with the dreary subject of Acids, Bases and Salts but developed within ten minutes into the collection and examination of specimens of soil from all parts of the estate, the discussion of soil acidity, and a hunt for new indicators. The History and Geography teachers are going to co-operate in the development of this project.

Animals were involved also. We had begun to keep pigs, to make use of the scraps from the kitchen, and the children took part in the care and feeding of these and other animals. These two, Tweedledum and Tweedledee, were a source of much amusement and they developed athletic prowess. They occupied a stone stable on the far side of the courtyard with access to an open run beyond it. They began to leap over the fence. A member of our Advisory Council later to become the governing body, came to help for a week. He was a university lecturer in mathematics and he set about a methodical addition to the height of the fence. But he ought to have used multiplication rather than addition, for after the fixing on of each new board and his departure for a meal those pigs learnt to jump higher. We were tempted to see how high they could eventually jump. We beat them in the end, but just before that we were bellowing with laughter at the sight of two great fat pigs leaping on to the top rail and rocking on their tummies till they fell over the other side.

My wife and I and a few staff and children used to walk the four miles to Bentham Friends' Meeting on Sunday. On one occasion about half way home, we met Tweedledum and Tweedledee trotting towards us side by side, sleekly and tubbily self-confident in their road-worthiness. On another occasion they were found, again side by side, ascending the great staircase from the entrance hall.

7. *Oooo! You're rude!*

CHAPTER VII

Goats, Pranks and Discovery

THE PRECEDING CHAPTER was to have been wholly about children. It ended with pigs. An education concerned with reality is full of paradox and surprising confrontations. Now for thoughts about the oscillation of spirit we experienced, the laughter and tears, the evidence of good and evil.

The attempt to establish a caring community soon meets the contrast between the affection and need that draw people together and the insensitiveness and intransigence that drive them apart. Exasperation can result from the cumulative effect of the trivial, such as the fact that hitherto house-trained people will become thoughtless in community and leave a hot coffee mug on the polished surface of a piano – an act that would have angered them in their own home. They become careless about the condition of loos and wash-basins. More serious, they can do destructive things to each other, stirring up a trivial chip-on-the-shoulder to become an intensely paranoid attitude, which is then projected on to anyone in authority. One person can become parasitic on another and sap energy, destroying trust and loyalty overnight.

What is happening in the community experiments of the seventies? Do they find, as we did, that women adjust themselves less happily to communal living and tend to draw their husbands into the tension they create? When the School became less of a commune and more of an established boarding school, with more leisure and better accommodation for staff, women were then more at home in the School and gave energy and understanding generously to it.

Frances and I often felt inadequate to deal with the problems of relationship among the adults, and sometimes felt resentful about the deflection of our energy and attention away from the children. We had to remind ourselves that these two areas were not in fact separate, but intimately related. Like the other married couples, we had only one room to call our own, and there were many occasions when we retired to it, slammed the door, flopped on to the bed and wondered why on earth we had made ourselves responsible for this crazy venture. We were always restored by some expression of liveliness or affection in the children, the calm reliability of a particular man or woman, or an unexpected development in someone hitherto unresponsive.

Sometimes stress was so mingled with the ridiculous that we almost laughed and cried at the same time. Such an occasion was the slaughtering of the pigs after they had reached an enormous size. We decided that this ought to be done but did not anticipate that the local butcher would do it on the day before the beginning of term. So while the parents were arriving with their children, Frances and I stood looking in dismay at the kitchen table, covered with about four hundredweight of dead pig, in bits.

A local farmer gave us instructions on salting and I had a good stock of potassium nitrate in the lab wherewith to pack the bone marrow. So we set to work with a sack of salt and all that pig – not to mention brains and blood – having to wipe our hands now and then as we rushed from pig to parent. It was a hectic occasion but followed by a period of enormous gastronomic pleasure. Much had to be eaten immediately and for a week or two the school (with the exception of the vegetarians) lived on roast pork, including the most delicious liver we had ever tasted.

So much for pigs; but we also bought two goats. We had been told they were no trouble; their milk was always safe. The white one soon produced a kid which became a pet of the children and found its way round the School even to the extent of going tittuping up the stairs to the dormitories. We set about milking the mother; she gave milk reluctantly and after a pint had collected in the pail she either kicked it over or put her dirty hind feet in it. Only my secretary proved capable of handling her. My letters had to wait.

The other goat, a big Saanen, began to ail. I went into the outhouse. It lay there utterly inert. It had had a copious evacuation and I saw what was wrong; its gut was a mass of intestinal worms. It died a few hours later. That night the art master and I dug a deep grave on the bank behind the School and when it was ready we lifted the gaunt leaden corpse out of the filth on to a hurdle and staggered out with our burden through the postern gate. The sky was an appropriate back-drop for tragedy. The battlements were silhouetted against black storm clouds driven by a north-westerly across a fitful moon. As we tilted the hurdle, the corpse hit the bottom of the grave with a sickening thud that echoed in one's own belly.

How ambivalent we are about children's pranks! A headmaster can become so tired that he feels it needs only one more thing to make him go and jump into the river. When it happens he feels almost murderous. But three months later he is telling the story gleefully as though he wouldn't have missed it for worlds. One boy, the trout-tickler, was always up to something. The main boys' dormitory was on the first floor and under it an equally big room in which the girls slept. He was mainly responsible for the hole punched in the floor through which jets of water were frequently squirted from bicycle pumps. His worst misdemeanour was more serious. Our fire alarm was a policeman's whistle. One night he stole the whistle and after dark he blew it vigorously. The girls beneath them all filed out hastily on to the cold dark terrace while the boys gurgled with sadistic satisfaction between the warm blankets.

I had enough of that boy. I sent a telegram to his parents warning them I was sending him home. They replied with a long telegram, begging me to give him another chance. By that time I had cooled down, and feeling stupidly soft, relented. I never had cause to regret that I kept him; he became one of the most intelligent and thoughtful of our pupils, and one of the several good professional artists the School produced. Nevertheless, I said to the School that the one clear cause for expulsion was any action that endangered the lives of others: and a prank that cast doubt on the genuineness of fire alarms was in that category.

Our great staircase was an impressive part of the building and had its temptations to mischief-makers. One day there was a yell from the top and a large laundry basket came slithering and bumping with tremendous noise from the top to the bottom. It didn't remain quite still on the hall floor. I opened it and found inside a boy curled up, miraculously unhurt. But generally speaking there was little misbehaviour of a malevolent nature during those early years. More than a year passed without a theft; then a boy stole half-a-crown but did it so clumsily that I quickly identified him. A great deal of aggression was worked off in the wooded slope behind the School. There were many dens, dug out in the earth, covered with scraps of corrugated iron, surrounded with stockades and firing points.

Tents were put up for sleeping out. There were two clusters in front of the building separated by fifty yards, one for boys, the other for girls. One evening a boy unknowingly provided a charming entertainment. The staff had come up to our room to drink coffee, about sunset. Looking out of the window, I saw a boy wriggle out of his tent and move like a snake through the tall grass towards the girls' tents. I called the rest of the staff and there we all stood, looking down on the young Scot, so intent that he never thought of looking up. He was carrying something in his hand that we could not identify. He paused for a moment at the opening of the girl's tent and then began his wriggling journey back. In the morning I walked casually past that girl's tent looking out of the corner of my eye. There in the opening was a rose, standing in water in a baked bean tin.

Sometimes I unintentionally provided humour myself. When I first took up bee-keeping, I was unafraid and opened the hive clad in shirt and shorts. But I bought an additional stock, arriving in a box by rail. Completely self-confident I opened the box in front of an empty hive. Those bees were not friendly. They dive-bombed me in mass formation. I transferred the combs and ran, my face black with bees. After three days of enforced seclusion the headmaster who emerged was still hardly recognizable.

Another incident was more public and the cause of more hilarity. A charming young woman I knew slightly had applied for a teaching post. I met her train in Lancaster and we got on to the Wennington branch train by jumping into the last carriage just as it moved. It was a long train and several coaches did not reach the platform at Wennington. I assumed that it would move up and stop again, but as we passed his cabin, the signalman saw me, leaned out and yelled: 'It's not going to stop again. Pull the cord!' No doubt many railway passengers have shared my life-long desire to do just that, and I yanked on the cord with glee. We heard the brakes hissing but perhaps the driver did not realize what was happening, for the locomotive puffed all the harder. Eventually the train did come to a halt, about half-a-mile above the station. The Wenning river ran alongside the line with a clear pool deep enough for bathing. The School used it when they couldn't be bothered to go all the way down to the Lune. It was full of boys and girls that afternoon and the train stopped opposite.

I leapt down on to the line. If you have never done this you will not realize how far the footboard is above the ground on an embankment. I looked up at the girl hesitating far above me; and held out my arms: 'Come on, jump'. Skirts at that time were not very long and they were wide. She jumped and I caught her. There were yells of joy from the bathers. The guard was stumbling down the line towards us, bursting with anger. I argued, of course, that the signalman was the final authority. It took some time to live down the teasing that followed. Such humorous events helped us through, but if you recognize that we were only up to 7s. 6d. a week in pay by 1944 and had saved no money whatever to safeguard the future of the School, that we owned no furniture or kitchen equipment, you will understand that our spirits were sometimes plunged into depression.

However, most of the time we left the material future to take care of itself, for after all, until the German reversal at Stalingrad, we did not know if there would be a future for any of us. What preoccupied us was the need of tomorrow and next week. This depended so much on finding a creative way of dealing with the unpredictability of human beings on whom 'community' was making heavier demands than ever had to be faced in a private home and ordinary work. For those in our present world who see the establishment of communities as a remedy for the alienation of man in the impersonal corporate state, I would say: Yes, have a go at it! But be ready for the discovery that *alius,* the other person, can be terrifying when you are thrust together with him, and you can be terrifying to him. We are all born ambivalent, to hate as well as love, to reject as well as accept, to hurt as well as caress. The dark side, the Shadow of Jungian terminology, is always there within us. We can't expel it or destroy it; we have to come to terms with it so that it no longer threatens our conscious purposes and may even offer us its energy. This is what we human beings are like; to wish our nature were otherwise and that we were wholly loving and co-operative, is to render ourselves incapable of dealing constructively with the jungle we call humanity.

In the early bulletins there were often references to tiredness; and we saw that it is not weariness of body that destroys a man, but weariness of spirit. There were times when our shoulders seemed to be carrying all the weight of the universe and our energy insufficient to do the least thing properly. At other times we did much more work with less fatigue and less impatience. Occasionally at the worst times I went off with a spade or a seed box and came back with a vast weight lifted. This is what an act of religious worship ought to do. It is what we claim for a Friends' Meeting – but how often it falls short of it! In facing innumerable practical emergencies the emphasis had been thrown almost wholly on the aspect of our faith expressed in: 'By their fruits ye shall know them' – that is, by the way they clean lavatories, prepare meals, sweep floors and care for each other. That must always be the final test, but it is not the whole of life.

I see that in one bulletin we dared to mention God, and almost apologized for this. In some progressive circles it was then, and still is, embarrassing to find God mentioned, almost indecent.

(April 1943)

> We have gone a long way on our spiritual reserves, but to avoid the weariness of spirit that sometimes assails each one of us, we must achieve a deep and common consciousness of God. This statement could easily be misunderstood. It is not that we have to make a common admission about the place of God in the universe, arrived at by argument. No, we have to achieve an awareness of God working in history and in our lives. Real education is founded on a stubborn faith, making it possible to struggle against the tide of destruction that sweeps through humanity both in peace and in war. In some that faith is implicit, but there comes a time when it

> must be consciously realised and confessed if our strength is to be adequate. This consciousness gives us direction. Mere 'progressiveness' gives no sense of direction, only an illusion of it. In this we see the weakness of progressive schools in general, where their philosophy fails. Our community has to go a long way before this common faith is achieved and recognized. There is no short cut. Ordinary methods of convincement and persuasion do not apply to the situation. It must be the result of a search and an accepted discipline. A consequence of these conclusions is that if they are right they limit the extent to which this system of education can be imagined to spread. If its success depends upon the shared experience of a closely linked community, what hope can there be of it in large schools established by an edict from above and not from a common impulse? Perhaps there can be no real development in education until the whole country has passed through an experience that gives its people a new social consciousness and a sense of direction.

That was written thirty years ago and here we are in the seventies in a crisis of affluence, greed and stupidity, full of plans for social and educational *organization,* but perhaps no nearer to a sense of direction.

The discovery of direction and meaning was at the heart of our purpose: *discovery,* because that is how direction is found, the consciousness of it growing through accumulated experience. We were Christians, but we never offered a religious package deal backed with promises of simple solutions. The social projects of the thirties and the thinking that accompanied them had prepared us for the difficulties that human nature throws up when anything new is expected of it.

More will be said later about direction in education; but for the moment it should again be made clear that we were not hoping for the realization of some ideally chosen objective. It is stupid and injurious to direct a community, or society in general, towards a social plan if you do not know whether it is related to the kind of being man is. What we were trying to do was to enable adults and children together to discover what it would mean to have life abundantly, to be fulfilled, to live creatively. We often referred to the development of awareness and sensitiveness: to the need to know yourself and the world and to know how to direct your energies without blundering and exploitation. *Direction,* therefore, was more concerned with something growing and intuitive, with movement over the terrain you could see, rather than the reaching of a distant peak.

Religion is often thought of as something that is either left out of life or added to it. Some may look upon it tolerantly as a lubricant of social life, one that with more rationality can be improved. To us, religion was not something we could have or not have. It was the wholeness of our effort, the endeavour to deepen all our relationships, to achieve insight and free ourselves from fear of the world and each other, to accept all that came to us as the kind of experience for which human life was made.

If it had not been for the mid-week Friends' Meeting held at the School, the adults would never have held together. To that meeting came several Quakers from Bentham, including among them Charles Ford, who ran a silk-weaving mill in Bentham. His own experience made it possible for him to understand ours. He had long ago turned his own business over to profit-sharing and he expected little for himself; he and his wife lived simply and he never owned a car – he always bicycled to work. His life was a demonstration of his repudiation of capitalist ethics, of getting rich on the work of others. A simple, lovable man of great integrity, never evasive or defensive. Yet he had found that to abandon the normal owners' control of a works had by no means solved all the problems of human co-operation. Normally the director of a business, though aware of criticism and hostility, can to some extent shut off the impact of these from himself. But Charles Ford, stepping down from a position of power, became vulnerable and had to take the impact of the still unresolved tensions in human personality. He never regretted this; it was a creative situation although often a painful one.

He and his friends from Bentham came every Wednesday evening to sit with us in Quaker worship, bringing with them steadiness and affection. Often the hour was wholly silent but in it we were helped to face our own tensions; our problems did not melt away but we learnt to accept them with greater humility and courage. When we would otherwise have become fragmented in individualistic defensiveness we learnt to live with our difficulties with more compassion for each other.

CHAPTER VIII

From Despair to Renewal

IT WAS WITH THE INITIAL HELP of Charles Ford that we solved the problem of the School's constitution; he referred us to his brother, Gervase Ford, a leading solicitor in Leeds. Although my wife and I were, like every one else, receiving only a few shillings a week, one parent was circulating a rumour that I was 'making thousands'. So in 1944, we were turned into a non-profit-making limited company registered as a Charity and several members of the Advisory Council became the unpaid Directors of the Company and Governors of the School, under the Chairmanship of Professor John Macmurray, who had been watching closely what we were doing and visiting the School when possible.

This was a bold move in view of the fact that we were given notice early in the year to vacate the building at the end of it and that we had no money in reserve and hardly any household furnishings and equipment of our own. The Grey Court Fellowship, owners of Wennington Hall, were hoping the war would end in 1945 and that the building would once more be a holiday centre.

How could we have dared to think that this venture could survive, this small school of only sixty pupils occupying such an insignificant position in the whole pattern of national education? I went so far as to put our problem before Mr. Lester Smith, Director of Education for Manchester, and Sir Percy Meadon, the Director for Lancashire. Both showed real interest and the latter invited me to Preston giving me a large part of his day. These men could not materially help us but were emphatic that there was a place for independent educational effort of this sort and we were encouraged to think that there might come a day when practical co-operation with national education would be possible.

So we struggled on. The war had taught us to live without security but with irrepressible hope; and the experience of a community – for all its difficulties and disillusionments – had given us strength.

We were also driven by our feelings of responsibility for the children. The responsibility had become an intimate one; it could hardly have been greater if they had been members of our own family. To close the School would have been to deprive many children of the only stable family life – if it could be called that – and the only security they had known. I included in the February 1944 bulletin an illustration of this fact, in an account written by Frances, of her attempt to help two girls.

> Gretel and Jane – these are not their real names – had been troublesome all day. In the evening they were reported to me as being in a hysterical condition. They came to our room weeping, both tense and one pale and shaking. 'What is it?' I asked gently. Gretel burst into louder sobs for a moment, and then said that she had been bottling it up all the term and couldn't hold it in any more. 'I want to murder everyone in the world and start afresh with just Mummie and myself'. It soon came out that recent removal to the outskirts of London had taken her parents into the raid area, and Gretel had experienced a great deal of frightening noise in the last holidays. 'I could bear it better if I could be there with her' she said. Gretel is eleven, a lovable, passionate, and most interesting child. Jane, aged nine, having heard Gretel's outburst had associated herself with her. 'I feel that too' she said. This child went through an agony of distress last term; in her background there is the tragedy of a broken home, the all-too-common story of moral standards crumbling in the social chaos of war. For a while I sent her away and talked to Gretel alone.
>
> Gretel was emphatic that the world was horrible; it was going all wrong, and there was nobody worth keeping. 'I should like to start it all over again with a new Pandora's box that we could keep shut' she said. We sat quiet for a little, and then I began to tell her about all the good that has happened in war-time, in spite of the war, sometimes even because of it; some little children being cared for as never before in hostels and nursery schools, doctors discovering new ways of fighting infection, ambulance men going out to rescue the wounded under fire, plans and hopes for rebuilding towns. 'Evil is so noisy,' I said, 'with its bombs and murder, and good is so quiet that it is easy to miss it!' 'But the balance is all wrong' she said. So then I spoke about the balance of good and evil in oneself, how each one can overcome evil impulses and encourage good ones: how she has been sent to safety by her parents in order that she might get ready to tip the balance over towards good when she is old enough to do a job in the world; that it is not as though she were helpless. It is just people like this sensitive far-thinking little girl who, lovingly directed, will feel the greatest responsibility as they grow older. I pointed out that her idea of murdering everybody would be a bad start – that Pandora's box was unreal, since

evil is not in a box or let out of a box; it is in oneself, to be understood there; and it was not an impossible thought that she could begin now to build up the sum of good in the world.

These ideas about doing something definite to help determine the future seemed to be just what she needed. She told me in her emphatic way, next day, that she felt much happier. The other child is much harder to help. How can one comfort a little girl who suspects so terribly that her mother no longer loves her? The thought is not put into words, but it is behind all her anxiety and tears. In her association with Gretel's violent imagery there is a disillusion that is terrible in a child of nine. This child was brought to me the next night after a bout of lonely weeping in the bathroom. Her small hands wrung each other ceaselessly as she talked and wept. I held her on my knee, giving her as much love and comfort as she could accept from a woman who was not the lost Mummy. We collected together what little comfort we could. We tried to translate together the meaning of 'Absence is no divider of hearts', trying to help her to understand the need to keep her own love alive. How much worse it would be if she herself had not this loving heart, if she didn't care. We sat for a long time by the fire until she felt a little warm and comforted, and her restless hands were quiet in mine. Yet this child looks happy enough, almost carefree during the day. Both these children have great courage and potential character. How can we make their suffering, cruel in children so young, a means of strength and not a weapon that strikes them down?

As we watched Jane biting her nails and twisting her fingers in misery, trying desperately to be brave and hold back her tears, we realized that here was the responsibility we could not lay down. If the School closed, for that child the last thing that had any permanence and her only friendships would be gone.

There were many other children to whom the School was necessary. A deeply hurt child was a refugee Jewish boy who had seen a horrible demonstration of public cruelty to Jews and later seen his own parents torn from the home never to return. Though this was a few years after the event, he was still suffering from bewildered distress, unable to give himself to anything. We tried to cheer him up, to tell him all that was past; now he was loved and he could get on with life. This had no effect whatever on his frustration. It was a Jewish psychiatrist, himself a refugee, who helped us to understand his need.

You are doing all the wrong things, he said. You want him to forget, when what he needs to do is to remember and assimilate the past. He needs a catharsis. He needs to feel and to pour out his grief. You say he doesn't ever cry; then talk to him, help him to feel and help him to cry. It worked. I would not say that he recovered fully from the abominable injury done to him. But he certainly became happier.

There was another consideration in the matter of survival: the possible value of the School as an educational and social experiment, a piece of research. It had not reached a stage when we could draw conclusions as to the success and possible extension of our system. Of some things we were certain; and the development of the School had been steady enough to give us a vision of what the School could achieve when some of its worst difficulties were surmounted. But as an example to form a basis of practice for others it had not gone far enough yet. If it came to an end now, it would have no significance for the rest of the educational world; it would be significant only for what it had achieved in the minds of those who worked in it. We who started it would be able to look back upon it as a personal discipline and a valuable experience, but would feel about its objective value as a laboratory research worker would who saw the work of four years destroyed by an untimely explosion.

In one group – the children who came to us at the age of eight, three years ago – we were beginning to see results. This group was outstanding for the vigour of their thought, for their application to work even when unsupervised, and especially for the quality of their feeling and imagination. In their work we had closely woven general history with the history of religion, and they had a rich background of myth and folk-lore. It was this group that in an earlier stage lived so fully in the story of the Iliad, and made it an educational project. Their writing showed unusual understanding and power of emotional expression. We looked upon this group as representative of what our School could do, and we longed to be able to keep them with us to see whether they came through adolescence without losing their confidence in us, without wasting energy in inner conflict, knowing how to use their freedom to creative ends. We felt that they would, but we had to know, if we were ever to make any claims for our education. It was not only necessary that the School should not be closed but that this group should not be reduced or broken up by the difficulties of re-establishment. Among other things we had to retain the parents' confidence in our ability to carry on in new circumstances without the quality of our education suffering.

Trying to face the uncertainty – often in the middle of the night – we could only shudder, as though we were about to embark on an adventure in which all our lives were in danger. The attitude of the boys and girls was heartening. We did not at first tell them directly that we had to look for a new building but soon they suspected and had to be told. They began to look forward to it as a pioneering adventure, and to hope that the great trek would take place in middle of a term, not in the holidays. Some of them, we were sure, would gladly have slept on the bare floor of an empty house if it had been necessary. So without material resources, we went on hoping and began even to think of mortgage – with not a penny to deposit. We felt like Moses, who could keep the tide of battle in his favour only when his friends held up his hands on either side. We had our friends, but so far no money.

We were nagged by the difficulty of maintaining an adequate staff. We begged our friends to help us find replacements for those who had to leave. Just at this critical time we lost the Bedales sixth-former who had come to help us – a tireless and endlessly versatile young man who had taken over all the handicraft teaching as though he had been born to it, who could cope with any repair work in wood or metal and plunged happily into any emergency. He was a conscientious objector, and when he went before the Appeal Tribunal, which I had hitherto respected for its wise decisions, he was directed to do land work. It seemed an irreparable loss.

Although I laughingly told house agents we hadn't any money, they provided information about country seats for sale. Frances and the Senior Master held the fort while I travelled widely. Wartime train services were poor; I went as far as I could by train and plodded the rest of the way by bicycle. I squelched through floods to reach Kipling Hall. The Army had used it and left unmistakable traces. Any new tenant had to guarantee to take care of the old masters that covered its walls. No – not for us!

There was a big house up in the remoter Lune valley, again with a plethora of paintings. Amazingly, that house had a private zoo and an elephant in it. Fascinating to me was the fact that far above it was a lake and down the steep slope came a penstock feeding water into a high pressure Pelton wheel. So the house had its own hydro-electric generating station. That would have been fun to manage. Then we heard of a really marvellous place – Gisburn Park, not far away, with its own railway station. 1,000 acres of farmland and the river Ribble, full of salmon, running through its woods! The price was only £100,000. Call it a million by present values. We thought it would be fun to inspect, and off we went. A beautiful building just about the size we wanted, with a glorious octagonal central hall with pillars covered in gold leaf. We came away from our dreams comforting ourselves with the thought that if we had been able to occupy it we should have lost several children by drowning, for the Ribble was deep and fast; there was a weir and a mill-race and dark depths of menacing water.

The year wore on with continuing uncertainty. We obtained a postponement of the notice to quit; we could now remain until the summer of 1945. One day a parent, an enterprising business man, called on Frances and they began talking about the problem of buying a building. We had hoped to offer for a building and perhaps 20 acres of land if we could borrow the money. The parent then explained that this was not the way to go about it. It was possible to buy a building without any money. We should boldly undertake to 'buy' a building with a large agricultural estate, get someone to lend us the ten per cent deposit necessary to hold it for a month and in the meantime put the farm land to auction in the hope that sale of this would provide a large part of the purchase money. Ingmanthorpe Hall, near Wetherby, well suited to our purposes, was for sale at £36,000. But what about that ten per cent? Just when that problem seemed insurmountable, the parent of a pupil telephoned to ask if we could make use of £3,000.

We did not go ahead with this hair-raising scheme without the assurance from our solicitor that it was a reasonable procedure. Then we plunged in. Our agent got the price reduced to £26,000, and we put down the £2,600 deposit. The farm was quickly sold for £14,500 and a detached bit of land for £1,250. Now it seemed that the net cost to us of the house and remaining 80 acres was to be about £10,000. But there was another reliable asset, mature timber, beech and sycamore, in the 30 acre wood. My agent came to me with a pleased face and said he thought there would be at least £500 worth, but he had yet to measure it up. By the end of a week with a measuring tape, it had become £3,000 worth. That reduced the expected net cost to £7,000, and my good Quaker lawyer had no difficulty in persuading Barclays Bank, on the security of the remaining estate and building, to advance that sum. In fact it provided twice as much, to enable us to make alterations and additions, especially for the housing of staff and essential furnishings. So that is how we acquired all we needed without any money of our own.

The whole prospect changed for us, from the seemingly inevitable closure of the School to the opening out of a new phase. The effect on the spirit of the School can be imagined. So many other clouds were lifted at the same time. The war in Europe came to an end and the black-out was lifted. At night we switched on everything in Wennington Hall and all the School trooped out into the field below the building to gaze in ecstasy at the light pouring freely through every window on to the terrace, the trees and the bushes. In anticipation of this we had been collecting old timber and great quantities of dead brushwood from the wood behind the School and we were able to light an enormous bonfire round which we all capered until we dropped from exhaustion.

The children's wish to take part in the removal could not be gratified, for obvious reasons. The summer term had to end earlier than usual. Our goods filled eleven loads and we were surprised by the amount of school property we had acquired in four years. The worst complications were the beehives of which I now had several. I had closed them the night before but when I lifted them I was furiously attacked and had to run for it. In two of them, wood had shrunk underneath, leaving gaps just big enough for the bees to emerge. I ran to the house for my smoker, gloves and veil, only to find that by mistake the removers had taken them with the previous loads. I had to do something. I cut two holes in a small cotton flour sack and put it over my head. On top of that I put on a gas-mask – the more elaborate type with a corrugated tube emerging from the mouth piece. Thus armoured I went down the staircase, passing on the way a group of visitors who had, unknown to me, come to inspect the building. Their eyes recorded bewilderment. I identified the cracks and late that night sequeezed in wet clay from the pottery (very useful for beekeepers in this kind of emergency). I travelled with the hives the next day, holding my breath; but there were no further escapes.

When we transferred the School to Wetherby, we decided not to break the link with the past by adopting a wholly new name. We simply dropped one word, and Wennington Hall School became Wennington School. The decision would have been different had we known that Wennington Hall was not destined after all to become a guest house again, but to be purchased by four county boroughs and reopened as a school wholly for maladjusted children. For a few years there was occasional confusion because of the similarity of names.

Ingmanthorpe Hall was a very different kind of building. It was basically Georgian though built in Victorian times, and it stood on the site of manors dating back to Domesday Book. We had bought it from a Leeds brewer who had lavished a great amount of money on its interior. It was in immaculate condition. There were about thirty-five rooms in the main building and behind there was a large courtyard surrounded by many stone-built garages and horse boxes; still further behind that more rows of horse boxes, for with the Wetherby race-course opposite the drive entrance, the wealthy owner had made horses a hobby. I might have been worried about the temptations of the race-course, but my mind was eased by the fact that the drive was a mile long.

There was a big room, large enough for whole-school assembly and dining, that had been called the music room; it was very high, large windowed, facing south and west. Opening from the other side of the entrance hall there was the ideal headmaster's study. But what caught our imagination when we first inspected the building was the recently built swimming pool, elaborately paved and terraced, surrounded by rose pergolas and ringed with lamp sockets for fairy lights – which had presumably been switched on only in pre-war days. We traced an electric circuit running right down to the 30 acre wood over a hundred yards away; evidently this orgy of romantic lighting had been carried right in among the beeches. The pool had three big central heating boilers to warm it and a large circulation and chlorinating plant feeding a fountain beyond the west end of the pool.

The interior counterpart to this luxury was the so-called onyx bathroom, the most outrageously lavish among the several expensively built bathrooms. It had a huge marble bath, fit for a Roman Emperor: three feet deep, made like a miniature swimming pool with steps and chromium plated hand rails leading down into it. It was edged all round with green onyx and beyond that the room was paved with black marble and surrounded by walls of pink Carrara. The use of large mirrors made the room seem to extend endlessly in all directions. In corners there were a shower and a bidet. We were told that all this had cost £4,000, pre-war.

On the last evening of the removal I heard a riot going on in this bathroom. I walked round to it and swept open the door. There in the water, with their heads and shoulders emerging, were the eight van drivers and assistants! The snag about that bath was the fact that it used up, in one go, the entire supply of hot water. The next time I heard the noise of communal enjoyment in that bathroom was just after the beginning of term. Then it was the heads and shoulders of all the older girls, their eyes glowing with wonder and excitement. They had not asked permission of course, and no one else got a bath that night.

We tried advertising and selling that bathroom. £4,000 bathroom for sale! Call that thirty or forty thousand – the modern equivalent – and you will realize the stir it made. It became a radio joke and was printed in the *New Statesman's 'This England.'*

We could laugh with a little superior detachment at all this luxury, but the gardens overwhelmed us with delight. Acres of orchard, a one acre walled garden with what seemed like a hundred yards of greenhouses along the north end. Ten vines in one half. Four great peach trees fanned out under the glass in the other half. Nectarines on the walls, and at one end – oh joy! – a fig tree with its suggestively shaped leaves covering a great quantity of small – but growing – green fruit.

Few of us got any time away from the building that summer. Beds and bed-linen had been ordered, dining tables were being made, stacking chairs were on the way. We went to auction sales to get chests of drawers quickly and cheaply. Builders came to start building downstairs lavatories and flats over the garages. We were lucky in that the mother of one of the girls was the director and owner of a Leeds building firm; she had put up a great deal of much needed housing in Leeds and could take over our smaller projects without delay.

There was a centrally placed room on the first floor with a balcony overlooking the terrace to the south. It was a delightful room but had been called the boudoir – which literally means sulking place. Somehow it got called our drawing room. That, of course, strictly means withdrawing room. Sometimes we used it for that purpose but much of the time it was the social focus of the School; we certainly tried to make it a place of welcome for everybody. My paintings were ready to go on the walls, but furniture was a bit scrappy. Later, when Mr. Ercolani became a Wennington parent we had the aesthetic satisfaction of furnishing it wholly with Ercol furniture, which just suited it.

We had to sell those huge peaches; they fetched half-a-crown each, and at the best as much as 7s. 6d. The only difficulty was getting them in to the luxury shops in Leeds and Harrogate. I made many journeys with a carefully packed crate in each hand. We needed the money!

It is bewildering to recall how during the summer and autumn after the end of the war we began to buy and plan, and to recognize that the ability to do so had been created out of nothing, by human goodwill. We had at once to put in labour-saving machinery – Aga stoves, electric mixer and dishwashing machine – and to begin to convert stables and garages into classrooms. The stables were already on the central heating system; and they were lined with heavy pitch pine which, when stripped off, was sufficient for all the new window frames and other necessary joinery. There was already an estate workshop and a large circular saw, so we had all the amenities for using our own materials. Everything seemed to be happening suddenly and progressing fast.

8. Ingmanthorpe Hall

9. The youngest enjoy a communal bath in the fabulous bathroom

10. A great harvest of grapes — Muscat and Hamburgh

11. Before mains water came, we used a submersible in a deep well. When it failed, the water squad had to pump water from one roof tank to another

12 and 13. Juniors provide an impromptu entertainment

CHAPTER IX

The Surge Forward

THE BEGINNING OF THE AUTUMN TERM was hilarious. The boys and girls had not seen the building; they had only had it described to them. They rushed all over it. There was an internal telephone system connecting the bigger rooms and a push-button call system that worked indicators near the kitchen. The first thing the boys and girls did was to press every push button – so that the bell in the domestic corridor rang continuously and every indicator on the huge board was kept wagging until the transformer was switched off.

We brought sixty pupils to the new building and within a term we had a prospect of thirty more. But never before had we been so badly staffed. The senior master and his wife had returned to state school teaching and we had only two fully qualified teachers of secondary subjects apart from myself. The children weren't worried; they were busy exploring all their new opportunities and everything for them was exciting. Huge sycamore, beech and oak trees were being felled in the wood and dragged out by tractors, a daily dramatic spectacle. There was a big flat field ready for games – we'd had only an undulating and rock-infested one at Wennington Hall – and the boys almost unanimously chose soccer, which then flourished without needing staff organization. When we had mastered the running of the motor driven chlorinator and filter the swimming pool came into use and several boys and girls responded to my challenge to a dip at 7 a.m.

The January term brought new difficulties. For the first time – and the only time for many years to come – we were smitten with epidemics: flu, chickenpox and scarlet fever. Flu knocked out several adults, and it was one of the rare occasions when, though still on my feet, I was confined to our room for a day or two. My wife, who had already taken on the work of two matrons and was beginning to ail herself, called the remnants of the School together. She explained that the ship had lost most of its officers, including the captain, who would soon be followed by the mate, and that the crew must now appoint its own officers and run the ship. A Committee of twelve was immediately formed by the boys and girls, certain members directed to take charge of classes, others to help the senior Matron, who was just about to return to work. I was soon in action again, but there was no need to take charge; for the next fortnight the children ran the School without any serious lapses. Their organization was excellent and the experience was enjoyed by all. We were being carried through a period of great difficulty by a tremendous wave of energy and confidence in the children.

About this time there was a growing enthusiasm for music. It was difficult to provide enough pianos for those who wanted to learn; four out of ten children were learning piano or violin and we found a superb wind teacher, who continued in the School for twenty-five years until his retirement. At that time symphony concerts were broadcast regularly on Sunday afternoons and our drawing room floor was usually covered with prostrate listeners. There was yet more help from visiting musicians. Paul Hamburger and Esther Salaman were coming nearly every term, giving us week-ends of almost continuous music, piano and singing. Paul was always asked to play the Waldstein Sonata; performed by him it was a specially moving experience and it was listened to with the closest attention. Esther sometimes sang over forty songs in an evening performance, responding to request after request. Such was their personal relationship with the children that the latter did not feel they were being played at but included in the act of musical creation.

The hunger for music and startling development of musical sensitivity was illustrated by the memorable occasion when the B.B.C. broadcast Toscanini conducting Beethoven's Ninth Symphony. A large number wanted to hear this. The drawing room was in darkness save for the dim light from the radio and the floor was packed tight with pyjama-clad boys and girls lying wrapped in their rugs and listening. Three of them fell asleep in the third movement with their heads pillowed on the marble curb and at the end we tiptoed out smiling in amusement at the angelic sleeping faces of three boys, who in their waking life we all knew were far from angelic. Another occasion was the broadcast of the Messiah; three quarters of the School wished to listen. We put the loudspeaker in the entrance hall at the bottom of the staircase well, so that bed-putting could go on as usual and children could listen as they took their baths in silence. It was an impressive sight looking down from the top of the house, to see boys and girls in their dressing gowns sitting on all levels of the stairs or standing silently in the semi-darkness of the landings. Gradually, at the appointed times, they slipped away to bed, there to listen through the open dormitory doors. To some people I am sure it would have made ours seem a crazy school.

During the summer of 1946 we held our first Parent's Day. The weather was appalling but the building was thronged with parents and other visitors; it was difficult to move about. We had been at work on a project that involved the co-operation of all the subject teachers: to show by charts, maps, models, etc., how the essential needs of mankind were satisfied at five successive stages in history. The output by the children was tremendous and on Parents' Day the walls of the assembly room were covered with their work. The group that got to work most quickly was that studying the development of the legal systems; they immediately produced models of every instrument of correction, punishment and torture that history books and encyclopedias recorded. Even under the best conditions there remains a dark corner in a child's unconscious where sadistic impulses lie in wait! There were illustrative paintings of huge mural size, encouraging a vigorous broad treatment.

One day while the project work was in progress a local man called on business and was waiting in his car in the courtyard. I passed the time of day with him and he seemed puzzled, but amusedly so. 'Is this really a school? Doesn't look like one to me – the youngsters look too happy.' I invited him to take a look into the art room. What he saw there astonished him even more: about thirty boys and girls of all ages, furiously at work, whistling, humming or chattering, but not wasting a minute. It is interesting that the ordinary man, once he sees this sort of education, recognizes it as right and good, for this is the way any group of people in real life sets about a job. Only in the abstract or by unthinking habit does the common man respect the formal education of desks and drills and uncreative tasks. It is encouraging to remember that most of the parents were ordinary folk, a cross section of the people who carry out the essential work of the country, not the intelligentsia or the self-consciously emancipated. Few had boarding schools in their tradition. Most were reacting from the mass culture of the large secondary school, from its impersonal and institutional treatment of children, and they were seeking an education more personal, more inclusive, more practical, carried out in a social unit small enough for the child to comprehend and value.

I once heard a representative of the Advisory Centre for Education in Cambridge describing the independent schools as places to which middle-class parents could send their children so that they would be educated only with children of their own class. This was never to be true of Wennington. We claimed to be a classless community and we took, with help of local authorities, children whose parents could never have afforded the fees.

Several paying parents were Yorkshire and Lancashire manufacturers. The use of adults' Christian names did not seem so odd to them, for it happened in their own works, and their experience disposed them to understand the close relationship between *thinking* and *doing* that we practised. We encouraged them to feel they were part of the venture and several responded in a useful way. Rolls of cloth began to arrive, substandard but excellent for our purpose, ranging from canvas suitable for stage backcloths to patterned material for curtains. Having seen the potholes in our long drive, a parent brought his road-workers over a weekend and filled them up. Redundant lathes arrived from engineering works, and for photographic blocks I could turn to one of the best photo-engravers in the North. A trawler skipper arrived one day with a huge halibut over his shoulder. A contribution of a different sort came from a mother who was the leader of one of those large choirs for which north-country towns are famous. She brought her whole choir.

The Parents' Day I have referred to was an encouraging experience, making us feel, as Professor John Macmurray emphasized in his speech as Chairman of the Governors, that the School was now really established. We knew we had the friendship of a large body of people, giving us confidence in making known to a wider public the fruits of our experience over the previous six years.

Early in the same year this statement had been made by the Minister for Education in the Labour Government, Ellen Wilkinson:

> The Minister also expresses the hope that there will be progressive development of full-time boarding school education, not only for those whose homes are for one reason or another unsatisfactory or remote from the type of education suitable for them, but also for those other pupils for whom, in the opinion of their parents and the local educational authority, boarding school education is desirable. (*Times Educational Supplement:* quoting Circular 90 of March 8th 1946.)

The Education Act of 1944 enabled local authorities to pay for boarding school education where it was desirable and some local authorities were planning boarding schools of their own. Wennington had a challenge to put to such authorities. Were they going to submit the under-privileged children to the experience of being 'guinea pigs' in schools for the privileged? Would their own boarding schools, with the lapse of time, become as middle-class and divisive as the Public Schools, which come under so much criticism on this score? Or would they recognize that in establishing boarding school education for those who would not otherwise get it, they had a unique opportunity to provide children from the anonymous, soulless conurbations with an experience of stimulating and responsible community life?

Trevor Huddleston, when Bishop of Stepney, commented on the contrast between the kind of social life he found among Africans when he was working in Kumasi and that of the East End people for whom he later became responsible. The Africans were by any British standard desperately poor but they were a community in the full personal sense of the word. The people living in the East End of London were increasingly being housed in vast concrete beehives, victims of an impersonal industrial culture, reduced to units and deprived of any encouragement to discover an identity.

Ivan Illich would say that the Eastenders were the victims of a manipulative society and that what we need is an education that restores an experience of the convivial, of doing things together as an expression of the spring of life that is within each human being, encouraged and developed by friendship and mutual responsiblity within a real community. Our experiences in the first few months of 1947 illustrate in a dramatic way what it means for a school to become a community in which all daily activities are inherently significant.

The winter of 1947 was a dramatic crisis for the whole country and for us specially exacting. For over two months deep snow lay and only for brief periods was our mile long drive passable. The few deliveries of coke were only a small fraction of the fuel supply necessary. But the 30 acre wood was littered with the lop-and-top left after the beech and sycamore trunks had been dragged out: every twisted branch, everything less than a foot in diameter. There it all lay, poking up from the drifts of snow, scattered among the white domes that hid the jungle of rhododendron.

In the course of an ordinary day's work we sometimes had doubts about independent boarding school education, twinges of conscience when we recognized how we had taken children out of their own environment and were trying to educate them away from their fellows. But the experiences of that winter term throw up in sharp contrast the opportunities that a boarding school provides. For the day school pupil the fuel emergency happened over his head. There was little he could do. 'They' were responsible and 'They' ought to put it right. He could be careful with electric light, do his homework in the kitchen with his coat on, or have an unexpected holiday if his school closed. But in the community of a boarding school, the emergency was an opportunity that of itself brought a training in social responsibility and initiative. Electricity and fuel consumption graphs, and the arithmetic involved, became significant in the crisis, and every department of the community's life came under review. The consumption of electricity fell to one-third in some weeks. As to provision of fuel, there was for the children something that could be *done.* During the whole of those two months we had to depend on wood. Every day there were groups out among the trees, cutting lop-and-top into suitable lengths, loading them on the 'Cronk' – our £12 lorry – and bringing them to the sawmill.

At first the shortage of saws was a problem, but after being told about the wood-frame bowsaws used on the Continent some boys set about making frames to take Bushman blades and in less than a day we had many saws ready for use. The work was tough, but the boys and girls worked with undiminished cheerfulness throughout the term. They worked knee-deep, often thigh-deep in snow, and sometimes, when the work was specially urgent, in blizzards. They wrenched branches from beneath the snow and out of frozen soil. Their wellingtons rarely had time to dry, so their feet were often wet; but they did not catch cold and health throughout the term was good. Sometimes our old lorry was out of order or had dug itself deep into drifts; then we turned out the whole school to carry the sawn-off branches. Several such days were interludes of bright sunshine, and it made a wonderful picture – the long line of a hundred or more boys, girls and staff moving to and fro over the winding track into the woods, some of the tougher seniors sharing a huge branch and here and there an eight-year-old hauling a toboggan load.

We got in at least a hundred tons of wood, but never keeping more than two days ahead of the furnaces' needs. It was a tremendous enterprise. As a physical achievement alone it was remarkable, but its ultimate value lay in the experience it brought to the children of dealing directly with an emergency, or carrying the School's upkeep in a literal sense on their own shoulders. Where else but in a small self-supporting boarding school could children get this experience of practical responsibility and have its value confirmed by results? Am I exaggerating its value? There is no conclusive answer to this question. One of the difficulties in educational research is that those qualities we most earnestly seek to develop are the ones we are least able to measure as results. Even twenty years hence when perhaps I shall be able to point to the careers and social action of old boys and girls, evidence will never be definite beyond doubt. Our assessment has to rest upon a faith that is in a sense religious: that a co-operative action for the good of the whole group, undertaken with enjoyment and fulfilled with satisfaction, provides one of the chief foundations of character.

Even in some of the winter's worst difficulties there was a great deal of fun. The pressure of snow sliding down the roof formed great slabs of ice

15 and 16. Fuel for the furnaces, 1947

completely blocking the wide gutters behind the parapet. When the intermittent thaws came, the water found its way up under the edge of the lead flashing, and poured into the buildings. Emergency squads at work on the roofs had the wettest and dirtiest work of all. One girl, the strongest of her group, found satisfaction in heaving great slabs of ice over the edge of the parapet to send them crashing on to the terrace below. With Heath-Robinson inventiveness we tried every sort of dodge for shifting ice, such as salt and hose-pipes with hot water, but muscle and physical endurance remained almost the only effective agents.

In the midst of all our strenuous activity and enjoyment we were not neglecting studies. The loss of a class every day in the fight for fuel did not slow down classroom progress, rather the reverse. Every school has to fight lethargy, to stir up life and eagerness. Anything that makes life as a whole more meaningful and calls for response, will act as a tonic to the mind. We were coming to the end of the School and Higher Certificate era, which was replaced in 1950 by 'O' and 'A' level G.C.E. Our examination results were good in spite of the fact that several pupils were not of 'grammar school ability'. In 1948, for instance, 66% of the subject marks were over the credit level. But we wanted a more discriminating and educational assessment of the quality of our work and therefore asked for a full inspection by the Ministry. This took place in the Summer Term of 1948.

It was a happy experience for the School and apparently for the inspectors. We avoided formality and asked the boys and girls to behave as naturally towards the inspectors as they did to us. As a result the inspectors easily got into personal touch with them. They taught some classes on their own and the boys and girls enjoyed this. On one occasion, when Frances was taking a class, the chief inspector, whose own subject was English, sitting at the back quietly wrote a sonnet and submitted it for examination by the class – a philosophical poem on the swimming pool, reflecting the life of the School.

The conduct of the inspection and the spirit in which it was carried out were most encouraging, giving one good reason for pride in this department of British educational administration. There was no tendency to criticize from an orthodox angle; the inspectors were as interested in progressive methods as we were and found reason to urge us still further forward. They came with no preconceived notion of what the School ought to be like, but with the desire to understand our aims and then to discover how far we were achieving them. As Mr. Allen, the Chief Inspector, said, what he wanted to do was to hold a mirror up to ourselves. We had claimed that an education was not just what happened in the classroom, but concerned the whole of our life in the school. So the group of inspectors came at 7 a.m. and sometimes left quite late, leaving their homework, as they called it, to be done in their hotel after a 12-hour day.

They brought in additional inspectors to discuss details of household organization. Their intention was not to criticize in a destructive way but to make sure that we knew and took advantage of all the special provisions made for schools, in, for instance, the matter of rations. They looked at the gardens and the woods and made suggestions for the further development of these as part of our educational plans. The scrupulous way in which everything was done is shown by the fact that no criticism of the work of other staff was made to me that had not been made to the staff themselves, no criticism made to the Governors that was not already made to me, and the Governors told of everything that was to be reported to the Ministry. Perhaps the most pleasing thing that the inspectors found was that our children accepted them in a fearless, friendly and direct way but without ever being cheeky. They were eager and responsive in class and conversation. It seemed that we had achieved basically what we set out to do. The inspectors thought, however, that we ought now to try to add more in the way of finish and style. If we could do this while preserving the basis, our children would be really outstanding in their personal quality. We agreed with this, and it was for us to find out how to do it. There was an interesting epilogue to the inspection. A fortnight after the general inspection was over it was announced in morning assembly that the art and craft inspector, who had not come before, was due to arrive in a few days. When it was said that Mr. Allen, the chief inspector of the panel, was coming again with him, a spontaneous cheer broke out.

The final result was that the School was recognized as efficient by the Ministry, in the grammar school category. This began to raise problems of the status of teachers and their salaries. We were still egalitarian, receiving two pounds a week each, and did not feel by any means poor. But it became difficult to replace teachers who left. A person who had not lived in the community could not imagine that it could be so carefree financially; he naturally wanted Burnham Scale and regular superannuation payments.

At the next Parents' Meeting two parents took this in hand: a Labour peer and the secretary of a trade union. They said it was time we paid proper trade-union wages and put a firm proposal to the assembled parents that the fees should be raised to make this possible. This was passed unanimously. It did have an effect on replies to advertisements of staff vacancies. Of this I was glad but my feelings were mixed with regret. We could not raise the pay of the domestic and house staff in the same proportion, for this would have been to make the cost of running the School intolerably high; but there was no definite evidence that this injured relationships.

We tried to maintain social unity between the teachers and the other staff. We wanted to avoid the social division that in other boarding schools encouraged pupils to speak of domestic staff with implied contempt. We kept the common room open to all comers, but at the time of 'elevenses' this broke down. The domestic staff – mainly women coming in daily from Wetherby – got there five minutes before the teaching staff and monopolized the newspapers for the whole twenty-five minutes, so that the teachers, who had collectively paid for the papers, could not read them. We had to arrange a later mid-morning break for the domestic staff!

Another traditional gap that we tried to bridge was that between the School and its Governing Body. We did not want the Governors to be distant V.I.Ps. who appeared once a term, made decisions about the School and vanished for three or four months. John Macmurray, the Chairman, was now heavily occupied, having moved from University College London to be Professor of Philosophy and Dean of Arts at Edinburgh. Nevertheless, he did find time to help build the shelves for our Library and always when he came for the termly meeting he continued to have meals with the staff and meet senior children for a discussion. He often also addressed the whole School on a Sunday evening. For a few years we were privileged to have Dr. Tylor Fox, a long-established friend and a Quaker, the pioneer in the treatment of epilepsy. Also near at hand was Dr. Alfred Schweitzer, then assistant to the Professor of Physiology at Leeds. He was a refugee who had become wonderfully anglicised, one of the most vital, intellectually brilliant and inspiring men I have ever known and it was a delight to have his enthusiastic stimulation while we were building up our science department. Before long he became Reader in Physiology at University College London but this did not lessen the contact. My own scientific interests were moving towards biochemistry and physiology and whenever I was in London I spent some time watching him at work in Gower Street – seeing, incidentally, some of the dramatic experiments, done on dogs, which contributed to the development of the heart-lung machine. Whenever he came to the School he was in the middle of everything: talking about his researches or about mountaineering and joining the School musicians in a string quartet.

In the summer term in 1952 he was doing all these things for a fortnight, staying with his family in the School. He spent much of the time swimming and helping advanced biology pupils with dissections. He left after that fortnight – it was just before the end of the term – making us all feel toned-up by his participation in our life. He went almost at once to climb in the French Alps with a friend. A week later I was sitting on our drawing room balcony watching the shadows of trees lengthening across the playing fields on a golden summer evening. The telephone rang: a lecturer from Leeds asking if I had any news of Alfred Schweitzer. 'No, why should I?' 'He's missing in the Alps; that's all I know. I hoped you'd know more.'

My son rang from London next morning. Alfred and his companion had been found frozen to death on a glacier below the summit of *La Meige.* They had been caught in an unexpected summer blizzard. With them there were the shreds of a nylon tent, and not far ahead the refuge hut they were no doubt making for but could not see. Our grief was almost uncontrollable. This, and profound shock, were shared by many others who knew him. For a while the future of the School seemed a blank; his fertile mind had contributed so much and together we had explored so many possibilities.

Some Governors were parents. Gertrude Bray was one – the woman builder whose advice and help was so useful. Another parent was Eric W. Cockcroft of the Todmorden textile firm and brother of the nuclear scientist. The Quaker element was well maintained; we had Alfred and Madge Bayes, well known in the civic and political life of Hyde, Reginald Cox, the Sheffield University mathematician who taught the pigs to jump, and Constance Dearlove, the Southampton teacher who came out of the blitz for a term. Later these were joined by David and Mary Medd, senior architects at the Department of Education and Science.

We were blessed for a while with the help of Hugh Leech, Senior History Tutor at Keele. He was one of those dons – there are not enough of them – deeply interested in the needs of students as persons. Hugh could never refuse a request for help and to sit in his room at Keele was to hear a succession of taps on the door. He took out of himself more than his body could stand and he died, like Alfred Schweitzer, all too young, when a host of people depended on him.

As time passed the School lost other Governors by retirement and new ones were added. A high level of expert knowledge was maintained but, because of the long distance the members had to travel, not such a degree of involvement in the life of the School.

CHAPTER X

Classwork and Community Jobs

To proceed with a strictly historical account would make this book too long. 1948 can be taken as the point when the School became established and took a form that remained stable at least in outline. What remains to be said is best dealt with in the form of topics. For some years the demand on children's time and energy in meeting the domestic and outdoor needs of the community remained unchanged. Later the amount of domestic work, especially in washing-up, was reduced because, so the argument went, the children were too tired by it. In the course of years, still further efforts were made to curtail it. Seen in the light of the School's whole history, however, the argument is open to doubt. Teenagers are always ready to look tired; but give them an incentive and they are capable of incredible feats. Further, the period round about 1950, before there was any reduction, was one of the outstanding peak periods of achievement, in academic work, music, drama and constructional work. There is no evidence that reduction of the community demand in later years released boys and girls for other achievements.

The day began at seven in the morning, some being roused to prepare vegetables, some plunging into the pool, a few doing both, going in and out of the water in one movement like dolphins and racing back half-dried in their dressing gowns. Others got up more sluggishly by 7.20, to sweep corridors, tidy up classrooms, see that pottery and workshops were ready for use, clean glassware in the laboratories, cycle to Wetherby for the papers – and perhaps even seize a moment to play a piano or an oboe. Breakfast was disorderly but quieter than most other meals; people dropped into chairs, ate quickly and were out – except a minority who sat slowly chewing slogs of bread and marmalade, deliberately infuriating the squad appointed to clear tables and sweep up crumbs.

Beds were made after breakfast and the dormitories swept. Assembly was at 8.45; it was a time for announcements, followed perhaps by poetry readings, a movement from a symphony, a psalm read not for its piety but for its poetry, a passage from the Gospels read in two different translations, or, once a week, a quarter of an hour's commentary on the news.

Our teaching time-table was not unorthodox: five periods in the morning and two or three in the afternoon, but with the outdoor time in the winter put after lunch, while there was daylight. After tea, at seven, the evening was flexible, within the system of assignments which, as explained earlier, was the permanent legacy of our attempt at the Dalton system. Instead of a piece of homework or prep to be done at a particular time, there was an assignment to be handed in after a fortnight. This system made it possible to ask for an element of research in the work; making use of library books and other resources, and it made it possible to fit drama rehearsals, debates, music practice and any other sporadic activity into an evening, without disturbance to classwork. Sixth-formers were encouraged in this assignment system, to behave as students rather than as school-children doing limited bits of work for particular occasions.

We sometimes asked ourselves why we were not more wholeheartedly enterprising in our teaching-learning system. Why were we not getting away from 'subjects' towards something nearer to real life and its problems? Weren't we in the classroom following habitual lines and failing to make contact with lively ideas being practised elsewhere?

To answer this, we said that we could not experiment on all fronts at once. The heavy demand made on the staff by the fearlessly open kind of personal relationship we encouraged – and the need therefore for a different kind of discipline – was quite enough for a young teacher to face without having to make teaching experiments at the same time. Anything new would have to grow out of the life of the School, not from the imposition or adoption of ideas from elsewhere, however enlightened. This may have relevance to the breakdown we hear about from time to time of pioneer experiments in state schools. We tend to assume (often it is my first impulse!) that the wicked Establishment has crushed the pioneer; but it may be that the pioneer was asking too much of people, that they were being expected to put into practice with their heads ideas that their hearts and their habits were not ready for. Perhaps a headmaster's job is not to offer plans that ought to be put into practice next term, but to be at work as a catalyst among his staff, helping to speed up their own processes, increasing the awareness of what is actually happening in children, in the classroom, the discovery of faults and possibilities, so that when new ideas come they arise from the group, are based on experience and are supported by competence and desire. Every new project requires its own discipline; the newer and more challenging the project the more severe the discipline may be. The thought that all you have to do in pioneer education is to set things free, is one that has left many people floundering in pathetic impotence or blaming adverse circumstances for their failure.

What did happen at Wennington was that projects every now and then burst out of the time-table. A young historian who came to us straight from Cambridge, and who is now Head of the Department of War Studies at King's College, London, soon had his pupils scouring the neighbourhood for historical information and taking the record of our estate right back to Domesday Book, to William de Roos and Dame Agatha Tresbutt (whose crest carried three buckets representing the three wells on the estate). The boys and girls had to learn to interview old people and vicars engagingly and courteously, even using the word 'Sir', which they never used in a school of Christian name habits.

This was followed by the School's biggest project ever: the Mediaeval Fair, which swept every one of us, from the oldest to the youngest, into mediaeval clothing. The project was introduced in a series of morning assemblies. Two women started girls off on the preparation of the enormous wardrobe. Groups went to York to investigate mediaeval art and pottery; others delved into drama and the musicians got together mediaeval music. Troupes of acrobats and tumblers were trained and some of my science pupils translated their chemistry back into alchemy. I made mead from the product of my beehives. The historian watched over us all and did special research into the Court of Piepowder, a court held on the spot, therefore of dusty feet, *pieds poudres*.

On the great day my wife and I, Lord and Lady of the Manor, were heralded by trumpets and made our proclamation opening the fair; the musicians played, the tumblers tumbled, the performing bear (a boy inside a real bearskin) was frighteningly convincing and a woman caught selling bread adulterated with sawdust was tried before the Court and put in the stocks. She was released quickly to have a bath – to remove the two or three eggs with which she agreed to be pelted. The mead was sold to parents only (it was very potent) but a surprising number of children afterwards commented on its quality. The Fair ended with a peal of trumpets and a proclamation requiring citizens to disperse quietly and not to lie about drunken in the streets.

Many years later an equally ambitious project grew out of Geography classes and expanded to replace not only these but also the classes in English, History and Domestic Science. It involved only forms 2 and 3 (12 to 14 years). It was an extensive neighbourhood survey and began with a preparatory study of a dozen topics including farming and land utilization, industrial and traffic problems, community and social services, recent and more distant history, local churches and battle sites, archaeology including the birth and death of the local railway line.

There was a build-up in which local residents and the Wetherby Historical Society helped and the work of the District Council was studied. For field work separate groups investigated forms of land utilization and the growth of industry, the contribution of the York Museums, the relation of churches to cultural history, the work of the police and the new telephone exchange, the care of old people, the educational facilities. They did not stop at the stage of recording and understanding, but tried to make suggestions, for instance as to the use of the disused railway track.

In the final stage of writing up there appeared an immense amount of information about Wetherby's traffic problems; exact information for instance about the number of lorries coming through the middle of the town instead of using the by-pass, and the drivers' reasons; about the parking of cars for short or long periods and the relation between the provision of parking space and the amount of shopping actually done. Useful advice was passed on to the Council affecting their decisions as to a one-way traffic system; it is probable that our evidence prevented a plan that would have been clumsy and possibly dangerous.

This project brought Wennington's boys and girls into a mutually appreciative contact with local officials and local residents expressed surprise at the keenness and precision of their observations. More than anything else, perhaps, it mitigated the critical reaction that many people had previously felt towards the School.

The half of the afternoon (tea was at six) not taken up with classwork or its developments was given mainly to outdoor activities. Thursday afternoon was wholly free, a half-day, and everyone had one other part-afternoon free. Of the remaining three part-afternoons, one was given to games and two to 'outdoor work'. This latter activity could better be called community work, for some of it became indoor work. The Estate manager might have forty boys and girls to allocate on an afternoon, with the assistance of two or three other staff, and an elaborate list appeared on the notice board as to the work and place for each of them. Some were routine jobs, such as the replacement of light bulbs, the examination of chairs and other furniture for needed repairs, clearing the grounds of waste paper. Others were more adventurous, the felling of trees and logging. Yet others were ambitious constructional projects.

We tried to vary the allocations, so that no one got too much routine work, but sometimes a boy or girl liked to be responsible for a permanent routine job. One boy for a long time cleaned all the loos, going round with a bucket and one of those hideous brushes. (He later became an artist.) Some people became 'specialists'. Four boys made all the furniture for a new classroom, two built an extension to the pottery, some became stage electricians, and a group reclaimed an old car and built it into a lorry. The biggest projects were the sewage plant and the hard tennis courts. The estate manager was originally a civil engineer working as agent for one of the biggest firms. He was accustomed to planning the work of building power stations and graving docks; but with his daughter at the School he became so involved and interested that he gave up these vast enterprises for our humble tasks. We thus had the services of a man who knew all about techniques, materials, processes and planning. In 1958 the value of his experience was dramatically shown in enabling us to take on the building of a very much enlarged sewage filter bed in ferro-concrete. This involved many months of work for large numbers of people and the final stage, filling it up with the filter stone, was carried out by old scholars during a summer holiday.

Even before the coming of this useful member of staff we tackled some big jobs. We justified having two workshop teachers in our small school by the fact that they gave half their time to repair and construction, using groups of children. The value of this was shown in the way we tackled the building of a stage. At that time our only room big enough for drama was the dining-room, still called the music room because it had been so labelled by the previous owner. At first we acted at floor level, but later aspired to a proper proscenium and lighting. So we had to plan a stage made of movable nine-foot square sections, thirty inches high. There was a big area of our wood under larch and several of the trees had been blown down by wind. The two teachers got together a group of competent youngsters, sawed enough trees into nine-foot lengths, got them up to the circular saw, sliced them to the required sizes and then began putting them together. (Pupils were not allowed to go near the circular saw in use. Only the handicraft teachers and myself were insured to use it.) They started on a Friday, worked all through a weekend, and on the Monday afternoon they were nailing down the planks on to the frames packed together at the end of the room.

Perhaps what I enjoyed most was the estate work, trying to keep the trees thinned out by felling the smaller ones, and the fruit-picking in summer and autumn. The tree-felling was tough work but it was possible to employ girls just as well as boys and there was always a sense of exultation in the cry of 'Timber!' as all were warned to stand aside before a tree crashed. We could employ large numbers on this work; there was so much clearing, sawing into sections, and hauling to be done.

Apple-picking extended over six weeks or two months in the large orchard. At its heaviest the crop could be five tons, but in later years it diminished because of the deterioration of the older trees. A generally enjoyable task was the picking of strawberries and the children were extraordinarily well controlled, providing at intervals there came the permission to eat one. One year the crop was embarrassingly large, nearly a thousand pounds. The children became bored with them and we had to give them away to old people's homes and hospitals. A more normal crop was two or three hundred.

A point needs to be made here about the supposed difference between boys and girls, in view of the fact that many educators, including even A. S. Neill, assent to the idea that there is a sharp difference between their interests. Neill's girls seldom went into the workshop, but at Wennington, not only were girls equally present in definite workshop classes, but there were many also at the voluntary sessions at week-ends. Neill does however admit that perhaps the School inevitably reflects the habits of the outside world, this implying, as many Women's Lib. members now say, that women could vie with men in many fields if they were not conditioned otherwise from birth. I would say that a school *need not* reflect the world in this respect. It depends on the teacher's relationship with the children. Wennington's first craft teacher came from Bedales, where girls were taken seriously in the workshop, and he maintained this attitude without even having to think about it. One of Wennington's best woodworkers was a girl, capable of the highest degree of precision, and she became the woodwork teacher in a secondary modern school. The man who married her has an exceedingly capable and useful wife.

It should be added that at times (but not continuously) boys were equally included in domestic science classes without difficulty. They certainly enjoyed cooking and they were not unwilling to sew.

Is it necessary to say much about the educational value of the community work that has been described? Are there any readers to whom its value is not obvious? An American student who left the School in 1968 has just come to see me, full of appreciation about his experience in the School. He saw that he and his friends could feel that Wennington was 'our school' because they made things for it; if they broke things they mended them in the workshop. They saw the consequences of their actions and had to take responsibility for them. He compared Wennington life with the utter anonymity of New York. As he put it, if a man stepped on the foot of another in the subway, what did it matter; who was he anyway? That's what life in the mass does to people. But at Wennington, if you hurt someone in body or spirit, you had to come down next day and meet that person at the breakfast table and face what you had done. Wennington was the kind of place where you could not just leave it like that.

Then there is the training in all-round resourcefulness that the community work provided. A former pupil who is now an outstanding scientist said, in the course of some encouraging remarks about this part of the School's work, that although he could not remember any particular stage of development in classwork, he could recall clearly the dramatic moments when he learnt to tackle a practical job requiring enterprise and originality.

This kind of community work makes a demand on the staff as well as on the boys and girls, and it requires organization and some expertise. There is a tendency in schools, where it has been important in the past, to allow it to become voluntary; it is sometimes argued that if the work is voluntary it will be better done. The effect of making an activity of this kind voluntary is relative to the total situation. Unconsciously and sometimes consciously it is then felt to be less important than those things on the time-table that remain compulsory, the classes for instance. But in fact the sharing of community work is the sharing of the basic tasks of physical existence, and to do anything to diminish their importance would have been to give in to the educational pressures the School had resisted from its foundation and to break the unity between thinking and doing.

Further, it is well known to teachers that when volunteers are called for to do an urgent job, the people who offer first are those who are already busy – the ones who could rightly be given a respite. Those who need it most, as an experience in personal development, are usually the ones to hold back, the emotionally disturbed whose previous experience has made them ill-adjusted to their group and unco-operative. It was evident that our practical community work was a therapeutic experience for such children; it put them back into relationship when otherwise they might have sat about doing nothing.

There is a case for permissiveness perhaps if the school is small enough, when the head can be in a creative contact with every child; but then to be consistent everything should begin by being voluntary. Under these conditions the unco-operative youngster can be brought into activities by a new spirit growing within him. But the size of a school limits this approach. I watched with great interest the way the boys and young men at Finchden Manor ran their own community life, doing even their own cooking, and being patient for long periods with those who were unwilling. But they were delinquents or seriously disturbed lads who needed a respite from adult domination; there were never more than forty, and George Lyward and his colleagues were quietly aware of all of them.

As a school increases in size there has to be increasing organization to guard against the consequences of human fallibility, to keep the staff up to scratch as well as the children. As we have seen, with increasing organization there comes the danger of manipulative education. We have to make some kind of compromise, and the effort at Wennington was to try to put into these obligatory jobs a quality that made them in some measure 'convivial', an experience in which it was fun to be working together.

The use of that word *fun* brings a sharp reminder – that life in the School was far from being all fun. As will be shown later, in a school that encourages fearlessness and does not use a regimenting discipline, the whole of human nature comes to the surface. In writing the history of a school, as in thinking of one's own life, the memory of positive achievements tends to swamp the memory of failures, frustrations and painful experience, and to the casual reader the account may seem vainglorious. In honesty, it has to be admitted that our organization rarely worked smoothly, that we had to find in ourselves – that is, in the staff and the senior boys and girls who co-operated with us – the toughness and resilience to survive the moments when individualism and waywardness threatened to make organization unworkable.

17. The late George Lyward, Director of Finchden Manor — a welcome visitor and adviser to Wennington

18. The Potato Plot 1944. Maureen Reed facing camera *(see p. 188)*

19. Hauling a tree for planking to the local sawmill at 'Old Wennington'

20. New Building. Polishing the Hall

21. Peeling apples

22. Sewage plant — building ferro-concrete walls

23. At work on interior

24. Two former pupils (medical students) finish the job on vacation

25. Tree-felling in the wood

26. *Girls at it too*

27. *Taking an axe to it*

28. *Sampling the 1954 strawberry crop (750 lbs.)*

CHAPTER XI

Organization and Participation

TUESDAY EVENINGS WERE RESERVED for staff meetings. These were regularly once a fortnight for routine business, and sometimes on the other Tuesdays for discussion about a single matter of interest or urgency. As far as possible everything was settled by common consent, but the staff were glad that the headmaster should take responsibility for a number of final decisions to avoid endless discussion.

Once a month, three times a term, a report form was filled in for each child in every subject, giving a brief indication of effort and achievement but not by numerical marks. The purpose of this was to see that every child was thought about in a complete way, at least by his or her form master, and then discussed if special attention were necessary. Teachers, like all other people, have their weaknesses and they need some kind of system to 'keep them up to it'. Group behaviour and every aspect of School life came into the picture.

It will be remembered that early in the School's history, self-government was temporarily abandoned; pupils were not ready for it. Within a year or two whole School meetings began to be held and, as a result of this 'Council', responsibilities began to be taken over by the School or by particular members. Again difficulties began to arise, for the whole School meant over a hundred and there was 'too much talk' and great difficulty in arriving at decisions. The School in general did not want prefects in the accepted sense but there was a development from *ad hoc* responsibilities to more general authority. 'Counsellors' were instituted to help to develop a more reliable spirit in the School and they had the job of keeping reasonable order, but with little recourse to punishment. Usually, though not necessarily, the Counsellors were the oldest people, the Upper Sixth and a few others. They were not elected by the School, but at first selected by the staff and later nominated by their predecessors each year.

Soon there grew up the need for a representative committee to reach decisions without so much talking. It consisted of representatives of all the forms, and of the staff, and it included the principals and Counsellors *ex officio*. The Chairman and Secretary were always boys and girls and they had complete control of the meeting. This was called the Senate, for to call it the Council would have been to confuse Councillors and Counsellors. At first it was held informally in a sitting-room, but it was discovered that this led to slackness in decision-making and recording. So a strict committee procedure was adopted, with chairs formally arranged (no armchairs!) and motions to be put and seconded. An attempt was made, however, to use the Quaker procedure that avoids voting and therefore to some extent avoids producing a dissident minority. It attempts to get the sense of the meeting and move towards unanimity. So we had voting only if disagreements could not be resolved. This method required much patience and a good chairman; but in spite of the difficulties it was good training. Minutes were carefully recorded, in a weighty leather bound book, and a card-index made of all the issues debated, so that when discussing any topic there could be reference back to earlier discussions.

Most of the rules and the general conduct of boys and girls outside the classroom were under the jurisdiction of the Senate. They were wise about such matters as the bounds for children of various ages – which varied from three miles up to unlimited distances. They were concerned with the care of each person's property, and instituted an insurance scheme which worked well. They kept a record of thefts and damage, assessed their total value, and adjusted premiums accordingly, appointing a committee to examine claims. The work of the Senate was not always successful; indeed it often came near to hopelessness and defeat over the care of bicycles. This, and other apparently insoluble problems, every now and then drove the Senate into the doldrums. Faith in it diminished – until some crisis called it into action.

I had a veto and I had to be honest about that, for as headmaster I was under legal contract to parents to safeguard their children and see that work was done. Rarely did I ever have to use it for this reason. I had however to use it sometimes to protect certain people. Children are always in a hurry to complain about food, and sometimes it was necessary to intervene. For a long time we had Italian or Spanish cooks who were warm-hearted and hard-working, but they were not represented and did not want to come to the Senate. We could not allow them to be criticized when they were not there to defend themselves; indeed we did not want them publicly criticized at all; it risked rumours reaching them with consequent hurt. So all complaints or requests had to be privately channelled through Frances, to whom the Spaniards were devoted and who knew how to communicate with them.

On the other hand, boys and girls *could* make complaints about staff failures outside the classroom, e.g. failure of a master-on-duty to be available or of the maintenance staff to put up a new and louder fire alarm bell. The complaints, if supported, were duly recorded in the minutes and it was the secretary's job to see that the appropriate person was informed.

To prevent any accusation that the Senate was going into a huddle on its own, provision was made for a public gallery, so that non-members could attend, remaining absolutely silent, and see what their representatives were doing. A full gallery meant general life and interest, an empty one a period of deadness.

Probably the most interesting project the Senate ever undertook was the re-organization of bed-putting. Bed time had been supervised by a master on duty assisted by a senior boy and girl, forms going to bed at half-hour intervals. It was a noisy and irritating experience for all concerned. There arose a suggestion that people should just go to bed when they liked. This was debated at length in the Senate and I raised no objection. What followed was interesting, because as soon as they accepted the principle they had to face the practical difficulties, including a system for regular baths and the need of examination candidates to get enough sleep. What they had indeed to do was to work out a new *discipline* to make greater freedom possible. What they decided was tougher than anything the staff would have imposed.

The younger half of the School had to be in bed by 9 o'clock and the older half by 10.30 p.m. They all had to go to bed in silence so as not to wake up those who had chosen an early bed, and the silence had to extend to the corridors and bathrooms. Moreover, after the first person had gone to bed in a dormitory, the light could not be put on again lest he should be wakened.

The first week was marvellous. People crept up to bed with the stealthy feet of Red Indians and the whole dormitory area was completely silent. Boys and girls said in the morning what a wonderful night's sleep they had had. But then the strict self-imposed discipline began to break down and after another week there was noise and lights were on. There being no-one else about I went on to the corridors to remind them of the Senate's decisions. But it was wrong for me to be doing this. The Senate then met and appointed a watch-committee, with power to suspend the scheme, to call in the staff and revert to the old arrangements if there was serious breakdown. For quite a long time this worked fairly well and I think that for a year or two it was certainly better than the staff-constructed scheme it replaced.

In the end it lost its impetus, and steadily more staff supervision had to be introduced. Does this mean simply that it was a failure? No. They learnt a great deal through this experiment about the relation between freedom and discipline. Further, systems set up in this democratic way should not be too permanently established in a school. If there is breakdown when the supporting spirit is no longer there, a new generation can have the experience of tackling the problem in its own way. The foundation of participation in school life is not laid in any formal structure; it is provided by free discussion and consultation taking place at any opportunity, and of a kind that makes each person feel that his view is respected. Sometimes quite young pupils, eleven year olds, produced wise ideas and it was a thrill to hear them courageously voice them in the formal Senate.

Form masters and mistresses were encouraged to hold form gatherings to get to know their boys and girls, but some were slack; too easily defeated by difficulties in social organization and finding means of enjoyment. Frances and I made a point of getting to know the Sixth-formers and they came up to the drawing room after eight on Friday evenings regularly. It was a social gathering into which business could be introduced, general discussions about the School or the world started, music listened to, or things read that were of current interest. When the group broke up, after perhaps an hour, the Counsellors remained. Then we often plunged into the deepest problems of school life and we came to depend very much on their knowledge of the problems of particular children. Without ever calling it psychology, we were together finding out how individuals 'ticked', how they made relationships with each other, or failed to make them, what developments raised or lowered the quality of the community's life. They discussed, often as perceptively as any of the staff could have done it, how people could be helped and punishment avoided. They went to bed very late on these occasions. By eight o'clock on a Friday evening I was often tired and my shoulders sagged as I thought of the sixth-formers coming and the counsellors' meeting. If it had not been an absolutely regular event it would often not have occurred. Yet it rarely ended without our feeling refreshed and glad. There was so much evidence of cheerful concern and wisdom and of the growth of affection in their feelings towards each other.

Participation is very much in the air these days, but we should ask carefully what it means and what it is achieving. Perhaps the words 'in the air' express just what its weakness may be. What happens in a school pupil or a university student when he or she joins a governing body? Is it all just a matter of talking, or is it followed by developments in conduct? For true democracy is not just a matter of exercising rights and sharing power; it is a way of developing new feelings towards the business of living and working together; it is sharing at the personal and practical level as well as the administrative.

Did we achieve this kind of democratic participation at Wennington? The positive evidence is in the amount of really arduous work undertaken by the counsellors and the aides. The aides, by the way, were people who might become counsellors in a year's time and had specific duties only, no general control. The head boy and head girl were nearly always back at School three days before term began, and with them most of the counsellors. They had to plan the allocation of domestic jobs for the term, to go through the School list to make up squads, with careful thought about the compatibility of people in them and the kind of leader necessary for each. It was not necessarily the head boy and head girl who drew up the final list; if there happened to be someone else among them who was good at it, he or she would spontaneously take it on. The lists were always there, without prompting from me, covering the notice board, before the flood on the first day of term. Throughout the term they saw to it that the system worked, that the vegie-squad did get up in time to do their work and that a hundred and twenty boys and girls all over the School buildings did their particular jobs before breakfast; that wash-up squads did turn up after meals, defaulters were dealt with and quarrels resolved.

More often it was the head girl rather than her colleague who got a grip on this kind of organization that required wisdom about persons. There were many occasions also when she prevented the headmaster from neglecting his duties and from remaining in ignorance. Her head would appear round the study door: 'Look, Kenneth, there's something I think you ought to know', or 'you promised to do so-and-so, and you haven't done it yet!'

At lower age-levels there was evidence that the amount of practical participation demanded of boys and girls was not causing them to become 'browned-off'. Many beside counsellors wanted to come back before the beginning of term to help in preparations, to paint dormitories or classrooms, to prepare beds, to do minor repairs, to clear out the swimming pool. Often too many wanted to do this, more than could be properly used and we had to hold them back. There was no doubt that they felt it to be *their school.*

29 and 30. Teaching, house and office staff, 1959

31. *Clearing swimming-pool of the winter's dirt*

32. *Eleanor Spray, Head Girl 1951-52 (now the author's wife)*

33. Some of the Counsellors, 1957 (unusually well dressed!)

34. Overseas pupils: nine nationalities

CHAPTER XII

Science and the Arts

IT HAS BEEN ADMITTED that we were not obviously enterprising in the curriculum. To have shaken up the traditional pattern of school subjects would have been to create too much insecurity in both scholars and teachers. It may be good for us at times to face what seems total insecurity or to rethink all our ideas, but more generally it is true that there must be a basic security behind our most hazardous adventures. The child who has the security of his parent's love is the one best equipped to face unexpected and demanding situations.

Learning is a moving forward into the unfamiliar, and in most children there is inadequacy and consequent anxiety. A little anxiety is not a bad thing; it is part of the tension in which we generate the energy for a drive forward. But it can become an inhibiting fear. In the learning situation the teacher needs to be reassuring. The more demanding the work the more important it is that the child should feel that the teacher really knows what he is doing. The most 'popular' adult in a school may be the least mature and he is rarely the one most valued as a teacher by the pupils. The teacher most valued is the one who is well prepared, has insight into what he is doing and maintains sufficient order for work to be done. It is precisely this kind of teacher that can dare to be adventurous.

There should be no idealistic compulsion to be progressive. The teacher who rebels against traditional ideas in education and substitutes what he imagines to be freedom, may be as remote from the reality of children's lives as are those he rebels against. He may simply be taking children from one prison and putting them in another. When I visited Finchden Manor and moved among the forty delinquent or intensely disturbed lads there, I was fascinated to see how in the apparently casual conversations he had with them, George Lyward was sowing a seed of confidence and nourishing growth. He might puzzle a boy by an equivocal remark – he often intended to – but I can imagine that the boy, walking away from the encounter and scratching his head, would be asking himself what on earth George meant, but at the same time sure that it was relevant to his condition; it was something he had to get to grips with.

George Lyward was not only a remarkable, intuitively effective therapist, but also an efficient and inspired teacher. When one of his lads had worked sufficiently through his emotional problems to want to study, George could set him on a path that made extraordinarily rapid learning possible. It was not any kind of cramming; it was made possible by illumination, by finding a focus of meaning so that apparently ill-assorted or otherwise ill-understood things fell into a relationship that could be remembered. This was an act of perception and imagination, tapping resources at an emotional level, not just an intellectual exercise.

I once spent an evening or two with him discussing the presentation of subjects and we examined a number of topics in English and History, to see how this procedure was relevant. I remember, however, that he added two severely practical precautions. They were to this effect. Never overestimate your pupil's ability to understand what you are talking about; return time after time to the basic and the simple, the seemingly elementary. He emphasized this specially in relation to sixth-form work, in which the teacher is apt to create an intellectual structure on frail foundations. The other advice was this. Give your children at the outset a picture of what you hope to cover in a definite period – say a month or a term – so that they do not feel they are merely wandering on indefinitely, so that they can feel that each thing understood is a step towards the achievement of an objective they can hold in their minds.

This is an approach to the teaching-learning situation that draws together the emotional and intellectual, that creates and continually re-creates the security within which discoveries can be made and adventures undertaken. It is a way of growth, in which not only do flowers appear, but roots grow deeper. It is an approach that can be effective within the traditional subject-classification and at the same time allow a movement beyond its limitations.

We may be so dissatisfied with the traditional curriculum that we decide to break away. We may say that life itself is not a matter of subjects. Life presents us with whole situations to which this departmentalism is irrelevant. So let us bring life into the school and study it. In real life the sciences are not separate; they work together; so we must have General Science. Similarly we must have Social Studies instead of English, History, Geography. Now this is good, provided the teacher and his pupils can get imaginatively right into the situations in which the subjects are unified. This may not happen. Perhaps more often than not it does not happen. The example I am best qualified to deal with is General Science, in which I could once claim to be something of a pioneer and in which I continued to believe in spite of the failures I observed.

True General Science begins from the awareness that you cannot understand biology without understanding physical and chemical processes, that you cannot understand chemistry without knowing physics; further than in our lives we are physical, chemical, biological, psychological creatures in dynamic relationships with a complex environment. But how do you teach or study this in school? With all too many teachers, and in text-books, General Science became a scattering of information about physics, chemistry and biology in the hope that the child would somehow use it all some day in his understanding of the world. It was not a really unified scientific discipline, approaching problems with coherent thinking. When at Bedales I arranged for a special syllabus to be accepted involving this kind of coherence, but the examiners insisted on dividing the school certificate paper into three sections – physics, chemistry and biology – and the different sections were sent to different examiners.

Other groupings or integration of subjects may be even more open to the objection that the teachers may not really know what they are doing, because the subjects are less precise than the sciences. In our enthusiasm for educational planning, we must beware of the danger of breaking away from one kind of intellectual pattern, only to find that our new scheme is yet another *intellectual* pattern of the teacher's that does not relate to the children's imagination and emotional life.

This is not to diminish the value of experiments in curriculum reform, but rather to emphasize the need for a true readiness in the personality of the teacher, for a real assimilation to have taken place in him before he puts new hopes and intentions into practice. The quality of the teacher and the nature of his relationship matters more than the plan of the curriculum. A teacher of chemistry who knows and *feels* the relationship of his subject to biological problems (he ought not to be teaching chemistry if he does not!) can by an occasional reference and stirring of the imagination in his pupils, establish between the subjects a bridgehead over which their thoughts will subsequently pour.

So perhaps what actually happened at Wennington was right: the acceptance of teachers as they were, trained in certain habits, inevitably the products of their own education, not expecting too much of them all at once, but providing the encouragement to break out of their strait-jackets at intervals.

One thing we were able to do right from the start. We recognized the importance of the education of the emotions; this was a leading implication of the philosophy of John Macmurray. It must be remembered that he attributed many of the ills of society and the world to the fact that we have attempted to train the intellect while leaving the emotional life undeveloped and primitive. The problem was not simply to release the emotions – for that might mean to release a horde of devils – but to encourage them to grow up rationally. That does not mean adjusting them to our logical processes as though these were still to be dominant, but allowing them to become object-centred rather than self-centred, making sure that they are about what is real, not merely an expression of our own impulses, longings, sentiments. By developing in contact with what is outside ourselves, with what is real in other people and the world, the emotional life becomes enriched and more sensitive.

We set the stage for this move towards emotional maturity by giving attention primarily to the quality of personal relationships right through the community, to achieve honesty, directness and fearlessness. In the curriculum we gave ample space to those activities that were creative and imaginative, that arose from direct intuitive experience. It meant giving music, art, craftwork, poetry and drama an equal status with the more usually important academic subjects. These were not to be temporary activities that gave way to supposedly more important examination subjects as pupils became older. But how, it will be asked, did we find time for all this? By not being in a hurry to get pupils through their 'O' levels, by making the examination genuinely a 16+ examination, by refusing to think of sixth-form work as the only important objective, for which you have to 'get rid' of all but three subjects.

The exciting development of pottery has already been mentioned. When we moved from Wennington Hall to the new building at Wetherby, the wall between two stables was knocked down to provide space for four power driven wheels obtained from a commercial pottery closing down. The activity developed with great enthusiasm and Wennington was one of the small group of schools first to submit pottery as an 'O' level subject. But why make a creative subject like this yet another victim of examinations?

The solution to the problem of examinations is never as simple as propagandists imply. For many reasons I would like to see them abolished. But while we have them we should use them as constructively as possible and if it is thought that pottery is as important as a more academic subject, the good potter has a right to become qualified in it just as a good linguist or a good mathematician becomes qualified. The task then remains for the teacher to see to it that the work remains creative, never accommodated to spurious or conventional standards, and that the examination authorities are severely challenged if they misuse the examination. We can say that the examination in pottery never destroyed its creative quality or injured the attitude of the children. The large majority of boys and girls took it and passed. In 1956 the School shared the first prize in the crafts section of the National Children's Art Exhibition in London, a distinction resulting from the work of four of the School potters.

In art and pottery we had the same teacher, Louis Jones, right from the beginning, maintaining a consistent standard. He can now think of many studio potters and teachers of pottery, artists and teachers of art, who first found joy in this work by his side. The pottery and art room provided a superb example of convivial education.

Music teachers fluctuated with the coming and going of different teachers – for musicians are restless people – but music was always a significant experience to the children. Not long after the move to Wetherby, musical activities received a vigorous stimulus from the advent of Noelle Barker who, at nineteen, came with an Aberdeen M.A., qualifications in music and a vast 12-cylinder open Lincoln. She gave us a very lively year, and then departed to become a professional singer – coming back at intervals to entertain us.

Sometimes we were able to keep two full-time music teachers very busy as well as the visiting wind teacher. Sometimes 'O' level music had an enthusiastic entry, sometimes exams were not important. Once there was a meeting in Leeds of heads and music teachers from many schools. The chairman asked what proportion of pupils took the 'O' level music exam. He started at five-per-cent and got a show of hands. As he went above 25 per cent the hands diminished quickly to nil. There was a gap, but he persisted to 75 per cent, and the Wennington hand went up. That was a high figure even for Wennington, but at periods when it was less, it did not mean that music was less important. Always there were large parties going to concerts in Leeds or Harrogate. Some readers may think that this musical achievement is not at all exceptional, and over a fairly large group of schools, this is now true. But in general the battle for the recognition of music is far from won. A Wennington boy from a musical family became a player on several different instruments, took an honours degree in music and subsequently a research degree. He was dismayed when he became director of music in a grammar school, in a prosperous new city, to find a high degree of philistinism towards music, so much so that a girl who was a promising violinist gave up because her fellows made her ashamed to be seen carrying a violin case.

On the other side it can be claimed that Wennington did not produce the precious type of musician who isolates himself within a cultural circle. One of its pupils became a composer, but he is also capable of doing his own plumbing, bricklaying and joinery.

It is not inconsistent to diverge at this point to talk about science. There are not, in essence, two distinct cultures, the one artistic and creative, the other logical and scientific. The outward appearance of a distinction is created by specialization, segregation and the demands of technology. Among scientists now turning to the history, biography and philosophy of science there is a rapidly increasing emphasis on the personal, creative and imaginative activity in science; and the fertility of original thought among scientists is seen to depend upon something as non-logical and intuitive as the painting of a picture or the writing of music. The concepts that provide a theoretical structure for science come from the unlimited resources of the human imagination.

It follows that science should not be taught as though when entering a laboratory the pupil must leave the rest of himself and his studies behind him; also that the scientific environment should not be so completely tailored and ready-made that it seems to limit thought and activity. Slowly building up a laboratory in a garage was a good discipline for the imagination. Two or three of our best scientists came out of that period. There came often a point when we just had not the apparatus necessary for a particular purpose. We browsed around our shelves of junk, or we saw some oddments on a table, and things seemed to come together, intuitively taking the shape of something that would do the job. There must have been many such experiences in the 'sealing wax and string' period of the Cavendish Laboratory in Cambridge. I think Noam Chomsky was right when, thinking about the creativity of the scientist, he wrote: 'We need humility. We don't know a damn thing about human creativity, about intuition and about nearly everything else'. But it seems not unreasonable to suppose that imagination and intuition can be nourished if a stimulus is provided throughout the whole of a child's development. Perhaps what happens in a child painting a picture, or making a mobile in the art room, will have an effect on his ability to face problems in the laboratory.

There came a time when we had to have a purpose-built laboratory. We raised £15,000 by donations and covenants and got help in design from our two governors who were architects at the Department of Education and Science and who introduced me there to a colleague who had original ideas in laboratory design. Dr. Goodier, in charge of science at Eton, showed me how he had made Industrial Fund grants go much further by do-it-yourself methods of bench construction. So my dream of new laboratories was at last realized. Was this the end of the discipline of necessity, the encouragement of imagination by scarcity?

It was not. What I had wanted, and now achieved, was space, plenty of room to move about. For the modest sum of £15,000 by good planning, we had three large laboratories and two ancillary rooms, built next to the School workshop. The basic equipment and apparatus were provided too, but not the cupboards full of expensive items of apparatus looking like museum pieces and to be hauled out once a year for demonstration purposes. It was still necessary to be inventive and to make much use of simple apparatus. We had been working towards the adoption of the Nuffield Science Project and the new laboratories made it possible. This project, which had been tried out as a pilot scheme in a fairly large number of schools, was an imaginative break-away from orthodox text book teaching. In that form of teaching, experiments were merely illustrative of an established structure of fact and theory. If the pupil was told about the effects of acids on metals, he afterwards went away to the bench to show that what he had been told was true.

The heuristic method, which has been mentioned in connection with my experience at Christ's Hospital, was one which threw up a number of problems to be solved by taking actual situations met in everyday life, such as the experience of floating on water, or in the history of science, such as the problem we now think of as oxidation. It guided the child to think of ways of attacking a problem, knowing what would be likely and having the apparatus ready. Although in a sense the course was completely planned in advance, it did encourage a research attitude; it aroused wonder, provoked puzzlement, created a tension, instead of allowing the child to feel that when he entered the laboratory he had started on a package-deal tour with a guide who had learnt it all by heart.

The Nuffield project made use of the Christ's Hospital development, and it should be mentioned that one of the driving forces behind the project was Professor Eric Rogers, who had been a boy at Bedales and a teacher there just before I arrived. The project broke away from conventional school apparatus, was much more imaginative, took notice of what was happening in modern science and the world now; and, even though it provided a course to be followed, it allowed loose ends to proliferate as they always do in real scientific activity. It might be thought that in this last respect it violated an important principle that a pupil should be given the security of knowing what he is to cover within a reasonable time. It could go wrong in this respect, but it need not. It remains possible, for instance, having stirred a group up by asking questions and provoking an argument that raises problems about atmospheric pressure, to say: we are going to investigate this and it will probably take us this next month; if we need a bit more time we'll take it.

Yes, that question of *time!* Elaborate and very good guide-books (they should not be called text books) were issued in connection with the Nuffield project, and these of course indicated what was to be got through in the term or year. Here a serious difficulty arose. To many teachers there seemed too much to be got through in the time; perhaps the course presupposed more periods per week than a particular school provided. So one heard of teachers either abandoning the project for this reason, or hurrying by skipping over what may have been essentials. If there is one element we *must* keep out of the teaching situation it is hurry; the anxiety it produces is wholly destructive. Pupils and students must never be so hurried that they cannot assimilate what they are doing, really put down their mental roots. No good gardener works in a hurry; if he did his plants would die.

Another problem was the quantity of apparatus required if the course was to be followed in full detail, apparatus much more diversified than that of an orthodox laboratory. At the outset the cost of re-equipping was estimated, I think, at £700 per year of the course, i.e. £3,500 to cover a five-year course. With inflation the cost must now be very much greater. Laboratory suppliers leapt on to a profitable band wagon and new firms came quickly into existence manufacturing the range of Nuffield apparatus. The effect must have been depressing to teachers working in schools unable to afford this. Further there was a tendency, reappearing, for the equipment to dictate the procedure. The pupils were to carry out an investigation as described in the book, and in an appropriate place in the laboratory there was a slot out of which the apparatus would appear, a package in which all the items were ready for use.

It was a shock some years ago, though it ought not to have been surprising, to find that in some schools there were as many children bored with Nuffield-taught science as with orthodox teaching. Even in this new method the book and the apparatus could take charge, and the child become subject once more to a package-deal tour. In some schools the project was given up because the teachers could not have all the specified apparatus. What was not fully recognized by many was that the originators of the scheme were trying to encourage a different kind of relationship between teacher and pupil, a provocative dialogue in which unexpected things might have to be thought about. That kind of relationship could still exist between a science teacher and his pupil if they were moved from a laboratory into a kitchen. I have mentioned how, when Wennington had no laboratory, I found I could provoke scientific discussion by messing about with a bicycle pump. When I talked with Edward de Bono about this, he warmly agreed, and began to demonstrate how much physics you could illustrate by playing with a postcard. If you exercise imagination and ingenuity, you can in fact develop fully the kind of experience the Nuffield project aimed at, even if you cover only part of the course and possess only a fraction of the apparatus.

So the fact that Wennington could not afford a complete stock of Nuffield apparatus was no deterrent. The important asset was access to a workshop, so that when ideas for apparatus came into a discussion they could be made. One of the major stupidities in the design of school laboratories is the absence of a workshop. A fraction of the money put into catalogue-type apparatus could provide what is required: a bench, a lathe, a pedestal drill, hand tools, taps and dies, and a stock of metal and plastic sheet, rod and tube. It ought always to be possible to say, in response to an idea and after it has been thought about: 'It might work – come on, let's make it this evening!'

The apparatus exhibitions that accompany the annual meetings of science teachers, show how fertile in ideas some teachers and their pupils can be, and the televised programmes of boys' and girls' own research work illustrate the inventive and resourceful qualities that ought to be the universal aim of school science. Reports from boys and girls at various schools suggest, however, that there are still many teachers who think that science, in contrast to other subjects, involves the handing over of undoubted facts in such a way as to leave little room for argument or imaginative discussion. How mistaken this is! Science is not a mass of knowledge recorded in print; it is a personal activity, and text books are an imperfect, often inadequate and sometimes misleading, means of communication between people sharing an experience. Because it is a personal activity, the teaching of science can be convivial – a dialogue, the evoking of feeling, of insight, criticism and doubt, of intrepidity of thought.

It must be open to what Edward de Bono calls lateral thinking, the creative, sideways, intrusion of fertile ideas. His concept of PO thinking should be remembered. We must not look only for the 'right' or 'wrong' answer to a question, the YES or NO. The PO answer, the odd, unexpected answer, seeming at first irrational, may be the beginning of original thinking and lively discussion. Edward de Bono is an inventor as well as a medical scientist. In an era of rapid technological advance, it is encouraging to recognize that when its leaders reflect effectively on the human qualities they need, they take us to the central questions of personality and its nourishment. *How to Invent,* by those scientist-engineers, Professors Laithwaite and Thring, has chapters that should be important to every educator, no matter what his subject.

35. Invention rewarded. Problem: to remove from a roof-top room a girder that once supported three big water tanks. Too huge and heavy to take down through the house or to drop vertically. Solution: two tall larch trees culled from the wood. The girder was rolled out until it balanced, then given a gentle push. It landed accurately on the bales of straw

36. Invention subverted. Building a new timber store and circular saw shed from heavy asbestos-cement sections. Problem: to set and hold sections in position while fixing. Easy! Back the school lorry on to the site and rope them tightly to it. But what happens when the impetuous maintenance man drives the lorry forward without releasing the ropes? The rending-and-crashing was heard all over the grounds

37. The garage-laboratory about 1950

38. Chemistry outdoors: a Thermit fusion

39. *Making thermometers*

40. *Convivial work in the art-room*

41. *Throwing a pot*

42. *Opening the kiln*

43. Of this quartet, one boy is now a composer, and the other a County music organizer

44. Two typical products of the pottery

45. Wood-turning lathe and bench made entirely of second-hand and scrap materials (by boy on right)

46. Robin completes her dinghy

CHAPTER XIII

Drama

No school activity could be more obviously convivial than drama, calling as it does on every resource of personality. Long before we had any of the accessories, we were producing plays and involving as many of the School as possible. For many years Frances was producer, with my support as stage-manager and often actor. We were not ashamed to stage the Shakespeare play on the year's examination schedule; indeed we thought it necessary to give reality to the study. Among some progressive educators Shakespeare had become anathema, because it was highbrow, supposedly not within children's interest or experience. Certainly Shakespeare had been ruined for many children by slavish attention to stupid examination questions, but this did not unfit Shakespeare for children. Again it must be emphasized that the result of such a study depends on *how it is done and by whom,* on the relationship existing in a particular room in any school.

An education without Shakespeare is immeasurably impoverished. I doubt if, relative to the human predicament, there is any insight or judgement however independent or radical, that was not anticipated by Shakespeare, and in the evocative kind of language that, like the pithy sayings and parables of Jesus, sets us looking for depth beyond depth of meaning.

Here is a very early record, a statement by Frances in the January bulletin of 1946:

> I am still the English teacher, a very haphazard one now, I fear. Often I come to a class remembering only that I am teaching at that time, but not whom or what. Luckily I can get children interested enough in an assignment to start and carry on in reasonable silence if I am not in the room when they arrive. This is a useful ability, but it does not make for original work. However, a wave of delight in Shakespeare swept over the senior classes, helped greatly by Olivier's film performance of Hamlet in Leeds. We found small girls of eleven and twelve declaiming Hamlet to each other in our large resounding music room. Sometimes when I

came exhausted to class from the larders or kitchen, the class would say: Oh, do let's read Macbeth today, oh do!' And I would sink gratefully into a chair with what the children took no doubt for a gracious smile, but really a smile of relief. Anyway, I said to my conscience, Shakespeare is the best possible teacher of English. How they loved Macbeth! We read it for the most part round a crowded table, but every now and then they would say: 'Let's act this scene', and we would clear the room and draw the curtains for the sleep-walking scene or sit round Macbeth's Banquet while our hair stood up again on our heads, and our spines ran cold.

We staged the whole of Macbeth that year and I was cast for this murderous character. It was the first long part I had ever taken, but what an impression it left on me, more I think even than Shylock, for the lines of Macbeth still come leaping into my mind thirty years later. But the great discovery in that play was the quality of the girl who took the part of Lady Macbeth. It was not surprising that after leaving school she went straight into the Manchester Theatre Workshop Company and stayed with it through severe disciplines and hardships. Later she went to Australia and worked for a time with its Broadcasting Corporation. She went on to a more arduous venture, taking Shakespeare to the outback, covering thousands of miles in a fleet of wagons.

In Sydney in 1971, Actors' Equity quickly put me in touch with her. She now had her own theatre there. Over the phone, arranging to meet us, she said : 'I warn you; I'm not what I was! I'm forty and I'm fat! I only do mature parts now'. Indeed she was, very generous and charming; and it was amusing to think back to the 16 year-old, to the skinny murderess coming on with a candle in her hand:

Out, damned spot! Out, I say! – One, two;
Why then 'tis time to do't – Hell is murky!

A contemporary of that girl remembers how she was among those fired by seeing Olivier's performance of Hamlet, when she was about twelve, and how they were passionately driven to declaim the tremendous lines to each other. At night she lay in bed, sleepless, with whole scenes repeating themselves in her thoughts.

The list of plays performed over the years, even if I can only recall a fraction of them, seems enormous. Sometimes groups provided five different short plays in one evening, repeated for three nights, involving the co-ordinated activity of nearly every boy and girl in the School. Different members of staff produced the plays and surprised us by their unsuspected talent. The deputy-head wrote some highly original plays in the modern mode and staged them.

One play stands out sharply in my memory for the quality of acting in one scene: Anouilh's *Antigone.* By that time my wife, suffering from increasing tiredness and rising blood-pressure, had handed over production to me. I had chosen for the parts of Creon and Antigone a boy and a girl who had not previously been thought of as actors. Both were tense people with considerable difficulties; the girl was in fact a Greek, with a pure Greek name, who had been fostered by an English-woman. The boy was in revolt against paternal authority and for a while included me in his rejection. The girl had frequently made urgent demands for help in her moods of distress but was not easily able to make use of the help I offered.

There is one very long scene in the play when Creon and Antigone have the stage wholly to themselves, and move round it, thrusting and storming at each other. I was able to leave the play to itself and go round to the back of the audience. I found myself watching something intensely real, and completely ceased to feel responsible for what was going on. Round and round the stage they went, never forgetting a line and putting a fervid intensity into their words. It was an obviously cathartic experience for them and in watching no other school play have I felt such a spine-chilling experience. They neither of them became actors, but that is not important.

In 1965, unexpectedly, the way opened to the construction of a theatre that would take away all the inconvenience of using the dining room. At a parents' meeting, Frances had humorously expressed her intense jealousy of all the good things heaped upon her scientific husband (i.e. the laboratory) and said that she would never be content until her own ambition was realized – a purpose-built theatre. A few days later we had a letter from a firm of solicitors, acting for an anonymous donor who had given £5,000 to the laboratory fund. Now there was £10,000 for a theatre! Our very knowledgeable estate manager got to work. I had thought of an ordinary school hall and stage, but our two Department of Education architects on the Board of Governors showed me quickly how out-of-date I was. The theatre architect, Norman Branson, was called in to design for us a modern studio theatre adaptable to any kind of drama work, from the traditional proscenium type to theatre-in-the-round with audience participation. The estate manager's estimate came to about £20,000 and so accurate was his forecast that one of the tenders came within nine pounds of his precise figure. At another parents' meeting held a few months later we made an appeal for a general subscription to raise another £10,000. But within a few days the anonymous donor had offered the whole of it.

So there we were, a year later, in 1967, with a theatre built of stone, but inside like a box, with a flat floor, numerous entrances, and one end filled with a central control room looking down over the whole floor, flanked by balconies and backed by huge storage spaces. Under the roof trusses ran a grid that covered the whole ceiling area, slotted for the movement of flood lamps to any desired position and for the erection of proscenium curtains, backcloths, or cyclorama if we wanted them. You could walk over the whole grid and look down. Scattered over it were eighty mains sockets in groups of four (to provide for colour control) all of them wired back to the dimmer sockets in the control room. In my electrical junk-shop haunt, Lisle Street behind Leicester Square, Japanese autotransformers were going very cheaply and we bought all we needed of these, obviating the heat-waste of rheostat dimmers. All this extensive wiring and control system was built by pupils working under the estate manager and myself, and hundreds of pounds were saved. Further, we built a great quantity of wooden boxes, 6ft. x 3ft. x 1ft. for stacking up audience terraces, for a stage or for cubist scenery.

Our first big use of the new theatre was for the production of Obey's *Noah* the following year. Inevitably I found myself in the part of Noah, but undertaking it without at first realizing how appropriate the play was. The group, with the chief characters drawn mainly from the lower Sixth, were a delight to work with, responsive and eager, warmly affectionate and tolerant. Mrs. Noah was the one who slipped most easily into her part, adding a dramatic tension to her normal self: an affectionate and supportive Counsellor (due to be Head Girl) acting as though saying all the time under her breath: 'Don't worry, old chap, they're not a bad lot really!'

My chief worry was Ham. For this part I had chosen a real African, Alfred Oluyomi from Nigeria. Indeed I think I must have chosen the play with him in mind. I could not get him to act. His job was to be instigator of revolution and corruption in the Ark, the one who was cruel to the animals, whose hand was against Noah, who saw no point in preserving the animals, and who mocked at belief in God. But Alfred was essentially a lovable, warm-hearted young man who could not dislike anybody and who had not an ounce of savagery in his nature. I laboured hard to turn him into an insolent demagogue. 'Look,' I said, 'you're a Liverpool dock-side labourer and I'm the bloody boss. Come on, show me you hate my guts.' but Yomi just sweetly smiled – and continued to smile.

He seemed not to have the first idea about acting, and here he was, black, Hamitic in every cell of his body. I lunged about the stage, pointing over the bulwarks into the water: 'Look, there's a fish, a whopper. Point at it, follow it with your finger, move your whole body as it moves, chase it with your whole attention'. He just looked at me, slowly rolling his eyes, clueless.

I needn't have worried. As soon as he had an audience he became a different person. He remembered all I had asked of him and added more of his own. He became nasty to animals, sadistic in his desire to destroy fish, swaggering and insolent to me, conceited in the display of his fine black body, clad only in a loin cloth. He even remembered to sneer, though he could not quite obliterate his lovable qualities. He used all his muscles with every word and his eyes danced in his polished black face. He took the audience into his confidence and delighted them.

He brought the house down with his last action, unpremeditated. All the young people begin to disappear down the mountain after the ark has grounded, leaving Noah looking out on emptiness and desolation. Naomi and Ham are the last to go. Ham is carrying a big bundle. He looks round to give the audience a last look at his cheerfully insolent face. Then turning back to the road, he dumps the bundle on his wife's head and walks on ahead, jauntily free of all encumbrances. A picture you can see any day in any street in Lagos or Ibadan.

For me the play was additionally moving, because for the Headmaster of this kind of school it was very near the bone. Way back in 1940, when the bombs were dropping and we saw the distant sky whiten at night, we thought of Wennington as a Noah's Ark, riding on the destructive flood of war. And the problem of authority as it is put in the play is very like the problems of authority in such a school as this. When the crew turns against him, Noah, overcoming for a moment his dejection, says, 'You know, I don't care a bit about my command. Only over me – good Heavens, there's God!' One could cut out the word God and substitute a more universally acceptable phrase but the meaning would remain. The nature and results of authority differ according to the intention behind it. It can be used either for the satisfaction of the boss's desire for power or with the intention of setting people free – free to walk over a new world and make their own discoveries.

We had some much more experienced producers watching the performance and one of them who was also a psychiatrist wrote:

> . . . now the meaning of this performance is plainly revealed. The Ark and its passengers are the School, the fury of the Wild Man and the Storm and the strain of shipboard life are the tension, both destructive and formative, which stress all the community and none more than the man at the helm. Noah's faith in the worthwhileness of life and in the sacredness of relationships is the bedrock of the School's ethos. A voyage without charts comes to end as the School year finishes.

Though the performance of this play recalled poignantly the stresses of school life, it was perhaps the most enjoyable drama experience for me. We had always been conscious of the affection that draws together the members of a cast as they submit themselves to the intense demand on feeling and imagination that a good play makes. Never before had I been so conscious of this.

We had yet to see, however, what our new theatre made possible. A new teacher joined the staff who had been with us twenty years earlier, had subsequently worked at Frensham Heights for several years, joined George Lyward's work with deeply disturbed boys for a year and also taken a thorough training in the educational use of the drama. He began to take drama classes almost throughout the School, breaking up forms into small groups, getting them to explore situations and feelings and put them into dramatic expression in mime. After a year of this he was able to show us the meaning of flexibility in a modern studio theatre, and the value of dispensing with the picture-frame stage.

To introduce the principles of his production, he wrote:

> A *Theatre Workshop* – like a craftsman's workshop or an artist's studio – is an area equipped for a particular kind of activity. *Drama Workshop* is a technique for developing awareness, exploring situations, areas of experience, ideas and literary texts through immediate experience in which thought, emotion and 'physical being' are unified rather than fragmented. Its aim is free and spontaneous expression in a controlled and creative form. It uses the basic human need for play and drama as a means towards personal development, growth and expression. It is not concerned with the training of actors, nor – in the first instance – with the performance of plays before an audience. . . . The artificial mechanisms of the theatre – the proscenium arch, which divides performers and audience, elaborate costumes, props and make-up, and realistic stage settings, are reduced to a minimum.

Parents and visitors were invited to watch 'dramatic variations on the theme of sacrifice', under the general title of 'Heroes, Martyrs and Murderers'. The participants were dressed in 'workshop' clothing – jeans and vests. With a few individual exceptions the whole School was involved and the scenes included a wide variety: *The Princess and the Monster,* Aztec ritual murder, jazz improvization, rites of Spring, a very experimental approach to the witches' scene in *Macbeth,* a section from *Androcles and the Lion* and the killing of Thomas in *Murder in the Cathedral.* There was no curtain between scenes, just a complete black-out during which, if necessary, our stage boxes were moved into different positions.

So well was it all organized that the producer had made himself wholly superfluous. A girl whom he had trained as production manager sat in the foyer at the focus of an extensive inter-com telephone system set up by the stage electricians. She was in control of movements at all four entrances, and of the operations in the lighting control room and the tape-recorders. There was not a hitch during the whole two hours in spite of the large number of movements that had to be synchronized between people who could not see each other. To me – and to others, it was a convincing demonstration of the value of the open stage and audience involvement and of the absurdity of building any more inflexible halls and fixed stages. It does not rule out proscenium productions; they will always have their value, but it makes so much more possible.

The closing scene remains clearest in my memory. I had seen *Murder in the Cathedral* performed several times before, but never had I seen the chorus put into it such unusual and sincere dramatic quality as in this instance. Here we had the women of Canterbury not as a lined-up Greek Chorus, but moving out into the audience, each putting her own bodily movement into her grief. Here was shown starkly the difference between being taken into an experience and looking through a picture-frame into a world of fantasy. The end was intensely moving: an improvization, not suggested in the book and carried out in complete silence. Thomas lay dead, his body fallen on to the floor at the foot of the altar and lying diagonally across one corner, lit by a single spotlight. A little girl, smallest but one in the School, came from under the control room and through the audience, clad in jeans and shirt and carrying a candle, completely self-possessed but unconscious of her surroundings. She was not walking unusually slowly nor was she hurrying. She did not look stricken; if anything there was a quiet smile on her face. She walked as though we were not there watching her; she walked up the altar and set the candle on it, then moved a few feet back to a corner of the staging and sat down cross-legged to watch the body while the spot dimmed slowly to darkness.

I do not know who thought of this; it was a brilliant touch. For me, when I afterwards thought about it (at the time I simply saw and felt and was lost in it) it symbolized the undismayed encounter between innocence and evil.

47 and 48. Nov. 5th. Always an enormous bonfire and round it a general scrimmage. All adults not wearing a white kerchief were open to attack

49. The Studio-Theatre

50. Ceiling-grid nearing completion showing slots for floods, etc.

51. Control Room

52. *Anouilh's* Antigone: *Creon & Antigone*

CHAPTER XIV

Religion and Freedom

AT A CONFERENCE years ago we were in a small group including A. S. Neill and we were involved in a spontaneous discussion about personal relationships and the relevance of Christianity to education. Neill passionately broke in with his favourite exclamation: 'I don't know what you're talking about!' He went on to say: 'That's not religion! Religion is about Hell Fire, nothing else.' Frances turned to him: 'The trouble with you, Neill, is that you're not an atheist at all. You're a Calvinist standing on his head!'

Many Scotsmen have suffered under the dark shadow of this perversion of Christianity, with its evil doctrines of election and damnation. Even John Macmurray had occasion to complain about it. One day, in an uncharacteristic mood of depression, he said to me: 'If only I could get this incubus off my back!' 'What incubus?' I asked. 'Calvinism'. This pinpoints the major difficulty in discussing religion with children. Religion, like every other expression of man's passionate nature, is riddled through with contradiction and perversion; indeed more than other expressions, for where the light is strongest, the shadows are darkest. Young people hate the darkness, the shadow of the moralistic oppressor, the threatening, demanding God who is so interlocked with the Devil that he is almost identified with him.

It was a pity about this in Neill. I often felt that if only he could clear this shadow from his vision we could all get so much nearer together. Pioneer education does need something more – something beyond humanism – to give it direction and the kind of reliability that is not menaced by the immaturity of the self-consciously emancipated and the paranoid. The gospels are a challenge to search for that something, and it is significant that Neill saw Jesus as pro-life, pro-freedom and as the rebel who offered love. The continued exploration of this, without fear of being called religious, is very necessary in a period when 'meaninglessness' is a characteristic of modern society, with its frightening impulse to self-destruction.

Many of us loved Neill, but were so often frustrated (not necessarily for religious reasons) just when light might have broken into our discussions. I felt this more than some others, for now and then at the conference of co-educational boarding schools he said to me that I was the only one with whom he shared a common language. We two were interested in kids, he said; the others were only interested in 'O' and 'A' levels. He would get up and say, with his eyes narrowing over his eagle's beak of a nose: 'I don't know what you are talking about! That's not education!' He wasn't really fair. They, indeed all of us, were trying to see our way through the complexity of demands that faces every school trying to cater for an ordinary cross-section of parents, and knowing that we owe them some respect. But it is no good wishing a man to be other than he is, no good wishing that the penny had only one side. The way to get the best from what Neill, or any other innovator, has to offer is to avoid the temptation to detach the message from the person. It is by seeing the contradictions in Neill that we can get the truth – the truth in action – from him. The best effects of Neill's propaganda for freedom are seen when parents or teachers *assimilate* or *digest* what he has said and allow it to deepen their *own* insights. The worst is seen when they turn his communications into an ideology and then proceed to *apply* it to their treatment of children. We have seen pitiful and tragic results of this in families in the United States, a country where ideas go effervescing to the head all too quickly, and where Dr. Spock also has had reason to wish he had been more clear about the qualifications and caveats to a gospel of freedom. And there are disastrous results in the activities of some teachers in Britain who have turned Neill into Neillism and made school life a strain and a confusion to their colleagues.

Neill's detestation of the dark God was projected also on to many other forms of authority, including parents, the Ministry of Education, the Government, society itself and Them. Sometime in the late fifties there existed for a short time an ultra-progressive school, whose name I have forgotten. At the same time a manufacturer of chastisement canes was sending round to schools brochures extolling the virtues of thrashing, together with a descriptive list of the types of canes on sale – degrees of flexibility and durability. He offered to come to lecture on corporal punishment, and the school I have mentioned accepted. The boys and girls listened, then crowded up to him, bent him over a table and beat him. The school had a good deal of publicity, including additional details about its ethos and organization which would hardly recommend it even to the more progressive educators. Soon it closed down on the advice of inspectors who found its sanitary accommodation unsatisfactory. Later I attended a conference, and took a seat next to Neill. He turned to me and said, seriously, 'How are your W.C.s, Kenneth? Look to them, or They'll close you down!'

Having had most encouraging relationships with inspectors, I had no fear of being closed down. Nor had Neill any genuine reason, but he insisted on imagining it. I remember also an earlier conversation about two little children playing with each other's genitals. I agreed about its innocence and the stupidity of parents who use smacks and call it naughty. But his picture of the innocence seemed to me to verge on the sentimental, contrasting it with too black a picture of society and the wicked world.

Society is not imposed by a devil external to the human race; it is a product of our human nature, and in so far as it is evil, oppressive and stupid it is an expression of a dark side in all of us, a dark side potentially there in two toddlers investigating each other's anatomy. It was odd that Neill, who had been analysed, gave too little recognition, at least in his popularizations, to the fact of psychological ambivalence: the ambivalence of love and hate, of creativeness and destructiveness, of generosity and meanness, with which we are all born.

A result of this seeming failure in Neill is that although he admitted that a *Lord of the Flies* situation was possible in schoolboys left on their own, he saw the cause as coming wholly from something outside the boys themselves; a product of a vicious Establishment and its repressive education. We must admit that a different society and education could make such a nasty situation much less likely to develop; and many of us, like Neill, were concerned to hold back for a while the destructive social influences and allow children to grow up wholesomely.

Neill, however, did not face the ultimate problem. He wrote that man is not evil until he is made so by others; but where the evil in others came from he called a mystery. Surely, there are not two different species: men and 'others'? No, we have all got it in us to corrupt and be corrupted by each other. (That is why in any kind of society whatever, liberty must be safeguarded by eternal vigilance.) This makes no difference to our capacity to love each other. We can accept ambivalence as an objective fact; then there is no need to be dominated by a Calvinistic concept of sin, either in the acceptance or the *rejection* of it.

Neill's virtue was in his being, with his loving personality, 'on the side of the child', an inclination that at times he said he got from Homer Lane, that therapeutic genius who embraced in his personality far more startling contradictions, contradictions that Neill recognized. But taking sides has its dangers. If it is not taken up fully into something more radical and inclusive, it can be touched with paranoia and encourage children to go into the world anticipating hostility and feeding it in themselves, when what is really needed is compassion and understanding. The mother who says 'naughty' to the little boy playing with his penis may also be the 'Our Mother' of Louis Macneice's poem *The Kingdom,* the mother whose grim good humour was the daily tonic against despair, whose strength was 'the only cable that held the family together, self-respecting and sane'.

Everywhere, and coinciding with stupidity, even cruelty, there is some point of possible communication, of growth, however unpropitious the circumstance; and we should want our pupils to go out with compassionate imagination, hope and resilience, ready to find a responsive humanity among miners and dockers, yes, even executives and stockbrokers. For under all our labellings there are people worth knowing:

> . . . these are humble
> And proud at once, working within their limits
> And yet transcending them. These are the people
> Who vindicate the species. And they are many. For go,
> Go wherever you choose, among tidy villas or terrible
> Docks, dumps and pitheads, or through the spangled moors
> Or along the vibrant narrow intestines of great ships
> Or into those countries of which we know very little –
> Everywhere you will discover the men of the Kingdom
> Loyal by intuition, born to attack, and innocent.

Religion fundamentally means the experience of binding together and the discovery of freedom: the two apparent opposites that become united in friendship, the primary religious experience. We need love because we know that in finding someone to care for and to be known by, we are released from feelings of inhibition and unfulfilment. And in friendship we can begin to do things. But human beings are not content to have a good experience; they reflect, they ask how they can deepen it, diversify it, extend it to others. They talk about it, and because it goes beyond what is logical or rational, they use myth and poetry, music and art, in which to communicate. This effort goes adrift when the expression becomes dissociated from persons, when it becomes demanding and manipulative, when theology becomes more important than the experience of goodness in relationships, when as God's child you become God's victim.

I have said that pioneer education needs something beyond the limits of humanism to give it direction and reliability. This is true also of the whole social effort of humanity. It is not enough to hope only for individual and unconscious goodness. Every human activity needs a reflective coherent awareness of what it is doing. Many scientists use a sound method habitually without apparently needing to think about it. But at moments of challenge or crisis, when startling or disturbing ideas are offered, conflict may break out, pride or prejudice may interfere with judgement. Even scientists can be dominated by what is fashionable. So scientists have to be encouraged to establish a critical philosophy and some concept of the authority of truth. There have to be outstanding men among them like Medawar, Polanyi, Kuhn and Popper who try to answer the questions: what are we doing, what is scientific truth, what holds together theory and practice; is science personal, imaginative; how far is it objective; what can we as scientists say to the world?

We cannot leave any human activity to take care of itself. To survive, it has to bring what it is doing into the focus of conscious reflection. So pioneer educators must never cease to ask questions of themselves and each other: why do people matter supremely; why shouldn't we subject them to systems; where have we got this conviction from that the individual matters'? Do we need to strengthen this conviction or can we trust it always to survive? What kind of activities will strengthen it? Where did Neill get his concern for love from? How far into his own past could we trace it, how far into his associations, into his personal and cultural ancestry? Scottish Christianity, for all its dark Calvinistic shadow, had its positive values and John Macmurray could complain about the incubus yet pay tribute to the understanding of personal integrity his family religion gave him.

Many of those concerned in the building up of Wennington School had a Christian commitment as the spring of action and I think it was this that enabled us to hold to a steady course and prevent us from being lost in mere eccentricities, unconventionalities and rebelliousness. If the School has done anything outstanding or new, it has been related to a religious awareness and has had to stand the tests this has demanded. This has been our ultimate authority. The more we find external authority inadequate and the more we have to change its form and its impact on us, the more we need to develop an inner authority; and by inner I mean not merely within the individual, but inner to the community as a whole, holding it together in continuous discovery. This inner authority – both a point of reference and a point of growth – is what enables us to deal wisely and courageously with new stiuations as they arise, however unforeseen or daunting. It enables us not only to judge, but to savour and find delight, so that life together becomes both significant and enjoyable.

There was no desire to impose a religious consciousness upon the School; indeed that would have been futile. The important experience was in communication, in the dialogue between us, a dialogue in honesty and without compulsions. To explain why we had started the School and why we struggled on with it, we had to show how the effort was related to our Christianity. It was important to stress the effort to achieve the 'abundant life' and to make clear that to have life more abundantly meant, not something remotely 'spiritual', but the exuberance and confidence, the joy of the moment and the good things to be looked forward to, the sense of fulfilment that comes to those who 'have found a route on earth's true reckoning based'. That quotation is a line from Cecil Day Lewis's *Overtures to Death,* section 6. This and the associated lines, more concerned with life than death, we sometimes thought of as our signature tune.

My wife and I wanted to show our pupils that for us Christianity was not the acceptance of something restrictive, not being boxed in by rigid principles and morality, certainly not the recitation of belief. It was the way of discovery, the recognition of opportunities, both in moments of joy and enlightenment and in those of confusion and frustration. The crucifixion was not just an event that occurred once in history; it was a representation of something continuous in the experience of mankind – of the fact that man is made for difficulty, not for smoothness and ease, and that disaster can be the way to new growth. There was no point in saying this sort of thing if it was not evident in the way the School lived and grew – not by trying to achieve the comfort of a well-oiled mechanism, but accepting recurrent crises, failures, confusions as opportunities, and finding joy in resilience and resourcefulness.

The attempt to get children to think understandingly about religion is largely frustrated by their feeling that it is out-of-date, fusty, oppressive, confining. This situation is not helped by those who, while rejecting religion as the institutionalization of magic, admit that Jesus said a number of things in agreement with their own philosophy of life. Jesus thus becomes an example of something they already know; and was just one among many people enlightened in this way.

What would this attitude imply if we approached the truths of science in the same way? What would we think of the physicist or engineer who, accepting the laws of motion as habitual knowledge, thought of Isaac Newton as just another man who believed in them? A queer bloke who went to King's School, Grantham, but preferred to stay at home and play with clocks? What would we think of the nuclear scientist for whom the theory of relativity, with the relation between mass and energy, has become a daily reality, if he gave only a patronizing gesture towards Albert Einstein, another oddity who did not do very well at school, did not like wearing socks, talked a lot about the beauty of mathematics and now and then was a pacifist?

It does not diminish Jesus to put him in the company of Newton and

Einstein, and we could add a host of other men of genius, as I argued in my book *The Creative Imagination* (1963). The problem of communicating the significance of Jesus – especially as the magical and abstrusely theological appeal diminishes – is a matter of stimulating and nourishing historical and personal imagination. All such men or women were intensely involved with their world, whether in a particular aspect or, as in the case of Jesus, with life in its totality; and thus they were able to draw on the deepest resources in human nature. That is what 'incarnation' should mean: not something from outside coming in to take human *form* but a full realization of the transcendent possibilities in man.

Education often leaves the imagination flat and impoverished, leaves the child with little insight into the relation between the person and what he does or achieves. Subjects are just bodies of knowledge, which he is encouraged to think of as existing on their own, independent of people. The world and the universe are just things 'out there', instead of being seen to be *experiences* in the life of the living, feeling person.

The kind of feeling or activity I am describing as religious is not something that distinguishes 'holy writ' from any other effort to understand life in depth. It makes no distinction between religious poetry and other poetry, for all enduring poetry is an exploration of significant experience, an attempt to savour and intensify and relate life in its direct impact. The development in a school of a religious consciousness, then, is a growth in emotional maturity, in perception and discrimination, learnt through daily experiences. It is a growth in love, of people and of the world, in the power to direct action away from dead ends, away from what is unrewarding and inhuman, to what will open up life as 'a vast bundle of opportunities'. It is also a growth in awareness of the reality of evil, overt or latent in all communities, a recognition that we are all corruptible. No one who has lived through the rise of totalitarian regimes or who is aware, for instance, of the use of torture today, can doubt that evil is real and that fear might corrupt even those who claim to be proof against it; further, that it takes much the same form. All this can be evident, in miniature, in the crises of school life.

Yet there must also be a delivery from fear, so that a dangerous world becomes an exciting world to live in, not in itself a hostile world, but our home, for which we were made.

This description of religious consciousness is so all-embracing that in the School the word 'religion' might cease to have any specific meaning. But there remains the question of worship. I have explained that even in such activities as science, which seems to go along with its own momentum, there has to be a taking stock of what has happened and of trends, an attempt to answer the question: What are we all doing, where are we going? In the totality of our lives this is what worship is about, and it encourages reflection, a deepening of perception; it strengthens and clarifies the sense of direction.

Further, worship is a celebration; a celebration and assertion of the common life and of the identity of the community. It is an expression of the intention to go beyond individuality to become persons-in-relation. But worship, if it is to be properly related to life here and now, has become a difficult problem. Old forms have become dead. Too many hymns express an absurd theology or a nauseating sententiousness; they cannot be sincerely sung. We were never wholly satisfied with our gatherings on Sunday evenings; these were intended to be our one 'celebration', our coming together as a community, to ponder and express. What I remember with greatest satisfaction was the music played by boys and girls. We did not wait for perfection. Even the youngest played, if only haltingly; they did so with courage and they were listened to with sympathy. This sympathy was a test of the School's good feelings. There was an occasion when a girl seriously lacking in general confidence got to the point of being willing to play. She fumbled at a phrase half-way through her piano piece, tried the phrase again, failed and rushed out of the room. We went on with the next item – perhaps a reading. The moment it was over, the girl, who had remained behind the door, came back into the room, sat down at the piano and played her piece right through. Normally, there was no applause in such a gathering, but on this occasion it could not be held back; it broke out spontaneously.

We made much use of poetry at these gatherings, and it included a good deal of fairly modern material. I was fortunate in having as my deputy Brian Merrikin Hill, who was himself a poet. We shared a warm admiration for the poems of Edwin Muir and made frequent use of them.

We used brief drama-readings and much Biblical material, and any other appropriate sources of myth and legend. There was a talk of not more than twenty minutes given by a visitor, some member of the staff, my wife – or, too often, myself. This talk was a good way of testing the condition of the School; one could feel how they were accepting or rejecting, how they were reacting to stimulation, provocation or questions. In passing, it is worth mentioning that the reaction of a school to humour can be a good test of the relationship between children and staff. When you are working up to the critical point of a joke, in some audiences you can see the light dawning before your last words have been spoken, and laughter breaks out almost before you have finished. In others the faces are unresponsive, and laughter comes only after a pause – when, at last, it has sunk in. The quick response is, I think, an evidence of fearlessness towards the adult – a readiness to go out towards the other person, and therefore of freedom in relationship and feeling.

That brings me to more definite thoughts about freedom. Many years ago when attending a social event at a large Yorkshire day school, I was introduced to Lady Wheeler, wife of Sir Mortimer, as the headmaster of Wennington School. 'Oh,' she said 'isn't that the school where they do what they like?' It was one of the rare occasions when I had the right riposte. 'No', I said, 'it's the school where they like what they do'.

This is a moment to recall John Macmurray's philosophy of freedom, outlined in Chapter 4. A man is free only when he does what he wants to do, when he acts spontaneously; but only a *real* person can be free in this sense. He prepares himself for freedom by knowing what the world, other people and his own self are like, really like. So his spontaneous action depends on a discipline: the adjustment of thought and feelings to objective realities. The disciplined cricketer, aware of the condition of the pitch, the movements of the bowler and his own potential, lashes the ball over the boundary. He knows what spontaneity feels like. The undisciplined batsman loses his middle stump. To reassure us that we can hope to act spontaneously and freely without disruption, we see that man's essential need is friendship, the one experience he cannot do without; and that it is precisely in community that we can experience the personal discipline through which the spontaneity can be expressed without injury to others. It is in a caring community that the hidden things can come into the open to be known and dealt with, and the discipline – unlike imposed discipline or moralistic self-discipline – becomes part of the joy of living. In a school, the wisdom and experience of the adults, and the quality of the relationships between all of them, are of profound importance in the achievement of these conditions.

We have already seen that the achievement of freedom is not inconsistent with a school structure, a timetable with certain basic obligations and responsiblities. In the context of the religious and personal philosophy that has been outlined, freedom is not an experience we can take, it is one that is created and conferred. A child is not necessarily achieving any meaningful freedom when he decides that he will not take his turn at washing-up or refuses to go to school; for he is still caught within the situation, a negative attitude of mind. The boys and girls, who, as described in an earlier chapter, discovered how to make washing up efficient, were finding a freedom. It was no longer yes-or-no to a dirty job; they were getting on top of it. It was very satisfying to be told, then and many years after, that Wennington boys and girls staying in Youth

Hostels did the cleaning of the kitchen and the washing up cheerfully and efficiently without having to be reminded by the warden.

Children come to a school with varying degrees of unfreedom, resulting from past experiences and their own nature. It is for all the adults to create conditions in which fears and refusals, guilts and antipathies can be brought into the light and examined. What we tried to do was to make it possible for tensions to come out into the open, not to be hidden by a demand for correct behaviour. I doubt if children can, of their own accord, create these conditions. At strategic moments the adult has to challenge, to suggest, to ask questions, insistent or casual; he has to know when to let a situation develop on its own, when to intervene, in order to maintain the conditions for genuine discovery and mutual therapy between the children.

It is unfortunate that 'progressive' schools have attracted many people as teachers who are far from being mature or blessed with psychological wisdom: people who do not know themselves and are drawn to anything labelled as free in the hope of release from their hang-ups. Neill frequently complained of problem staff. A former Wennington pupil has very recently been telling me of her experience of helping in one of the 'free schools' that have been started in some northern cities. She says that their effectiveness is greatly hampered by the many men and women who are at odds with society and themselves, and who are projecting their own paranoid tensions into the schools. I have no means of testing the truth of this statement, but I have seen many such people in pioneer educational efforts. Sometimes they are not wholly disastrous, for their very immaturity can sometimes make a living contact with the children. But generally speaking they do constitute a danger; and their presence makes all the more necessary some kind of community exploration and assessment – call it worship or something quite different if you like – that demands humility and self-understanding and that seeks a direction that is more than just progressive or revolutionary.

We tried to make sure that this exploration and assessment went on right through school life, in the numerous consultations and the unrestricted dialogue. The Sunday evening assembly was the moment for drawing together, and it was not unreasonable to ask that every child should be present. But there was no case for compulsion where local church worship was concerned and we could not undertake to see that a child attended this. Several boys and girls, with an interest that rose and fell, came with us of their own request to the Friends' Meeting in York, and some entered Quaker membership after leaving the School.

* * * *

What follows is a kind of practical footnote.

When we think of the freedom of the young to make their 'own' choices, we have to recognize that there are very powerful forces at work in our commercially oriented culture that limit this freedom and often distort development. How does this affect our thought about the adult who refrains from using his authority because he believes that a growing boy or girl should make free choices and learn from mistakes? This is a convenient kind of psychology sometimes adopted by the adult who feels defeated, wants to avoid conflict and to find a reason to cover his impotence. The power of advertisements and of what is called the teenage subculture is far more compulsive and limiting than any parental authority. To secure freedom for the young we have to take responsibility, with all the knowledge and self-knowledge we can muster, even though it involves a repeated struggle and an occasional firm decision taken at the risk of hostility. It has to be seen that conflict is a form of *relationship,* whereas a defeated permissiveness is a breakdown of relationship and often an insincerity.

If the general quality of relationship in a school is that of mutual friendship, and if we, the adults, are clear about our own motives, we can in some matters say that we know better and that there are some forms of behaviour we do not condone. We can take smoking as an example. A crude doctrinaire psychology would assert that if we suppress a continuous desire we establish it the more firmly. The prohibition of smoking should turn people into smokers. But this over-simplification omits the factors just mentioned, the general quality of life and the motives. The old fashioned parent or teacher who smoked himself and denied the right to the young, tended to see their futive smoking as a snatching at adult privilege that could not be allowed. Within such a relationship a prohibition could hardly be effective.

At Wennington there were few smokers among the staff and their smoking was in private. The explicit reasons for suppression were the dangers of addiction, the waste of money, the public dirt and insensitiveness created, and the risk of lung cancer. To talk about the last of these was not as effective as might be imagined. Teenagers cannot easily imagine themselves in middle-age, so what might happen then is not real. But I do know that a few were definitely stopped by a medical visitor speaking on the subject.

At Wennington the struggle to enforce the rule was never-ending. It was possible to assess the ebb and flow of smoking by inspecting the shrubbery near the buildings; the number of empty packets told the tale. Over a long period the ebb and flow paralleled the rise and fall of stealing of money. Pocket money was limited to a definite amount for the various forms and it was not enough to match the rising price of cigarettes. If we sometimes felt that this use of authority was associating us with an outmoded educational attitude, we had to tell ourselves that we never intended to be classed in any category of progressiveness; every issue had to be judged in the light of the total complex in which it could be seen.

It was reassuring to find that in the long run the battle was worth it; it seemed to be won. Only a small minority of old scholars smoke. At an old scholars' gathering at about the time of my retirement, I looked round a room in which over sixty were chatting and I saw only two cigarettes smoked in the whole time. It might be argued that the smoking types would be the ones to avoid old scholars' gatherings; but the proportion of them would have to be very high to offset my observation, which was not the only one of that sort.

53. Alfred Schweitzer M.D., D.Sc., Doctor, Scientist, Musician and Mountaineer, (from his Alpine Club Membership Card; see p. 83)

CHAPTER XV

What Did We Do About Sex?

IN AN EARLIER CHAPTER I referred to the course organized at Bedales in preparation for sexual experience and marriage. A second book, *He and She*, covers the further development at Wennington. It was first published over twenty years ago and is still selling in the Penguin edition; but if rewritten now it would have to refer to a young generation whose conduct has been much changed by sexual permissiveness and the contraceptive pill. But the book continues to sell well; this is perhaps because it is fundamentally concerned with the acceptance of total responsibility for actions and is therefore relevant in any circumstances, whether formal morality is respected or rejected.

At Wennington, class discussions on this matter were not on the time-table. The School was small enough for it to become apparent when certain groups needed a discussion or wanted to ask questions. Questions of fact and even about personal relationships were arising at an earlier stage. Press publicity was largely responsible. Eleven-year-olds were to be seen poring over *The Times* discussion of the papal encyclical *Humanae Vitae*, and they were certain to be storing up questions. Because I always taught some science, I could now and then abandon chemistry or physics and invite these stored-up questions. They tumbled out, for the children had no reason to be guilty or afraid.

In their earlier years boys were more eager with questions than were girls. How does the pill work; is it true that there are safe periods; how are twins produced? It was difficult to adapt the answers to their inadequate physiological knowledge, but they were seriously put and had to be seriously answered, at the level their knowledge made possible. Some questions had a hint of humour. Do they always do it on Saturday nights? How long does it take? Such questions were not to be frowned at and sometimes an answering grin was appropriate. The questions from the girls were sometimes more personal and subjective; a serious girl would lift her face off her hands and ask: does it hurt? Answers to all these questions come best from adults who are at ease with their own sexuality, who have an intuitive feeling of the needs of children, who are not driven to talk sex by ideology or neurotic impulses from within themselves, who have no impulse to be daring.

It was odd that Neill should write: 'Personally I don't see the point in teaching sex' and in the same paragraph continue: 'Most children get their sex information from other children, and it is all wrong and pornographic and often sadistic'. It is precisely because popular sex information is so fouled up that we need to share with children what we have found to be good and reassuring and dependable. And sex is so intrinsically interesting! You never have an inattentive pupil when you talk about the length of seminiferous tubules, the bursting of ovarian follicles and the dramatic development of the embryo in the womb.

But of course scientific information is not enough. We must not fight shy of the emotional aspect of sex; and at Wennington we tried to establish the conditions in which this could be talked about and experience exchanged. It is over the matter of sexual activities that the generation gap is often most deeply felt and it is a good experience for young people if adults with some maturity can learn to bridge the gap. What we did was a simple consequence of an attempt to make education personal, to give an opportunity for a development towards genuine adulthood and emotional maturity.

One bright summer afternoon in 1951 when boys and girls in the swimming pool were revelling in the sunshine, suddenly and spontaneously they all threw off their costumes and continued their diving and swimming naked. We had not intended this as a Wennington habit and if we sometimes thought of it as a possibility we doubted if the parents would stand for it. Now that it had happened, it was, in the best sense of the word, innocent and we could not stop it without impugning its innocence. So it continued, but only at times when it could not be a peep-show for visitors or strangers: at the 7 a.m. rising bell and late in the evening.

Conduct at the pool was no different from that at previous times, the usual laughing and romping in the water, and never did I see a prurient look. I, or some other member of staff, had to be present sitting on the surrounding wall as a supervisor but this proved necessary only to make sure that the usual swimming pool safety rules were observed. Enthusiasm varied according to the weather. On a chilly morning perhaps only ten would appear and boys were more easily deterred. Bright sunshine might bring out forty.

Today, nearly thirty years later, such a practice may seem nothing to raise eyebrows. But then it was indeed an innovation. There were no objections from parents. As far as we could tell the children were discreet about it, did not claim it as progressiveness or emancipation; it became a normal part of community life. Occasionally I asked senior pupils, or old scholars, what they thought. Those who had come young simply accepted it throughout their time. Some boys who came late found it a release from furtive pre-occupations. For girls, the experience did not, as some critics might have feared, incline them to be immodest in later life, rather the reverse: nakedness was something to be enjoyed in a trusting community and exploitation of it for titillation became repugnant.

This practice had perhaps an important symbolic significance in Wennington life but what it achieved must not be overrated. Sexuality does not become completely wholesome by being brought out into the sunlight. Throwing off your costume doesn't guarantee a happy marriage later on. Each boy or girl needs to understand himself or herself at a deeper level. We must again recognize the fact of ambivalence – that not only are we born to love and tenderness, to caring and responsibility, but also with impulses to hate and reject, to hurt and exploit. The moralist, in relation to conduct generally and to sexual activity in particular, is driven to wish away the negative side, with the contradictory result that it tends to obsess him. What education has to do is to accept that the shadow is there in all of us and ceases to become a menace to our integrity in so far as it is looked at, understood, and its energy diverted and used.

So sex-education is related to the whole community experience; as much will depend upon the resolution of everyday personal conflicts as upon overt information about sex. Here we see the need for the adult in its true light. Being simply authoritative in trying to tell young people about themselves, does not lead to personal discoveries. The adult has to be a catalyst. As a chemistry teacher, I recognize how useful a word catalyst is, for a catalyst is needed in small quantities and its effect is to speed up a chemical process that would otherwise be too slow. The educator has to stimulate thinking, ask the appropriate question at a particular time, not to get the 'right' answer, but to set the young person looking for an answer that comes out of his own growing experience of relationships.

Years ago, if any guidance was given at all, it was in the form of straight talks based on the moral code. This will not take us far with teenagers of today, who know how the code is disregarded in the adult world and flouted in novels, films and plays. Forty years ago it was often assumed that most young men and women would find it possible to keep sexual experience for marriage. The assumption was probably mistaken then, as far as men were concerned, if not women. It is plainly mistaken now, and as the years passed it became obvious that if you talked about the direction of sexual activity in the belief that you could persuade the young to keep intercourse for marriage you were talking to a decreasing minority. Further, if you pinned your discussion of what was right on to the moral code, then at the first lapse all that was indeed good and wise might seem irrelevant.

There is still some resistance over this aspect of sex education and a simple parallel is useful to illustrate the limitations of moral codes. In Holland (I take this country only because I have spoken with some of the people concerned) there were committed Christians of the highest integrity for whom lying was, in normal circumstances, an unthinkable moral lapse. But during the Nazi occupation they found they had to tell lies in order to protect Jews in hiding, for to tell the truth would have meant death for them. Also, they had to play dishonest tricks with ration cards to ensure food for them. Obviously there was in these Christians a judgement, a concern, that carried them beyond moral rules. The complexities of sexual situations are greater than those of protecting victims of the Gestapo. Young people should develop something that will make a sensitive and responsible judgement possible in any complex of relationships, within the moral code or outside it. A sense of responsibility is important in a young man who has slept with a girl and made her pregnant or in a girl whose biological impulses have at an unguarded moment made her throw herself at a man. If two people decide to live together without marriage, the quality they put into the relationship and the way they meet difficulty and conflict are just as important as within marriage – even more important, for they have cast aside certain props which others have valued.

So a deeper morality is needed than the code provides; indeed it is not a morality; it is the spirit that takes us beyond the 'law' without despising its original intention; it is a sensitive guide that is much more than obedience to rules. This was the message of *Towards a Quaker View of Sex* which made such a stir fifteen years ago and split Christian groups in two. It neither condoned nor condemned departures from the code. Our research work had disclosed a great area of bewilderment and suffering and our effort was to establish communication with people in *all* conditions.

When we talk about a spirit, a sensitive guide, a light within, we are thinking about something that operates in all the activities of a person, that gives him integrity, makes him what he is. It is not just the limited sense of responsibility that makes him refrain from using the firm's stamps but does not prevent him from making improper use of his typist.

This is the kind of inconsistency that can occur when we think of responsibility as an independent moral virtue that is applied to a situation, instead of an expression of an integrity coming from within.

Fundamental sex education is concerned with the quality running right through the life of a community. What you do about your girl friend is thus not unconnected with what you do about your sweet papers; dropping these on the floor in the school common room for someone else to sweep up may be an expression of an attitude to other people, walking away and leaving them to bear the consequences. The development of this right-through sense of responsibility is connected with the acceptance of discipline. Too many educators in revolt tend to connect discipline with the disciplinarian and the authoritarian. Neill would substitute a concept of self-regulation, of behaviour coming from within. I think we should fight the disciplinarians by showing that discipline does not necessarily mean being forced to behave to a pattern decided by someone else; it is simply learning to do a job efficiently and well and accepting the necessary conditions. Self-discipline, as often advocated, could mean this, but it could mean a form of self-centredness; it does not emphasize sufficiently what is *outside* the self.

Learning to do a job well, making things in a workshop, growing things in a garden, doing research work, cooking a meal; these involve getting to know all you can about the material involved in the job, about the possiblities and limits of your own capacity and the way you adjust them to the material. The 'material' of sex-life is both 'self' and the 'other', and the other is not only the one other person but also the community, for we all grow up in a complex of relationships. There is no 'I' without a 'thou'. There is no such being as a totally isolated self. It is mistaken for any of us to say: 'I know what is right; do what I tell you'. But it is equally mistaken to say: 'It's up to you; make your own decision, do your own thing'.

At Wennington, as at other co-educational boarding schools in the present day, it was accepted that boys and girls fell in love and wanted privacy. They could wander off into the wood; they could disappear at ten o'clock on a Sunday morning, get away to the moors beyond Harrogate. Was this trust? Yes, but not in the sense of the words, 'Now I'm trusting you,' used as moral blackmail. It was the trust that, within the limits of human fallibility, relied on their remembering that they were members of a community and that the most private actions could subtly affect the spirit and direction of the School. Further, this trust included a recognition that the adults, especially my wife and myself, who discussed sexual conduct with them, were made of exactly the same stuff as they were, that we could talk about the details of sexual conduct (e.g. how far were they going?) without embarrassment, euphemisms or imputations of moral turpitude.

This is not to say we were never anxious. Again I recall J. H. Badley's remark that conducting such a school was like sitting on a rumbling volcano. There was, however, always humour and comedy, and never the feeling that, like Pompeians, we might be left with the taste of ashes in our mouths.

I have to recognize that conditions have changed rapidly in the ten years since retirement. The availability of the Pill, already referred to, increasingly prescribed at the request of parents, together with the publicity given to the 'freedom' it makes possible even in early adolescence, has affected every school. Ten years ago my wife Eleanor was working for the Inner London Education Authority, dealing with school-girl pregnancies and a wide variety of sexual aberrations and disasters in schools. It was still possible then to say that the co-educational boarding schools, because of the complete responsibility taken, were 'safer' than nearly every other kind of school. That may still be true, but it would be a self-deceiving Head who would claim that the new 'freedom' had not made inroads into his or her school. One senses a growing reluctant acceptance, but it is difficult to distinguish between the acceptance that recognizes the consequences that must be foreseen and thought about, and the acceptance that merely 'hopes for the best'.

Changes in culture do make inroads and do sometimes destroy good things. Though it may seem relatively trivial, the activity that comes to mind is dancing. Boys and girls, men and women dancing together – this is a sexual activity, though it is also much more than that. The dances were once the supreme social activities of the term, restricted to three, at the beginning, middle and end, so that they would have a scarcity-value and therefore be looked forward to as epic occasions. They were 'celebrations' of our community life and I could equally well have described them in the chapter on religion.

Great preparations were made. A special committee decorated the big room, choosing a theme and working intensely hard in the art room to produce original illustrative decorations to be fixed up on the walls. The theme might be 'Climbing', with mountain peaks, 'abominable snowmen' on the walls and skis hanging from the ceiling, or 'The Deep Blue Sea' with mermaids, pirates and highly coloured, gently moving fishes hanging above us, with an occasional octopus reaching out its tentacles. Everybody tried to make sure of getting a bath, girls got out their best dresses and the older ones took great care with make-up, having discovered that they could get away with it as far as the headmaster was concerned if it was so skilfully done as to look real. If a girl hadn't a best dress because her parents were poor or careless, someone would quietly report it, some material would be found or bought and she would be helped to run up something gay on a sewing machine. The boys scrubbed their faces, if nothing else, and put on good suits. Even the headmaster, whose attire at other times was apt to be somewhat miscellaneous, was seen on rare occasions in a dinner jacket. Another section of the dance committee prepared special food, ices and drinks.

The dancing was vigorous: quicksteps, fox-trots, polkas, waltzes, Lambeth Walks and that group exercise, whose name I have forgotten, in which you 'shake it all about'. In the art master we had a superbly graceful dancer, who set a standard for all. I was not a good dancer; I was apt to be beset by a reversion to my adolescent shyness, and the quality of my dancing was adversely affected by the slight failure of athletic co-ordination that lost me my position in the college first eight on the river long ago. But I could do fast waltzes – very fast. So when the first notes of the *Blue Danube* or the *Emperor* were heard I was usually hauled out of my corner by one of the more vigorous girls, in the expectation that she would be whirled round until she dropped with dizziness, and had to be supported to a seat.

There were many girls' choices, snowball dances, excuse-mes, so that everyone got a chance; boys were expected to distribute their favours, to pay attention to the shy girls and not to dance all evening with their special friends. Every subterfuge or form of persuasion was used to keep the dance on much longer than the planned bed-time and the seniors delighted in extending the Christmas dance to midnight and to a final drink of coffee with the staff. They went to bed, nearly always gasping: 'It's been a wonderful dance'.

The destruction of this most wholesome event began with, I think, the Twist; I felt in my bones that this would be destructive. It created a generation gap, for the adults were not inclined to it and the other body-shaking dances that followed. We tried to limit this kind of dance to a moderate proportion of the total, but it was a losing battle. As it moved in, the adults moved out, and some of the boys too. In a year or two the chattering, uproarious party, in which people looked at each other joyfully, joked and laughed as they danced, began to move towards the self-absorbed bemusing activity mainly for girls and ruthlessly exploited commercially. In the years just before my retirement, the only appearance of an adult at a dance was that of the master on duty, occasionally looking in to see that behaviour was tolerable.

54. *The morning dip. 'Race you to the other side'*

55. Wall decoration for a dance ('Deep Blue Sea')

56. 'Highland fling.' The Bursar, Ian Sellar (known as Hoots) was a genuine Scot. The others weren't

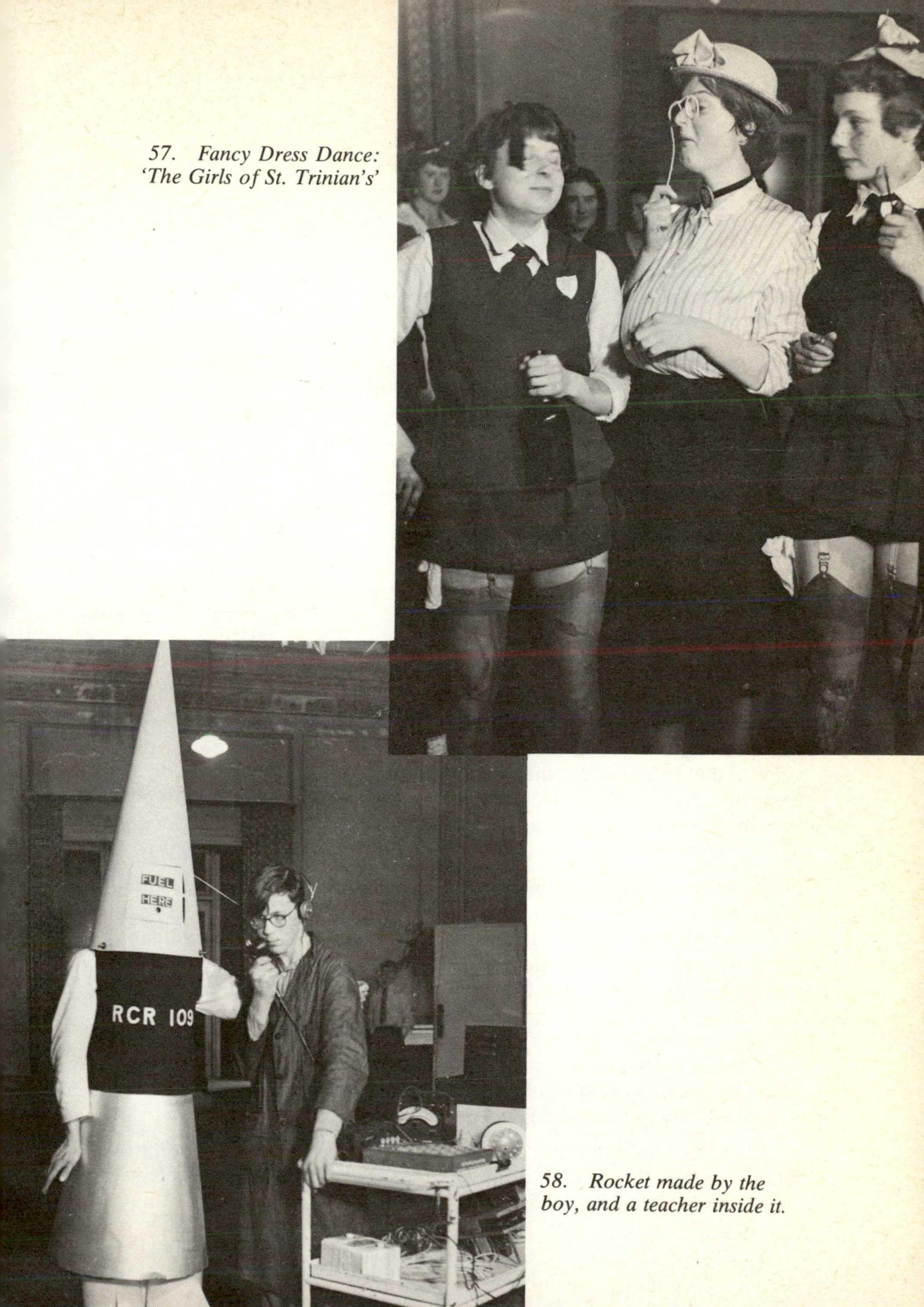

57. Fancy Dress Dance: 'The Girls of St. Trinian's'

58. Rocket made by the boy, and a teacher inside it.

CHAPTER XVI

The Unusual Ones

THIS CHAPTER WILL BE about those boys and girls who might have had difficulty in getting into most other boarding schools. The thirty per cent of children from local authorities, came some of them from homes that were very ill-provided for both as to physical conditions and personal care. A few had appeared before a juvenile court; some were school-refusers, some at odds with their parents. Hardly any were brazenly defiant, but nearly all had some reason for feeling ill at ease, frightened, uncared for or inadequate. Others among the local authority children did not suffer from any of these disabilities, but were sent perhaps because the parents' occupation made a settled home impossible or because a father had deserted, leaving a mother to earn a living, with consequent inability to meet the child's needs.

It may be remembered that Dr. Royston Lambert, then of King's College, Cambridge, made an extensive investigation of boarding-school-need, and it was used by the Public Schools Commission in its effort to make a recommendation about the future of those schools. He showed that five times as many children were in need of education away from home, as were in fact getting it. This number did not imply an equally large degree of maladjustment, but an unrecognized incidence of difficult conditions in which children were expected to work and grow up.

Besides the Public Schools, other independent schools, including Wennington, were included in the investigation. One of the assessments was of what I think was called totality. If a school had an assessment of 200 it meant that all the children were as alike as peas in a pod. If it had a nil assessment it meant that there was no trace of an imprint of similarity. Wennington had an encouragingly low assessment; the investigator, sitting at the dining table, found himself talking to boys and girls who were distinctly themselves, each with his own uniqueness, not echoing Wennington-cultivated sentiments and opinions, not reacting according to a code, but responding each from his own experience.

It seems reasonable to claim that these facts indicate a general condition in which the difficult or odd child had a chance to find his feet; he would not start off by feeling different, for he was in a community in which differences were respected and there were few patterns or conformities by which people were judged.

Some children sent by local authorities were offered on the basis of psychiatrists' reports that seriously underestimated the gravity of their condition; the doctors concerned were so desperate to get these unfortunate youngsters placed that they unconsciously gave them too good a report. Equally there were ordinary fee-paying parents who withheld information that might have made us reluctant to offer a place. There were times when we had to say we could not keep a child any longer. He was perhaps so sadistic that he was making life unbearable for the younger ones in his dormitory, or so disruptive in class that the work of the rest was suffering too much. There are some idealistic critics who will say that if we really loved each individual and understood his needs we should not have had to send any away. This neglects the significance of numbers. In an ordinary family, parents may be acutely aware of the frustration, even bullying, of one child by another. They cannot altogether stop it, but because they can be present much of the time, they can check and soften the impact. In a school of sixty or seventy you can see children sufficiently often to be watchful and not only to stop some of the unhappy impact but also to help the bully to see what he is doing. Beyond a hundred, and specially when there may be only one or two teachers who are therapeutically wise, certain problems become unmanageable. For the same reason heads of very large schools had a right to say to Wennington: 'All very well for you, but I've got a thousand kids to cope with!'

In general this leaves us with an irreducible dilemma. Repressive authority, tending to be encouraged by size, produces bullies and sadists all the way down the hierarchy of power. Nevertheless, the humane and sensitive heads of some large comprehensive schools, while admitting that size limits their personal contacts, do achieve the kind of authority that diffuses understanding, and minimizes conflicts.

We had two obstinate school-refusers. They participated in everything except classes and assemblies. One, a girl, would not come to a single class. We condoned this for a month. Then we tried persuasion, but it did not work. Her obstinacy was accompanied by a charming smile. One morning my patience snapped, and forgetting all psychological wisdom, I picked her up with the intention of carrying her to the classroom. She went rigid, stiff from head to foot. Then she reached for a broom resting against the wall, intending to whack me over the head. I admitted defeat and went away. Then Frances, suspecting claustrophobia, suggested that she should sit on a chair just inside the door of each classroom, with the freedom to rush out the moment it became unbearable. It worked. Gradually she joined in classes and it was she who, after sitting near the door in the Sunday assembly, came forward to play a piano solo, fumbled a phrase, rushed out, and came back in five minutes to play it right through.

The other refuser, a boy privately entered, gave us more trouble, and for a longer time. He chose not to go to certain classes, and changed his choice from time to time. My patience was mixed with bewilderment. But even he got to the point of taking 'O' level examinations. He played us some tricks, and with glee. At times he disappeared completely. On one such occasion another boy, noting my anxiety, said he knew where he was. He went off into the wood leading a posse of searchers, but came back later to tell me that the rascal would come out of hiding only if I fetched him. I was led into a very dense part of the wood, having to cross ditches and crawl under the arching branches of massive rhododendrons, to find a neatly constructed little hut, in which the boy lay curled up.

Once he disappeared on a cold drenching winter night. We had to bring in the police. But his outdoor clothes were not missing. Two concerned policemen got the help of the whole sixth form, who put on wellingtons and raincoats and searched every ditch and every dense bit of cover in the thirty acres of wood. They gave up at 2 a.m. When I tried to thank the police sergeant, he said he had youngsters of his own and he couldn't bear to think of a boy out on a night like this, and anyway it was a much more worthwhile job than hunting criminals. At 7 a.m. the boy was found in the changing room, soaked right through. He had been hiding in a dense clump of bushes up against the building while the many flashing torches passed him on their way to the wood. He didn't get pneumonia, not even a cold. He became a gifted pianist.

A boy of eleven came from unpropitious home conditions, in which he could never have achieved anything. He was a sensitive and creative boy; painted interesting pictures and wrote poetry. But as he moved into puberty he became assertive and tough. He was precociously intelligent and by the age of fourteen was walking around with a volume of Nietzsche under his arm. When I dared to test his knowledge of it, he replied with chapter and verse.

In the Sixth he became increasingly well-informed and articulate, but extremely assertive, so that in discussions, others, especially girls, were overwhelmed into muteness. Now and then I had to demand silence from him to give others a chance. In his last year he became a law unto himself, refused to do his share of duties, to go to bed or meals, to get up in the mornings. Could we keep him in the School? I couldn't bear to let him go;

I was convinced he was a valuable person. We provided a bed for him in an alcove. I sometimes had to go there at 11 a.m. to drag him out of bed. He was never nasty, but often surly.

The Latin teacher said that their roles were almost reversed, so rapid was his progress. Though he had missed many classes he did well in his 'A' levels, and eventually, without any further hitches, he took Ll.B., an upper-second. My precarious patience and occasional struggles with my own rising fury had been well rewarded.

When once I took a visitor into the workshop and talked about the background of some of the children present, I realized there were five illegitimates in that one class. (That was not an indication of the proportion in the School.) But no-one took the slightest notice of that kind of thing. Those five were with us because they had no responsible or visible fathers and the mothers were at work, perhaps serving in shops or charring. Two girls among them became headgirls one after the other and both got good degrees. It is doubtful that they could have had a chance of such self-fulfilment if they had not come to this kind of school.

Many adopted children came. Some had been fully loved, some had felt a lack. There was not one of them who did not at some time or other show the signs of insecurity; but it is good to be able to say that most worked successfully through to confidence. The oddest case of adoption occupied an enormous amount of attention for a month. She was a most attractive-looking girl, taken away in distress from a grammar school. Soon she began seeking attention from me. I began to find out things I had not been told; she showed me scars on her wrists as evidence that she had tried to commit suicide. (I did not take this too seriously. Such actions are often not really dangerous: just bloody enough to get attention.) She told me at length about a holiday in France.

She became distressed in the dormitory after going to bed and kept others awake by gabbling rapid French. Frances went in to see her. She begged for 'le professeur' or 'le maitre' to come and see her. When I came she reached up towards me and poured out a torrent of French with occasional lucid entreaties in English. This demand for attention after bedtime became somewhat embarrassing and hard on her companions. During the day she told me much about her family conditions; and although I had not mentioned any claim to psychological knowledge she began to pour out her dreams. Continued lapses into fluent French continued and I verified that it was good well-pronounced French though her record at the grammar school had not been outstanding and she had been in France only three weeks.

I thought we were making some progress, until we got a shock. The 'O' level exam was in progress in our assembly room, with my deputy in charge. There was always a hand bell in the room lest the supervisor should have to deal with an emergency and call for attention. I had been talking with this girl but had to leave her for a few minutes. Then I heard the bell ringing. I raced into the hall to see the face of my deputy looking round the assembly room door. 'Somebody's fallen off your balcony! It's a girl.'

She was lying on the gravel. I expected to find her severely injured. I verified that there were no limbs broken and got enough co-operation from her to make sure there was no spinal injury; that would have precluded movement. I carried her upstairs and phoned the doctor. He examined her with great care over the whole of her body. There was, as I thought, no fracture; there was not even the slightest cut or bruise. A veritable Joan of Arc! She had no idea how she came to fall from the balcony, which had a low parapet.

I had reached the limit of my know-how, and our good friend, Dr. Alfred Torrie, Superintendent of the Retreat, the Quaker hospital in York, agreed to take her. She stayed there a month, and during that time I had to go at regular intervals to assure her of my continued interest and affection. The psychiatrists were very interested in the full case-history supplied. At the end of the month it was thought reasonable to return her to school. Then occurred one of those mistakes which are perhaps inevitable because we cannot give all our attention to one person. She was returned on the day before Parents' Day. So there she was on the morning of that important day, with no parent of her own visiting her and myself heavily pre-occupied with other people.

She started walking down the mile-long drive. Half way she was overtaken by the Headgirl and her father on the way out to lunch. Ironically, he was a consultant psychiatrist. They gave her a lift into Wetherby. Just after they had set her down and she had vanished into the square, the Headgirl saw the light. She turned to her father: 'Daddy . . . that girl's running away!' They plunged after her, but it was too late. She must have found a bus very quickly.

What on earth will happen to her, I thought. All that time and attention gone for nothing? But some years later I had firm evidence that she had matured and had added self-confidence to her beauty.

At intervals between moments of congratulation, one has to remember the failures. Sadism has been mentioned. When nearly all the children were concerned about the development of atomic weapons, a boy plastered the school with posters advocating the bomb, with pictures of mushroom clouds and shattered bodies. This alone need not have been taken very seriously, but it was only one expression of his sadism, a cruelty unbearable by others. There was another boy whose joy was to wait, hidden round a corner, ready with a stick to thrust between the spokes of a cyclist pedalling past.

It was with a feeling of distress rather than mere relief that one had to reject such people because they endangered others. I tried to ensure that some better arrangements were made for them and I always felt relieved if I could turn to George Lyward at Finchden Manor. My conscience was relieved when he could take them; but there was no corresponding therapeutic haven for girls. We found that a girl referred as maladjusted for the first time at fourteen, might be too difficult to redeem. Her problem would be more definitely sexual than that of a boy of the same age. We stopped accepting disturbed girls of this age, but girls coming *before* puberty were often encouragingly responsive to an affectionate environment.

I had once been tempted to take a highly intelligent physically well set-up girl of fourteen who had been missing from her home for some months until the police traced her. No satisfactory account of her activities had been got from her, but she seemed eager now to make up for lost time. She was intelligently good-looking, pleasant and courteous, though detached personally. She settled down to work at once in every class, producing neat, ordered and fully completed assignments. Her work for me in science was near-perfect. This continued for a fortnight. Then I heard a rumour that she was seen packing some clothes. I quietly investigated; there was no sign of a suitcase or clothes being prepared. The next morning, a Sunday, my wife and I were driving down towards the gate and saw this girl ahead of us with a boy. They were carrying nothing, so I had no suspicions. They waved to us as they passed. That was the last we ever saw of her or of the boy. Somehow I learnt – I think through a letter written later to a friend by the boy – they had packed cases and hidden them some time previously in bushes on the road to York. There was no association between her and the boy in other respects. They had merely collaborated for this purpose.

That girl, as far as I know, was never found again. The police contacted the School from time to time to find if any letter might give information, but they dropped the case when her age reached sixteen. Her work was completed without any falling off right up to the moment of departure; she left her beautiful exercise books in her locker together with a pile of personal letters. These latter we had to read for the information of the police; they revealed a sleazy underground life among north London grammar school boys and girls with frequent references to 'queers' and to drugs – though I do not believe the girl herself took drugs. She was healthy to look at and too briskly intelligent. It is a story of bewildering contradictions and incompatibilities; and perhaps of tragedy.

Was it unwise for a parent to send a normally adjusted child to a school dealing with such unusual cases? The fact that we openly dealt with such cases, and did not try to hide them, must indeed have put off some parents. But it has to be recognized that all these problems are met in day schools and that contacts are made in the street between school and home, in the evenings or week-ends, of a sort that would scare parents if they knew about them; and things happen for which no-one takes responsibility – as that girl's letters revealed.

At Wennington the problems were acknowledged. The better adjusted boys and girls accepted what teenage relationships were like, but were given no excuse to feel superior or removed from others. They felt that the community was responsible for all its members, that problems existed to be resolved, that oddities and maladjustments were not to be wished away; they could be met with compassion, friendship and imaginative response.

It was far better that the School should be a therapeutic community than that I should be thought of as a therapist, and often a group was much more effective. Sometimes a dormitory group was clearly more patient. We once took a very intelligent girl who had a propensity for quarrelling with everybody, though she was affectionate in the intervals. One day, objecting to a teacher's criticism, she smacked his face – a real hard clout! When it was thought that I was coming to the end of my patience with her, the dormitory leader – who had to bear a lot of abuse from the girl – came to me and said: 'Don't send her away yet. Give her one more term; I think perhaps we can still do something with her.'

Thus the School provided an important experience for young people growing up: part of the educational nourishment that is more important than anything else, the beginning of a growth into accepting and understanding the complexities of human nature, and finding fulfilment in the adventure.

Sometimes I had to make quick adjustments to my discoveries and to odd behaviour. Contrary to my principles I clouted a boy in a fit of exasperation, felt depressed for hours afterwards, then found that through this I had at last reached a personal relationship with him! One day I was desperate to trace a theft of money; it was most important, not the least for the thief's sake, that he should be identified. I went into a room where a number of boys' jackets were hanging and let my eye run along them, wondering if anyone of them might be hiding the notes. I saw a wallet sticking out of a pocket and yielded to the impulse to pull it out. It opened as I did so, and out fell – a packet of three condoms.

The wallet revealed the name of the boy and I spoke to him, telling him what I had done and why, and asking him why he had the condoms. 'Well,' he said, in his curious, ponderous, half-shy way, 'these impulses come over a bloke, don't they . . . when you don't expect it? So you see, well, I wouldn't like to get a girl into trouble.' Poor rough, tough likeable lad; of all the boys of his age he was the least likely to get involved with a girl. But he was trying desperately hard to feel grown up.

There comes vividly to mind the first occasion when we took two children whose circumstances were so bad that they had to be taken into care. The social worker's description of them was alarming but also pathetic. At first we said 'Oh no!', but my wife had to go to London for other purposes and thought she ought to see the two boys. On the day she went I later had a phone call from her. Not only had she seen the boys but she was bringing them back with her.

I watched them walking with her across the courtyard and my heart fell. Oh no, I thought, oh no; it just will not work. That shambling walk of the inferior-feeling lad who has been in trouble with the police! But my fears were unfounded. No-one seemed to think of them as different, they were just like any other odd-bods who knocked on the Wennington door. One of them comes more clearly to mind than the other; he became an extraordinarily nice, responsive boy. If any crass politician asserts that independent education is necessarily divisive, I want to go back in time, take him by the short hairs and pitch him into the everyday whirl of Wennington for a few days after the arrival of those boys.

Sometimes children ran away, and caused us, and the police, a great deal of worry. Sometimes it might be a local authority child who disliked the country environment, who wanted to get back to the concrete jungle, the shop windows and the street corner. But much more often it was the child who knew that things were going wrong between father and mother; such a child had a pathetic idea that he, or she, could draw them together again. On two occasions, acting under this kind of impulse, children ran away in a thick fog and with inadequate money for fares. Again, I have nothing but praise for the thoroughness with which police helped us on such occasions, and with never a whisper of criticism of the School for planting such problems on them. Occasionally I told the children that the escapade probably cost the country some hundreds of pounds in phone calls and police-car hunting. In their state of mind this argument meant nothing to them.

In one revealing instance a boy of eleven was missing for over two days, in freezing winter weather with ice on all the puddles. He went wearing only shorts, shirt and jacket and with sixpence and a bar of chocolate. He never arrived home, and the temperature was such that we almost gave him up for dead, expecting a frozen corpse to be found in a ditch. Then we had a phone call from a motherly woman who had noticed a boy looking miserable in Leeds, and extracted information from him.

Two of us raced into Leeds to find him in charge of police officers. He had spent the whole two days in the open and slept under arches. On the way back to School I leaned over to him and said 'Look here, you've had your parents fairly crawling up the wall with anxiety.' His reply came without hesitation: 'That's exactly what I wanted!' Like the boy in the bushes, he didn't even catch a cold. There was no further trouble; that little boy became a six-foot honours graduate of London University and, like so many others, turned to teaching.

There is one other category to be mentioned, the epileptic. Our friendship with Dr. Tylor Fox for many years before starting the School made us familiar with the disease and the personal and social problems associated with it. One of Tylor's main concerns was to get the epileptic accepted by society without fear or revulsion and thus enable the epileptic himself to feel he could live a normal life. We knew what fits were like and the drug treatments Tylor had pioneered. So we often had one or two in the School, and we did what we could to make sure that other members of the group treated them with acceptance and sympathy. Some were specially eager to show themselves capable of a normal life, indeed they tended to overdo it. There was a projecting ridge running round the main building high up just below the top windows. Imagine my feelings when I saw an epileptic of about twelve walking round that ridge with his hands splayed out against the wall!

Another was anxious to be given some acting. He had not been successful in other school activities, but when I gave him a part in a Tchekov play he was superb and this was the beginning of an increase in self-confidence. As he became older, his fits became more severe. One day, whilst passing a boys' dormitory I had to respond to a sudden call for help. I found this particular boy was in the tonic phase of *grand mal,* unconscious and rigid. Three or four boys had caught him and got him on to a bed. Within a few seconds he went into the clonic spasm, began twitching and thrashing around. What was so impressive about the whole scene – which had a Rembrandt quality – was the quiet concern and tenderness on the faces of the boys standing round and sufficiently restraining him to avoid injury. An epileptic fit of this kind is ugly; a casual observer would call it repulsive. But there were no feelings of rejection on the other boys' faces. This is another instance of the fact that to accept into a school some children with unusual needs is to educate the others, in the development of acceptance and compassion.

The same boy wanted to come to our post-exam camp in Borrowdale and I consented, though uneasily. After a few days he had an attack, and did not recover fully. The group arranged to leave two of their members always with him while the others climbed. One evening he began to have successive attacks, hardly recovering from each before the next began. I knew enough about this to fear that it might be the dangerous condition of *status epilepticus* and got him first to Keswick and then to Carlisle hospital. He was later taken to hospital near his own home and the prognosis was bad. Eventually he did make steady progress and when he came to see me some years later he was almost free from the fear of fits and had qualified as a marine engineer.

Another interesting instance ended less happily. The boy concerned was even more anxious to prove himself normal. One day during the visit of a group to Malham Tarn, we were exploring Gordale Scar, where there is a great vertical cliff of limestone hanging over a waterfall, a cliff cut by horizontal fissures. I looked up and saw this boy crawling along a fissure near the top and looking over the edge. He was daring himself. There was nothing to do but wait till he came down safely.

This boy's great achievement in School was pottery; he was immensely good at it and produced superb pots, giving every minute of his spare time to throwing. We hoped there would be a career for him in this, and he was in fact accepted by a small commercial potter after he left School. But other people's fear of epilepsy stood in his way; and of course there was the danger if he had to be left alone among belt-driven machinery.

Richard's need to prove himself was always with him. Before he left School he saved a man from drowning – a man who had fallen into the Strid, the narrow gorge through which the Wharfe passes near Bolton Abbey. After that he took to skin-diving and came back after a holiday to show me proudly the Leica camera he had fished up from a Devonshire harbour (as well as an outboard motor). Skin-diving became a passion and again there was hope of employment, but only in his own mind, for the dangers were obvious. He insisted on offering his services voluntarily. A few years after leaving school he joined a group working on the Naburn lock, on the Ouse south of York. There came a moment when it was noticed that he had not come to the surface for some time after diving. Men went down to look for him; he was jammed between timbers under the water. It was difficult to extricate him and before this could be done his oxygen had given out and Richard was dead. His brief life had been one of great courage and enterprise, a triumph against adversity.

CHAPTER XVII

The Shadow and the Thief

MOST PARENTS HAVE HAD occasion to call their otherwise delightful children little devils. Even the most carefully selective schools have a variety of delinquencies to deal with, and eruptions of group misbehaviour into which the seemingly normal are drawn. We all have it in us to be anti-social, wayward, and stupid in the sense of being unwilling to foresee the consequences of our actions. A good educator is one who accepts that this is what human beings are like; he accepts the troubles that unavoidably arise and sees that they are opportunities.

Disturbances can, of course, become unmanageably difficult, the result of ill-directed administration and social conditions outside the educator's control. Much attention is being given in the press at present to behaviour problems in schools, especially to the alarming increase in certain areas where it is becoming difficult to keep teachers. I would hesitate to say what I would do if I were the head of a school where defiance and truancy are rife and where teachers do not turn up for their classes because they fear the rowdies. Bigness as we have seen, alters the aspect of such problems. I can only say how we dealt with common delinquencies in a community of a little more than a hundred. We accepted the challenge: this was nature as it always has been and perhaps always would be; and waywardness could not be redeemed by punishment, moralizing and regimentation.

The Jungian theory of archetypes proved useful: that we are none of us just one person but have in us a series of types of beings lined up behind the *persona,* the face we show to the public. We do not need to take this too literally. Like all theories, it is an imaginative way of thinking about personality and one that enables us to act effectively. For instance, there is a being in us that represents what we have got from father and his maleness, the *animus,* another from mother, the *anima.* There remains in all of us something of the *little child,* often disclosed privately in marriage, in the endearments the partners use towards each other and the cossetings they expect.

The word *persona* is the Latin for the mask worn in ancient times by an actor. It represented the character he was acting and it covered up his own real personality. We all to some extent put on a mask in public, and it represents what we want other people to think we are. But behind this is another self that contains the opposites to the contents of the public image. It contains a hidden feeling of incompetence behind our show of efficiency, a weakness that contradicts our show of strength, a cruelty that can sometimes come to the surface when we think we ought to be kind. This hidden opposite self is the archetype called 'the Shadow' and it is thought of as an active being in us because in moments of crisis or severe challenge it can take over, to the surprise of all around and even the person himself.

The archetypes need not be thought of as totally independent beings; they can incorporate each other. The little child can be part of the shadow of the strong, self-confident man or the gangster, so that when he is defeated he becomes pathetic and cries. The aggressive *animus* can be part of the shadow of the overwhelmingly loving woman, who, when her offerings are refused, may become thrustingly hateful.

Those who are responsible for the moral or educational care of others are dangerously apt to put on a mask of goodness, rightness and wisdom, hiding their own opposite impulses. The moralistic headmaster or magistrate can become viciously cruel to an offender brought before him for examination and punishment, can be taken charge of by his own shadow, that part of him whose hidden urges would prompt him to commit the very crimes he condemns in the offender.

Real growing up is an achievement of integration. To be integrated, to become one instead of many, to be made whole instead of being at the mercy of parts, requires that we should become aware of what we are made of and stop thinking that we are the mask we show to the world. It requires that we should discover how to make use of our 'archetypes' – the several active parts or beings within us. A woman who is dominated by her hidden maleness, the *animus,* the aggressive thrusting element, is a horror to run away from. (Some noisy women's-libbers are in this category!) But a woman who remains primarily a woman and knows how to make use of a vigorous impulse to get things done is immensely valuable to society. We need more and more of such liberated women; even when they seem formidable we can be grateful for their tenacity.

Now for the shadow. The problem of integrating it is a fascinating one. How can we incorporate the hateful, the destructive, the vindictive and the mean into anything we can call wholeness? How can we make friends with our devil? There is no wholly satisfying answer, for in spite of all the analyses of psychology, human nature remains fundamentally mysterious; we have to depend upon hints, on occasional flashes of illumination, on the awareness that somehow in the course of a human crisis something has happened. One thing seems reasonably certain: that the more we moralize, the more we condemn and try to expel this apparently threatening part of ourselves and others, the more dangerous it becomes; we increase disintegration and the power of evil, which is something beyond badness. The devil moves further into the darkness and becomes more active and malevolent.

It is interesting that the devil is thought of in the mythology of the Bible, not as an intruder from a different realm, but as a fallen angel, a rebellious member of God's kingdom. (And in Greek mythology, those who brought trouble to mankind were themselves gods or demi-gods, rebellious ones.) This suggests that the devil is to be dealt with, not by trampling him under foot, but by redeeming him, 'buying him back' into the kingdom to which he really belongs. Always the devil is thought of as associated with energy; always he is 'going to and fro in the earth . . . and walking up and down in it'. At least partly, the problem of making friends with the devil, bringing him into our integrity, is the problem of making use of his energy. He bears a smile as well as a sneer.

We should never think of redemption as the saving of man by thrusting down half his nature. It comes by understanding his make-up and his needs. We have to learn how to turn quarrelling into affection, grabbing into giving, the energy of anarchy into the eagerness of co-operation. There is no recipe for this; it is an individual and personal matter. There are, however, conditions we can try to establish that will favour this achievement. One is the recognition between the adult and the child of a common humanity, that we are all made of the same stuff, and a readiness to communicate at the level of experience and what can be learnt from it. Another is the removal of fear, which tends to drive energy into paranoid and destructive channels. And generally there must be a welcoming of the energy of the young, and the provision of a variety of modes of expression, not just the physical outlet in games, but a variety covering the many manifestations of feeling.

One of the commonest deliquencies in schools is theft. Once when I spoke about Wennington to a small gathering of heads of boarding schools. I was asked the question: *do you have stealing?* – as though I might have had some magic that prevented it. I had to answer: Of course! On several occasions we accepted children who had been referred to child guidance clinics for stealing, and boys who had been expelled from Public Schools for the same reason. Stealing is not the most worrying of deliquencies, nor is it the most difficult to remedy. The presence of a thief in a dormitory can be disturbing to the children's confidence in each other, but that is a situation that can be worked through constructively. Nearly all children steal or have stolen at some time or other and their knowledge of what it feels like can be appealed to in coping with the impulse as a general school problem.

Punishment is not appropriate; and the expelled boys who came to us really need never have left their schools. It is well known that much petty theft is an attempt to make up for some deprivation, especially the lack of love from a parent. The stealing of sweets is often a displaced appeal for affection, and adopted children, most of whom feel at least a little insecure, often did it. It is important to identify a thief, to get to the root of his trouble and to relieve the group of the unease and distrust caused by the thieving. Conventional school attempts to find a thief are pathetically stupid and ineffective. One has to learn to be a detective and to keep one's ear close to the ground, also to know the boy's or girl's state of mind. Girls tended to be more stealthy than boys. They did it in a small way, quietly and effectively and it often took a long time to find out which girl was stealing chocolates from dormitory lockers. Boys were bolder; they went in for it in a big way and left traces, sometimes comically evident.

When I think of particular instances, it is not always possible to see evidence of deprivation, and sometimes the fascination of a daring enterprise is what holds one's attention. I think at once of an interesting individualist who became, for a brief period, an accomplished burglar, but had such a convincingly innocent expression that he was known as Angel-face. Over the last twenty years and through various routes round the globe a somewhat hilarious correspondence has passed between us and I now know more about his exploits than I did when he was a boy. The larders were his unvarying objectives and he was out to show that he could defeat my detective activities. Once, after I had thought the larders to be impregnable, I found a large number of oranges arranged in a neat four-sided pyramid on his bed; he must have intended me to see them. Other discoveries that I made he now thinks to have been deplorable lapses in his efficiency, for they were associated with important enterprises.

Years later I heard the story of these. Five boys, all exemplary characters in other respects, formed a secret society which put on surreptitious and sumptuous parties in the most unlikely place – the school garden shed. Each boy was a specialist. One, who had a flair for science and as a cleaner and tidier had access to the laboratories, supplied Calor gas cylinders and bunsen burners on which to do the cooking. Our skilled cat burglar, using his secret route to the school larders, through neglected lofts and a disused trap door, supplied such staple provisions as eggs and butter. Yet another boy, son of a wealthy business man, was the banker, providing the capital to finance the purchase of such necessary outside items as cider. The binges were usually held between 1 a.m. and 5 a.m., and were cunningly timed to coincide with the school's frequent drama festivals, for on such occasions large suitcases, bulging with provisions, could be carried around without arousing suspicion.

Girls were always invited. A party without girls, they thought, would be pointless, for such events provided the opportunity to impress them. It was definitely a male display, a way of saying: 'Look how daring we were!' And there was a hope that this would excite a little adoration. They were not allowed to enter the garden shed until everything was ready.

What a sight then met their eyes! Gone were the mowers, rakes, spades and forks, and in their place was an immaculately laid table, illuminated by scores of candles and surrounded by extravagent decorations. To one side, and imparting a welcoming warmth, was the battery of bunsen burners, over which the 'cook' was busily preparing the first course.

At the end of each party the cutlery, crockery and glasses were conscientiously washed and returned to their shelves, the table and chairs returned to their proper rooms, and the laboratory equipment carefully replaced. Nothing was broken or damaged and although much cider was consumed, nobody got drunk. It was precisely this efficiency that protected these boys from discovery. Most other binges left spectacular traces, enabling me to track them down – if I wanted to.

The burglarious leader of this enterprise, now approaching middle-age, considers himself to be leading a life of unqualified respectability. He's a writer, and a lively one. As for his thefts, he found a way of salving his conscience in the end. He spent one summer holiday as a cabin boy on an Iceland fishing trawler, wrote up his experience and won the first prize in the *Birmingham Mail* essay competition. It was the latest 24-volume *Encyclopaedia Britannica*. He quietly presented it to the School library when he departed.

A daring escapade on the part of another boy was the robbing of the stationery cupboard. That was done by the clever manipulation of keys. If you steal large quantities of paper, exercise books, pencils, rulers and rubbers, you unavoidably leave traces all round you – and he was 'arrested and charged' by me within twenty-four hours. He became a policeman, and is now I think a detective-sergeant, if not an inspector.

Group stealing is a special kind of temptation. The individual prick of conscience can be eased if you share your guilt with others. A sixth-form boy was given seven pounds on his birthday and unwisely did not bank it at once with his form master. It was stolen from his wallet in his dormitory. The tracing of the thieves took some time, but it came through the technique familiarized in detective novels and 'Z Cars': getting into conversation with the more rascally types and putting in a casual question now and then. So I learnt that two boys had hired a boat on the Wharfe two or three times during the week-end, had had a big tea in the cafe and had bought a hundred cigarettes. It wasn't difficult to extract a confession. Careful calculation accounted for five of the seven pounds; where were the other two? Now there was confusion on the faces of the boys. Eventually, I got the reply: 'We put it in a wellington boot'. Off we went to the changing room and the boy produced his wellingtons. We shook them. Nothing there. Were the boys speaking the truth? I thought they were. Could anyone have found the money? But who would go fumbling into a wellington in the hope of finding pound notes? The boys were certain no-one knew of their hiding place. The wellingtons were wet, so I asked the boys if they had actually put pound notes into a soaking boot. Good heavens, no! This was odd, and it occurred to me that the wellingtons had been subsequently borrowed without the owner's permission. Much enquiry proved that this had indeed happened. The borrower had been larking in ditches but he was plainly mystified when I asked if he found two pound notes in one of them. At that moment the light broke; I pushed my fingers right into the toe of a boot and extracted the pulped remains.

Those two thieves lost a lot of their pocket money over a long period and they had to earn some by doing jobs; thus they returned the money. I do not think they continued to thieve. More worrying were instances of a planned crime against the school community; for instance a night raid on the school tuckshop by cracksman's methods. Again it was not difficult to trace the culprits. There was considerable general feeling against them; for the tuckshop was the pupils' 'own show'; they had built the kiosk, they undertook the ordering from wholesalers, they did the selling and kept the accounts, they estimated the profits and decided what charity or school project it should be given to. So it was with the backing and the extremely strong feeling of many boys and girls that I dealt with those two burglars, and subsequently kept a watchful eye on them.

It is perhaps right to say here that if you wish to be effective in tracking down petty crime in a school it is wise to be sure of evidence, to collect as much as possible before tackling the thief, and to keep some evidence up your sleeve so that if he tries to lie his way out of the situation, you confront him with yet more facts. This is not 'police-bullying'; it is common sense. It is far worse for everyone concerned if a teacher goes bull-headed at a possible thief, makes a great stink, charges him before he really knows and thus encourages him to find that lying pays.

The development of open access to goods has encouraged many young people to steal who would not otherwise be tempted. The first instance of shoplifting came after the first supermarket was opened in Wetherby. I was recalled from a Sixth-form post-exam camp in the Lake District to meet a detective inspector. He wanted me to do the investigating rather than bring the police and all the unavoidable melodrama into the School. He also paid me the compliment of suggesting that I should know better how and where to look for the stolen goods. A hunt revealed that several boys and girls were involved, all of them normally responsible people. A girl who felt badly about her appearance had collected a caseful of cosmetics; boys had got sweets and tins of food. One had a gramophone record. The inspector referred the case to his headquarters and it was possible that there would be a juvenile court hearing. Eventually, the decision was that the police would take no action if I would promise not to expel any of the boys and girls involved, in other words if I would take full responsibility for their future conduct and in treating their deliquency.

This was an instance of the unfailingly constructive and helpful attitude of the local police over the twenty-three years during which I worked in the School at Wetherby, from 1945 onwards. This needs to be said, for there is an inclination to take the proportionately few instances of corruption and bullying among the police as an indication of general unreliability and insensitiveness.

Police were more directly involved in a stealing incident many years earlier, a much more dramatic one. It was a year or two after the war ended. A friend rang from London to ask if I could take at once a boy who had been suddenly expelled from a Public School, one among several boys who had been expelled just before the School Certificate Examination. My friend said that she couldn't imagine what kind of mental state the headmaster could be in to take such peremptory and devastating action. As it happened, that headmaster was one of the few Public School heads whom I knew, and I respected him. The reason appeared almost at once in the daily press. A group of boys had stolen from a local army or airforce camp a quantity of weapons, including machine guns, and had hidden them in the school grounds. Perhaps it was by rumour that I heard that they had even been firing them; if true, this put them in the one firm category that I myself used as a reason for expulsion: any action that endangered life.

I heard at the same time that there was a fair quantity of army radio apparatus hidden under boys' beds in another of the co-educational boarding schools. 'Thank Heaven', said I, 'that we've had none of that trouble here.' The next weekend some instinct prompted me to stop and question a small group of boys who had just returned from a private excursion with loaded rucksacks. I stopped them and said, 'What? Come back already? And what have you got in those rucksacks?' 'Oh, just our stuff,' they replied. Well, it did not look like a rolled up raincoat and a packet of sandwiches, as I then explained to them. It was well crammed in, and knobbly. I did not then suspect anything serious, having too good an opinion of the boys. 'Come on,' I said' 'turn it out; I'm curious'. They demurred, but then sheepishly undid the strings and inverted the bags on to the stone flags. The contents made my eyes spin: electric drills, aero-compasses, rheostats, electric motors, lamps, optical apparatus, etc. For a while I could only gasp. Then I asked: 'Where on earth did you get all this?' They explained that they had collected it off the ground on the nearby R.A.F. airfield, a former bomber base. 'Go and see for yourself,' they said, 'it's all over the fields. Anyone can go and help himself.'

I collected the contents of the two or three rucksacks and then went to examine the nearest section of the R.A.F. station. It was as they had said; the ground was littered with thousands of pounds worth of apparatus and accessories and tools. Storesheds stood open and inside were piles of Dessouter drills, multi-range tests meters, capacitors, rheostats, valves – everything.

I went back and reluctantly loaded the apparatus into two big cases; reluctantly because we were just constructing a makeshift laboratory in what had been a big garage, and I was longing for money to buy apparatus! I drove round to the station and opened the cases at the adjutant's feet. 'Here's the temptation you leave lying around!' The Commanding Officer came in. He was genuinely surprised. He had only just been moved to this station; he had not looked around properly and he promised to look at the areas I described.

Well, that's that, thought I. Not too bad. The end of term was close upon us and I welcomed the coming respite from responsibility. But in the middle of the last mid-day meal I felt uneasy. I had a hunch that all was not well, one of the many hunches that from time to time led me to something. I walked out of the dining room and straight up to a boys' dormitory where most of the bags lay packed. There was a rucksack standing on the window sill. I put my hand into the neck of it, and my fingers closed on a revolver butt. It was a standard heavy service weapon.

I pushed in further and pulled out a second one, this time with the barrel sawn short and therefore for some reason seeming more malevolent.

I had the members of the dormitory up immediately after the meal. Everything was opened and turned out. One other revolver was revealed and also a pair of handcuffs. The two boys, it seemed, wanted to come clean. Yes, they had got them from the airfield, but like the other equipment they had been just lying around, asking to be picked up. The more normally responsible boy, a Sixth-former, offered to take me and show me the very spot where they had found the revolvers. He remembered that one revolver was pressed into the soil and left an imprint when he lifted it out. He would show me. I went with him to the very spot and he located it unerringly. Indeed he was very convincing. But there was no imprint. He suggested that rain had washed it away. True, it had been raining and for the moment I accepted his statement.

A curious thing happened on our way back over the fields. I suddenly asked him: 'Where did you find the handcuffs?' He was confused, said he didn't remember. For the first time I had doubts about his honesty. Surely handcuffs are such a romantic object that no-one could fail to remember the circumstances in which he found them. But I wanted to believe him. In all other respects he was a very good lad. I took the revolvers to the adjutant. As I went into the office a sergeant welcomed me jovially. 'Here comes the headmaster who looks after our stuff for us!' I handed out the revolvers and dumped them on the table. 'But leaving this sort of thing around is more than a joke!'

I explained how they had been found and where. But just then another sergeant came in – and his eyes bulged. 'These revolvers! The Police have been searching for them all week! Stolen from the armoury during the week-end'. I almost persuaded them that some local lads had stolen them, then dumped them and discreetly departed. But there were only three, and there was a fourth missing. The police were telephoned and I walked back to School to meet them. They soon found that the fourth was in the possession of a boy who had gone home a day early, to London.

The boys stuck to their story. But the boy in London was unprepared. The police got him out of bed at midnight and soon he confessed. They had indeed raided the armoury and stolen the weapons. So the whole truth came out, and I got all the details from the boys still at School. I had to inform the parents. The father of the most senior of the boys was himself a policeman; he was so upset that he went to bed for a day and turned his face to the wall.

On a Sunday morning two boys, strolling round the completely unguarded, chaotic airfield, had looked through the window of a hut and seen a box labelled 'Revolvers'. Through the window of the next room they had seen a cupboard full of keys with labels attached. They came back to School and told two of their friends of this romantic discovery. They returned to the airfield and debated the opportunity. Two wanted to steal. Two were doubtful of the wisdom and morality of the action; but these two nevertheless kept guard while the others climbed through the easily opened windows. And afterwards they were tempted and fell. The revolvers and the handcuffs, and indeed some other items, were distributed.

I was given an unofficial hint that if I made a special representation to authority the incident might not be brought to public notice. Some important boarding schools had been able to avoid court action because of the danger to their reputation. I refused at once, saying that whatever would happen under the law to any ordinary boy must happen to them. I was not being pious in this; I simply knew that any privileged treatment for these boys would be bad for them, ultimately. The detective was glad; he was sorry he made the suggestion.

So the boys duly came before the juvenile court in Wetherby. They were wisely handled. It was recognized that they had good school records, were not essentially delinquent; and the commanding officer testified that he had come new to the station and found equipment lying around, as I described it, in a way that would encourage stealing. The boys were put on probation for a year. This meant a monthly visit by a probation officer, who after a while was content with my own reassuring reports on the boys.

None of the four relapsed into any delinquency. One took a degree and a teacher's qualification. For a while he taught in one of the toughest areas in South East London, controlling boys armed with flick knives, and outlasting several other teachers who departed in defeat. Another entered chemical industry at a humble level and took a degree by evening work. The other two became craftsmen.

The end of the juvenile court episode was an absurd anti-climax. The stolen property had been resting on the table and included a beautiful white leather flying helmet found in the possession of the London boy. As the court rose, a policeman, in the hearing of us all, picked up the helmet and handed it to the boy. 'Here, old chap. This wasn't mentioned in the indictment; you can keep it.'

CHAPTER XVIII

What did they do afterwards?

EARLY IN 1971, Eleanor and I landed in New Zealand from Samoa and were promptly launched into the succession of TV interviews with which cities in that country and Australia welcome their visitors. After an appearance on the Wellington screen a telegram followed us to Christchurch. It asked me to contact a former pupil, gave a phone number and was signed by a Susan whose surname I only vaguely recognized. I rang the number, and then followed this conversation:

> Hello, I got your telegram, but which Susan are you? – there were so many of them!
> Oh, don't you remember me? I was the worst girl in the School. I didn't stay long; but that was because although my Mum liked the School, my Dad didn't believe in it.
> I still can't place you. What dreadful things did you do?
> Surely you remember! We had a cider party, and we stole the cider from Wetherby.
> Ah yes, that rings a bell. And I made you confess to the shop and pay for it. But your surname – it is the name you had at School? Haven't you got married?
> Oh yes, I've been married three times, but they were all idiots.
> You poor girl, that sounds very sad. But what are you doing now? How's life?
> I'm very happy.
> Really?
> Yes, I'm a barmaid.

Not often were the foundations of a career laid down at so early a stage. Young people today often leave their decision rather late, perhaps wisely. One boy left with no idea of what to do, but was soon visiting us and boasting of better pay than others of his year. He is a train driver, a militant member of ASLEF, a very active councillor in a London borough – and a staunch supporter of the School.

Girls who became nurses made the earliest decisions; they got their first experience proudly helping in the dispensary or sick room. Several determinedly pushed their way into the profession in spite of poor academic achievements; and they did very well. One with an I.Q. seemingly well below 100 suffered from dyslexia and this hampered her work dreadfully. She could not help having a poor opinion of herself. One evening, during a debate when the clever ones were scoring points, there was a moan from a corner of the room and a thump on the floor. The inert body was carried out. When Stephanie came round from her faint, she explained her collapse. 'Those clever ones; they made me feel no good. I couldn't bear it!'

She came into her own in medical emergencies. If anyone got a bad cut or other injury, Stephie was miraculously on the spot. If a matron was sick, Stephie was found doing her work – efficiently. She slogged at her classwork, fighting down discouragement. She began to get one or two 'O' level passes in spite of almost undecipherable writing. She found time to get to my sixth-form physiology classes, and her written work showed flashes of understanding shining through confused squiggles. She passed in that subject too.

Her smiling determination, and the insight of a certain hospital matron, got her into a good nursing school. She got through her exams by resolute hard work and her writing became almost normal. When she was in the middle of a midwifery course we had an amusing encounter. I was waiting at King's Cross booking office one day, when I heard a yell from the back of the queue. 'Kenneth!' She travelled with me as far as Grantham and talked the whole time. She was bubbling with enthusiasm for her work, and knowing my physiological and medical interests, she let fly about her experiences in delivering babies. The ears of the rest of the travellers got longer and longer, for Stephie could never talk quietly. By the time she got on to the latest suction method of delivery those ears were flapping. 'You just press it on to the baby's head and pull!'

When I next met her she had qualified as a midwife and was out on her own. She told a comic story of how she coped with a mother in a small Polish community in the Midlands. All the neighbours were kneeling and praying round the bed. Stephie just could not get near it. So she had to throw them out one by one before she could start her work. This, the girl who had fainted because she thought she was no good!

I ought to have remembered earlier that one of her helps towards self-confidence was learning to play the oboe, up to the point where she could play solos in the Sunday evening meeting. She joined the Society of Friends, and with Quaker encouragement went out to Mauritius to deliver babies in the chaos created by a cyclone. There she met and married a Tamil. They had a child, and later another. On the way home from our world-wanderings in 1971 we heard appalling news; Stephanie, her husband and her older child were dead, struck by lightning in a tropical thunderstorm. They had gone out for a picnic and failed to return.

There were many other instances of boys and girls who started haltingly and later did well; not so much through any conscious technique of teaching but perhaps mainly through being appreciated and encouraged. Another dyslexic became excellent at metal work and made a superb little watch-maker's lathe. He was madly interested in clocks so for a while I hunted up clock literature and got him to read from it for five minutes each morning after assembly. Still unable to write clearly, he was smuggled into a college of technology without having even 'O' level English. He won the Ingersoll prize for the best student of his year and is now established in the instrument-making industry. The dyslexia has gone.

Yet another dyslexic, after an inauspicious start, did so well in the workshop that towards the end of his time, to our amusement, he seemed to be aiming to instruct his teacher. He is now the chief production engineer in one of the Rank subsidiaries manufacturing high-precision optical instruments. In passing, it should be said that we did not claim to have specialist knowledge in the treatment of dyslexia. We did occasionally seek specialist advice, but generally success was attributable to tolerance, patience and the attempt to find activities that would bring achievement and the growth of self-confidence.

A boy was sent to the School, with his sister, by a local authority because there was tuberculosis in the family and it was wise to get him away from home. He was an ambitious boy but afraid of not being able to do what he wanted. I remember seeing him on the top diving board, daring himself to plunge but unable to do it. He was musical, began to work at the piano but again worked himself into a state of frustration. Then the moment came. It was suggested to him that he should try the clarinet – and he went straight ahead. At that time there was a boy's bedroom next to ours on the top floor. Hour after hour during afternoons or evenings we could hear bits of Mozart's clarinet quintet filtering through the wall. In the Sixth he became interested in composing. For this he needed peace and quiet, and it was a case for ignoring bedtime rules. If at midnight the light was on in the big music room and I opened the door to find him bent over the keyboard, the right thing to do was to smile, close the door and quietly creep away. The school choir sang songs composed by him.

He was accepted into the Academy, mainly on his clarinet playing, but later he turned wholly to composing. He won the Boulanger scholarship to Paris and studied for a while under Nadia. He found her too dominating, so he broke away, joined with another student in taking an empty house with a piano almost their only item of furniture, and gave English lessons to keep the wolf from the door. But he did not feed himself properly and had to return to England to let his tummy recover. Now he began to be noticed.

He was invited by Trinity College, Cambridge to become the first holder of its Fellowship in Creative Arts. The B.B.C. broadcast his works, he got commissions from it and from festivals, he wrote operas for Glyndebourne.

The School has produced many other musicians but nearly all of them teachers. It is not wise to encourage young musicians to become concert players unless they are exceedingly good, for the musical profession seems to suffer from competitiveness and jealousy more than any other; and the important experience is to *enjoy* music and pass on the enjoyment to others. I think our teachers became real musical educators. One who was so good that he might have become a professional player, instead became the organizer of classical music programmes for the Canadian Broadcasting Corporation.

Let us turn aside for a moment to think of the boy or girl who from the conventional school point of view is more ordinary. Sitting in class next to a budding scientist you might see a boy who looks cheerfully vacant; and he may go on like that for most of the day. Is he wasting his time? But put him on a tractor and he is absolutely reliable as also in many other jobs round the school estate. In many big schools he would have been 'streamed', so would the young scientist. Would this have been good? Did it matter that the tractor driver always felt a bit out of it in class? The boy I have in mind, after having become exceedingly useful to the School, went home to his father's farm and soon became its manager. Another boy was one of two brothers; the other was a high-flyer, got top grades right across the 'A' level report sheet and was accepted by his first-choice medical school. The less academic boy was fascinated by farming, listened to all the B.B.C. farming broadcasts and became a mine of agricultural information. It was therefore not surprising that when we were passing through Lusaka in 1970 we had news of him up-country in Zambia doing voluntary service on the land.

Another of our useful practical boys, one who learnt welding and helped to make our 'battleship bedsteads', went home to his father's enormous poultry farm (with the early prospect of a Wennington friend for a wife) and soon became capable of almost taking over. More boys than I expected became policemen and we can rejoice in that. I hope no one will ever call them pigs. One wrote an interesting article on the opportunities of police work.

It is more difficult to be definite about girls, for the careers of many have been diverted by early marriage in spite of my warnings against this. I used to say to them: 'Look, it's terribly important not to get married in a hurry. Wait until you've got more maturity, more judgement, more knowledge of yourself and of other people. Make it a decision, not a mere happening. And whatever you do, first of all get yourself a fully qualified job, capable of earning all you need, standing well on your own feet. You never know what the future will bring!'

Wasted breath? Not entirely. Many of the girls who got married soon after leaving did complete their courses after the ceremony. When I meet them, still seeming terribly young for the responsibilities of marriage, they do seem to have taken into marriage a lively, positive, practical and realistic attitude. They are not likely to wilt in face of trouble. I recently listened to two of them talking together some years after marriage, recalling how much they had been able to take with them from their school experience. They remembered how a cheerful and eager responsibility had been characterisitc of their life at School, how they had learnt to meet crises or problems without having to be told what to do, how they roused their colleagues to action, and sometimes their teachers. One forty-year-old woman who had married early, before getting any training, said that what she owed to the School was the eagerness and courage to respond to whatever life may bring. She felt she could never have learnt this through any other experience in her growing up. These words were the more impressive for my knowledge that she had passed through successive personal tragedies soon after leaving school.

How different was the career of another girl of the same group, one whose parents took her away just before she might have entered the Sixth, but not before the spirit of her enterprising group had taken charge of her. Some amusing letters came from her describing her first experiences. She felt very much a fledgling. She started training in domestic science and tried attending Quaker meetings. Then impulsively, and with just enough money for the fare, she set sail for New York. She had no job to go to, but someone told her that Leopold Stokowski was in need of a secretary. She boldly introduced herself and got the job, which she held for two-and-a-half-years, longer than any of her predecessors. She says that her spelling was a bit erratic, but Stokowski didn't mind that; he just ringed the errors and pencilled in the margin: Sorry, Wendy can't spell.

She went on to become organizing secretary for various orchestras and musical conventions in the States and then at the height of their fame, secretary to the Beatles. She nannied them through innumerable night-flights and near-riots. Then from her office in Eaton Square, she ran her own publicity agency for actors and musicians, orchestras and plays. Now she is publicity agent for the New York Metropolitan Theatre. She is the only Wennington pupil who could boast (but she doesn't) that a daily newspaper gave two whole pages to a description of her career. It piled on the glamour, but it is good to say that this kind of experience has left her unaffected; she remains as unpretentious as the day she left Wennington. Some of the *Evening Standard*'s comments are worth quoting: 'The point about Miss Hanson is not her qualifications but her qualities. She has qualities that rise above a mere ability to spell. She has one quality that makes life much easier and more agreeable for those around her; she has another quality that enables her to get on with a variety of human beings ranging from Mr Ezra Pound to the Moody Blues.

'She is just as good at organizing the canvas seat for the late President Kennedy to sit on in his motorcade as she is in shepherding Ringo round Asprey's. . . . The more difficult, the more temperamental, the more creative and the more powerful men are the easier Miss Hanson finds it to get on with them.' Wendy, says the article, 'was sent to what sounds like a splendid school, progressive and Quaker, in Wetherby. There were lots of poetry, music and politics. She helped to build a sewer while she was there – yet another string to her remarkable bow.'

Now for those who made the most of academic possibilities. It must again be emphasized that the School did not aim primarily at scholarly success, certainly not exam results. It aimed at general liveliness and emotional maturity, but it had good reason to believe that this development of personality would ultimately produce better scholars than did the deliberate intention to secure qualifications. In the School's early days we were unnecessarily humble. When a boy said he would like to go to Cambridge I told him that no one from an unknown school like ours would stand a chance. But he insisted on applying. Some time later he looked into my study with a paper in his hand. 'Who said I wouldn't stand a chance? I've got an interview.' He came back from his visit to Cambridge in a joyful mood. The Master of the college had welcomed him and they had sat down for a chat; but it developed into a discussion that lasted an hour. It was about history and not about his application. At the end of the hour he was accepted. Eventually he took an upper-second in Law, narrowly missing a first.

Wennington has been poor at keeping records of its old pupils, and many of them firmly cut the apron strings and did not bother to inform the

School. But of immediate results we could sometimes reassure ourselves. In 1967 we looked back over ten years and found that during that decade nine out of every ten of our university applicants were getting places at a time when the average for schools was five out of ten. The total number of pupils in the school during that period grew from 100 to 125, of whom at least one third would not have got into a grammar school.

The boy who went to Cambridge was soon followed there by two others. Two went to Oxford, three to Birmingham. Three were together at Keele in its early days and found the enterprising atmosphere of this new foundation very much to their liking. As time went on Sussex became the first choice and there were four together there.

The interesting fact emerged that our candidates were getting highly rated in their interviews and being therefore admitted even when their examination marks were moderate. The instance mentioned in a later chapter of the girl whose response was lively and articulate, and secured her an entry on two bare passes, was paralled in other cases. Further, the universities had no reason to regret this kind of decision, for most of the pupils so admitted obtained first or upper-second class honours. All through the years, degrees lower than this have been the exception. Linked to this is the fact that at a time when universities were complaining of a high rate of first-year failure, as much as 25 per cent, this was almost unknown among our pupils. Altogether I can remember only two instances, including a young man who fled incontinently into the army although his marks were good. This high survival rate can be attributed partly to the experience of self-planned work at school, preparing them for the freedom of university study, and to the fact that the boys and girls were not pressed so hard that they had no energy in reserve. They went up fresh, not tired. And it does pay to nourish the whole personality, to keep minds ranging widely, to keep the imagination alive, to keep thinking eager yet relaxed – not tense and anxious.

I had to keep a watch on myself lest I should contravene this principle. We had a boy who was an all round scientist with a passionate interest in insects. (I relaxed bedtime rules for him too; entomologists need to prowl at night.) He took the highest grades in all three advanced subjects and automatically won a State Scholarship. In a moment of kudos-seeking ambition I urged him to take the open scholarship exams at Cambridge. 'What's the point' he said, wiser than I. 'I've been accepted there and I've got a scholarship.' His subsequent career has been most interesting. He took a double-first in biology and became intrigued by the regularity of the pattern of hairs on insects. Why did apparently exactly similar cells on the epidermis remain ordinary for a stretch but at regular intervals turn into hair cells? What made a particular cell develop in this way, and why didn't it happen at random? Research into this earned him a doctorate, a Commonwealth Fellowship to the U.S. and a fellowship of Caius. He joined the molecular biology team of Francis Crick (of DNA and double-helix fame) and in co-operation with other workers the most fascinating questions arose. Understanding the differentiation of insect cells may be part way to understanding why the human embryo begins to take shape in a plate of apparently exactly similar cells. Why should the tail appear at one end, the head at another and the other organs in their right places? How do cells know where they are? In a recent Radio 3 broadcast he gave a lucid 45 minute account of his findings so far.

Wennington's scientists have none of them lost their interest in people and relationships. A contemporary of the one just mentioned was somewhat at odds with himself while at School and was transferred at sixteen to a day school with a high academic reputation. The contrast brought sharply into his mind what Wennington stood for; he then deliberately resisted all attempts at academic and social conditioning, and went on to London to take a first-class degree. This was followed by a Ph.D and a lectureship. He then became interested in his students as persons, found that they came up to L.S.E. very unfinished, underdeveloped, unready to deal constructively with personal challenges; and he made it part of his job to get to know them personally and to try to meet their needs for human contact and communication – much the same work as Hugh Leech did at Keele. The years have passed; he is now an expert in computer technology and one of his chief concerns is to prevent the misuse of computer systems to gain control of people.

One hopes that this reference to the quality of degrees and to academic success-stories does not seem like a re-introduction of scholarly snobbery and elitism. The references are necessary because a school that has to fight against misunderstanding and prejudice has to show to its critics that it can indeed 'do the job' they think so important, and do it without destroying the human sensitiveness that is so necessary. It has to show anxious parents that although it has earned such a reputation for dealing with personal problems that it is thought of by some as primarily for problem children, it is the school's attention to personal needs that prevents it from exploiting the highly intelligent to the point where they lose their originality.

Some parents did indeed think we could not do the job. In two instances very intelligent girls were taken away because it was thought we could not provide the conditions for the best Sixth-form work. Both went to schools where they were pressurized. Both went to Cambridge but their subjects failed to hold interest. They changed horses in mid stream and both took thirds. At Wennington we howled with rage. Not that the class of a degree is all that important. It was the whole pattern of events that made us angry and the final evidence of something gone wrong that need not have happened.

There was no talk about these achievements in the School; there were no honours boards, no prizes, no proclamations. Children meeting boys and girls from other schools during the holidays found it difficult to think of anything to boast about. They valued the School, but there were no easily measurable categories into which achievements could be put. It is often difficult to find out what old scholars have done. Two of those who left at the time I retired went to medical schools. One was brilliant intellectually and got top grades in all his science subjects. It has been only recently, after six years and persistent enquiries that I have been able to find out how well he has done. The other, a girl, had been a doubtful starter and needed a good deal of reassurance. I heard – again after this long length of time – that she had not only done well but was a gold-medallist in her year. I discovered her address and begged her for details. All I got in return was a Christmas card – 'with love'.

In one notable respect our pupils were failures. They have none of them, as far as I know, made money – or married it. This was borne in upon us in a sad way when we set up an appeal fund to help the School in an hour of need. By far the largest number go into teaching as their career. This urge to teach, from the human point of view, is a delight and a reassurance. Nearly all of them teach in state schools; they find conditions challenging and much to criticize, but they stick to it; they neither acquiesce nor destructively grumble.

Many have taken up art as painters, potters, or designers. In this it is difficult to measure achievement; often they have to struggle for a long time. We found a surprising instance in New Zealand. We had almost lost track of two brothers until we reached that country. Then we found that one (who had given us much to worry about at School) was the very well-informed foreign news editor of an important newspaper, a joy to meet. His brother, like so many other artists, had had a wretched time of struggle and deprivation in various countries in an effort to discover himself and achieve a style. He came even to the point of near-starvation. But in New Zealand, after some odd encounters with Maori culture, he emerged. A one-man exhibition of his works had been staged and every painting sold before the opening day. We found him in a remote part of North Island with his family, wearing very little, shooting his own meat, growing his own vegetables, building a new studio out of scrap timber, filling the house with big paintings, and looking after a distressed Maori.

Some gifted youngsters seem to have to make things difficult – or to have early adventures, perhaps in order to discover themselves. One such boy was accepted by two universities but impulsively threw up the opportunity. He took a potato-porter's job in Covent garden, lived in a Salvation Army hostel while saving forty pounds, then put a few necessities into a rucksack and started walking. He got through Turkey into Afghanistan and eventually to Bombay. Arriving there with only a coin or two, he got a job on a newspaper for a while. Then he worked his way south through Malaysia to Australia, where he spent some time as a tram-driver. Moving on to Tokyo he entered a business and was 'adopted' in the Japanese manner by the owner. At last he seemed likely to become repectable, a member of the establishment. But no, the next letter to me contained a whole page of the *Japan Times* put together by him; he had become sub-editor.

He married a Japanese girl, but moved on. It was exasperating to discover later that when we drove south from Auckland to Wellington, we had passed perhaps within hailing distance of his home. He had become another New Zealand newspaper editor.

Wennington cannot claim to have produced anyone outstanding in team games or athletics, but physical vigour has not been lacking in other ways. A woman and a man provide remarkable examples. The woman, now in her early thirties, began as an unusually sensitive little girl, easily upset; but as she grew up she got her teeth into life with a vengeance. She qualified as a graduate music teacher at the Royal Academy and now teaches in a comprehensive school. Alongside her regular teaching – which includes running a cup-winning madrigal group and a chamber orchestra – she has an astonishing record of voluntary activities into which she draws her pupils.

This began with work camp experience among black people in the U.S.A. and Uganda and was followed by a strenuous training in a variety of activities to enable her to become an instructor for the Duke of Edinburgh award: mountaineering, canoeing, sailing and survival courses. In 1977, with two boys from her school, she reached the summit of Mt. Blanc, and 1978 was crowded with other achievements. A term's sabbatical leave enabled her to set off with a rucksack for Moscow. She passed on through Iran and Afghanistan to the Khyber Pass, Pakistan and India. Through Katmandu and over the slopes of Annapurna, she reached 18,000 feet and descended into the deepest gorge in the world, Kali Gandarki, before beginning her return journey.

In the summer holidays of the same year, as a member of the Austrian Alpine Club, she went to Zermatt and climbed the Breihorn and Rimpfischorn. She tackled the Matterhorn and got within 150 metres of the top before being turned back by a summer blizard of the kind that killed our beloved Alfred Schweitzer. More recently she has climbed to over 20,000 feet in the Andes of Peru. She has bought a derelict cottage in the Welsh mountains for use as a climbing centre and has replaced all the woodwork and made the furniture, using the skills she learnt at School.

The man, of about the same age, has been seen on the TV screen, endlessly walking. He was uncertain of himself at school but became fascinated by mountains and dreamed of becoming a mountain guide. He met severe difficulties after leaving school. He had to pull out of his father's chemical engineering works because he was not really interested. After passing through saddening personal experiences he began walking alone. Christopher Brasher wrote about him in the *Observer* (5th March 1978) describing him as the most prodigious walker in Britain. With sixty pounds of tent, clothes and camera on his back, he has walked a thousand miles linking the Hebrides, another thousand round Orkney and Shetland, 1600 miles up the west coast of Ireland, 2000 linking all the National Parks and 1600 miles from Land's End to John o' Groats. He has just completed a carefully planned walk clockwise round the whole coastline of Britain, 7000 miles, covering up to 40 miles a day. He was joined by sponsored walkers at intervals, raising thus £40,000 for the blind. He has written thirty books and taken 30,000 colour slides, which he uses in lecturing, the winter activity that earns him his income. He is about to set out on the 2000 miles of the Appalachian Trail, from Georgia to Maine.

This endless walking might seem crazily obsessive, but Christopher Brasher found him eminently sane, so that he had to ask himself; 'Was it he who was so strange and unusual or was it instead the way most of us live, herded into rush hours, trying to beat the rate-for-the-job or wangle some material advantage over our fellow men? I did know that I had never met a man so at peace with himself.'

In recording achievements of this kind, usually described as tough, it should be emphasized that the School, while encouraging vigour, did not use physical exploits as a means of supposedly developing a pattern of character. It was the other way round; the adventures were the outward expression of what had begun in the personality, in the spirit. These two, like so many others, had to begin tentatively, first to accept what they were and then to grow into self-confidence from that point.

In reviewing what old scholars have done and trying to be honest about it rather than propagandist, there is always at the back of one's mind the awareness that many, perhaps the majority, have disappeared without trace. In general we do not know how they have fared; only now and then does a letter come out of the silence. No doubt many have experienced failure, for that is the commonest of human experiences. I have argued earlier that education should be for failure rather than success, for more depends on the way we assimilate our failures than on what we do with our successes: not only in the sense that we have to be resilient, but in that we have to take the frustration into ourselves and make it a means of personal growth. This is parallel to the way in which we have to stop judging each other by standards of perfection and have to accept imperfections as a necessary part of the material of love.

Failure can be implicit in success; perhaps it always is. The musician and the artist, driven by inordinate longing, may find frustration in the moment of apparent achievement, or looking into the quality of direct experience, may discover a terrifying world. The scientist, pressing ahead with seemingly innocent research, may see looming before him the possibility of biological engineering as horrifying in its moral implications as the nuclear bomb.

So perhaps the occasional letter from the humble nonentity who has nothing to be proud of, and who writes about life with a touch of heartbreak, reminds us realistically though poignantly of what our educational task really is and how unfinished it must always remain. Here is part of one such letter, written by a woman many years after leaving. She was a pupil at Wennington for only four months, left unhappily and seemed to be one of those whose needs we had wholly failed to meet.

> This will, of course, be just a bolt out of the blue, but it is something I have meant to say for such a very long time. The incidents that led to my leaving were the first of many, but it was several heartbreaking years before I realized that the only way to make any sort of life for myself was to come to grips with my emotional difficulties, away from home, and try to overcome them. This was after many outbursts and 'nervous breakdowns' and a shattering engagement. Gradually I got it all sorted out and stopped blaming my home and hating myself. I truly believe the most difficult part was admitting that the lack of stability was partly my own doing. But it never ceased to amaze me that the only part of my childhood for which I really blame myself is not being able to succeed at Wennington of all places. I must have been truly incorrigible if I couldn't make it there! My only excuse

> is that before I came to your school I had been quite unaware of what to do with freedom except to snatch at it and use it for myself.
>
> In the past two years of coping with life with average success, I hope I have gained that thing which shone through at Wennington – tolerance and an understanding of people whose needs are greater than one's own. I have always wanted to explain this to you, and the longer I've left it the more reason there seems to be in a school like yours. Without complaining, for I've learnt much from it, I've found a lot of bitterness and strife and deliberate ignorance on the part of most people. And when I've thought what is there in life, I've remembered that if one is tolerant and tries to understand *persons,* life becomes reasonable again.

An even more distressing story comes from a woman I met after having lost track of her for a dozen years. She came to the School at thirteen in a disturbed state with a history of truancy, stealing and hysterical behaviour. She desperately wanted to please both her peers and adults, to be cared for and loved. She would steal sweets and share them amongst her schoolfriends in a pitiful attempt to buy friendship. Throughout her life at Wennington her insecurity showed itself in strange behaviour, much of which she managed to conceal from others: bed-wetting, persistent stealing, fasting followed by overeating and vomiting. Whilst facing life at Wennington with a façade of bravado and confidence, eager to engage in 'adult' conversations with teachers and appearing to be in control of herself, she was going through 'a personal hell'. Yet she found there were others who understood her distress, teachers and children who had the sensitivity to accept and care for her in spite of it. Before coming to the School she had been rejected and ostracized, but now she was with people who genuinely cared for her. However, when she left at seventeen she was still unable to surmount her problems. She found society at large less sympathetic than Wennington – less willing to accommodate her strange and often overtly anti-social behaviour. The stealing became worse, she became obsessive about being fat, and developed something like *anorexia nervosa.* Yet she was still able to play the double game – never out of a job and much respected for her supposed competence and integrity. After about ten years there came a crisis, and she could no longer keep up the image of the competent, organized and respectable girl. Every aspect of her anti-social behaviour was slowly and hideously revealed, and she attempted suicide. She had reached rock bottom, but realized that the suicide attempt was really the first step on the road to recovery. She knew from her experience at Wennington that there could be people who would accept her for what she really was, and when she most needed them they appeared 'almost magically'. In spite of what had been revealed, she was trusted in a highly paid administrative post.

This was the beginning of renewal. She held the post for some time, her sheer ability enabling her to do the work well; but it was impersonal and her new development urged her towards work with people. Facing a severe drop in her standard of living she began training as a teacher. This was not so simple as turning over a new leaf. The past was still there, very real, but it added to her sympathy and understanding of others. She knows and admits that without her school experiences she would probably have ended in prison. Wennington showed her that people can be tolerant and loving. (Note the similarity here to the preceding account.) The School could not turn her from a little devil into an angel, but she sees now that the School gave her an inner strength, the beginnings of insight and the knowledge that even in the darkest moments she can find people who care.

She says, without conceit, that though she cannot undo her past, she is delivered from a crippling sense of guilt and can look to the future with hope and excitement. 'The very fact that I leap out of bed at 6.30 a.m., whereas previously I would hide under the blankets – sometimes for a whole week-end – is revealing. The abundant life is certainly worth working towards, even if it takes some of us quite a time to reach it.'

Since writing the foregoing, I have heard the last tragic news of one of our most lively and gifted girls. She was one of those who came during the early war years and she delighted in the opportunity provided by the first adventures in pottery. One of my most treasured possessions is a large ochre-coloured bowl made by her and decorated with trees and mountain tops on which little figures are dancing in the light of a radiant sun. Then about twelve, she did not realize what this foretold. She was brilliant intellectually and by the time she was fourteen I knew she had a university career and a first-class degree within her grasp. But then she came to me to say that Mme. Rambert had accepted her for ballet training. Her enthusiasm was immense and the prospect of that distant degree could not compete. We lost touch with her but eventually heard that in the course of dancing tours she had met a French engineer in South America and married him. When they came back to France, he left her. Then the original prophecy was fulfilled. She returned to England with her two children, struggled through 'A' levels, and at the age of nearly forty became an undergraduate and gained that degree. She was becoming established as an inspiring teacher of languages in a grammar school when the fate most feared by women struck. She had to have a mastectomy, but it was too late; secondary carcinomas were uncontrollable. Maureen had just a few weeks to tidy up her affairs and arrange for her children to go to the Friends' School, Ackworth, before she died.

59. Maureen's vase, the basis of the cover design

60. Young engineers casting aluminium multiple pulleys

61. Welding the 'battleship' bedsteads

62. Making the watchmaker's lathe —

63. — and the result

64. She could have become an athlete, but she was also a clarinet player and she married a Hallé trombonist

65. Sixth-form post-exam camp in Lakeland

66. *On the top. Sixth-form Lakeland Camp*

67. *What are they laughing at?*

CHAPTER XIX

Love and Hate: Joy and Woe

SOME YEARS AFTER RETIREMENT I was asked to return to the School to talk about its history and original intentions, and to explain why I was writing this book. A girl afterwards questioned me about the long cine film that we had put together over a period of many years. She was not more than thirteen and she spoke naïvely, as though an odd thought had just occurred to her. 'That school film; it all looks marvellous, they're all so good, doing things. They look so happy. Wasn't there any hate?'

This question was a perceptive one, and she would have had equal reason to ask it had she seen the two BBC televised documentaries about the School: Richard Cawston's production *The Teachers* in September 1962 which included Wennington as representative of co-educational boarding schools, and Peter Hamilton's *Incurably Human,* wholly about Wennington and shown twice in December 1963.

It has to be admitted at once that there had been unhappiness and hate. When I prowled round with a cine camera and saw something interesting happening, or a group laughing hilariously, I could cry: 'Hold it!' and get them to repeat it. But if I saw anger, even if I wanted to film it, I couldn't get them to hold it and repeat it. Unlike laughter, it was not easily reproduced.

Many parents said that they did not want their children to be too much burdened by exams or ambitions; they wanted them first to be happy. This however was something we could not guarantee; growing up was often a painful process. We wanted to avoid moulding children, conditioning them to use conventional responses; we wanted them to encounter each other with the mask and the armour off, as persons. But this made them vulnerable. Nevertheless, it was the only way to maturity, and it did provide, if not happiness and an ever-smiling face, an entry to the abundant life – a life in which opportunities could be seized and in which it was possible to assimilate disaster instead of being knocked over by it.

Looking back over the life of a school is like putting together the

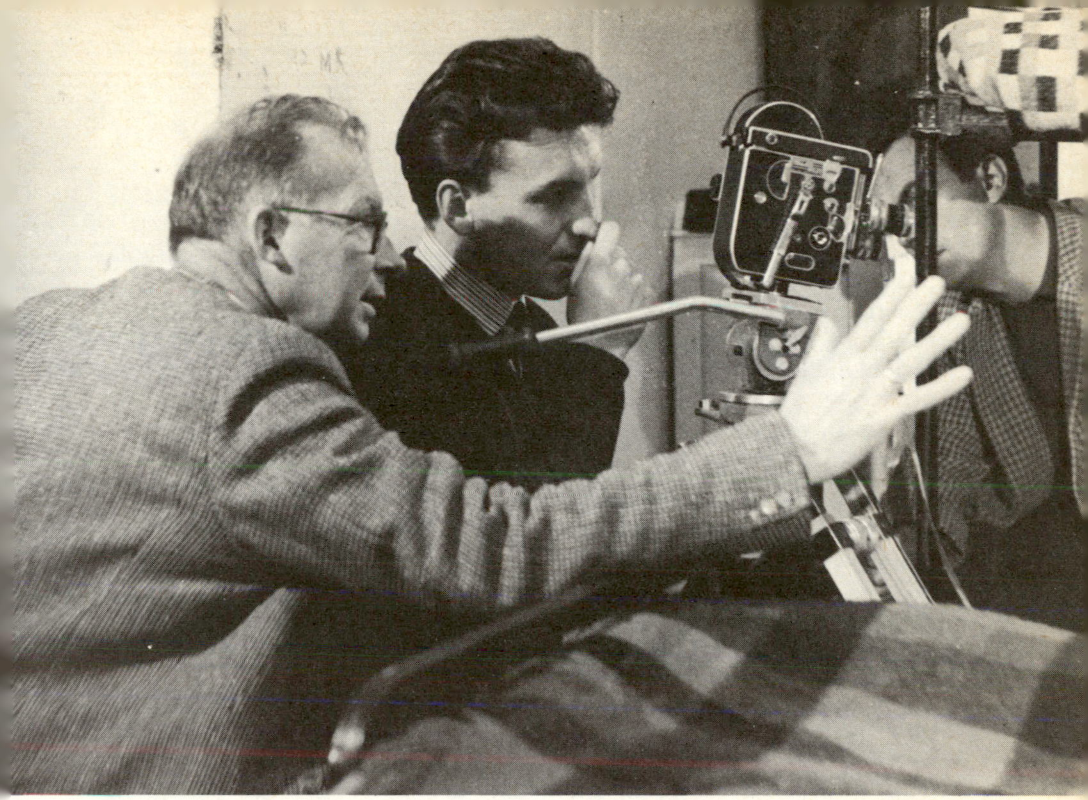

68. 1963. Peter Hamilton (Religious Broadcasting Organizer, BBC North Region) with cameraman, at work filming the School for the documentary Incurably Human. *Peter Hamilton later became chairman of the School governors*

69. Frances Barnes (taken about 1960)

School film. It is difficult to recall the dark side, the feelings of near-despair as they actually took hold of us, or to show how children sometimes tear at each other and go to bed in floods of tears. But few parents needed to be told that those things happen. What they needed to know was that their children were going to a School where they would learn resilience rather than a grim fortitude. Nevertheless to a visitor the School did look a happy one, because there was so little fear. There was no reason to straighten your coat or your face because of the entry of a teacher or any other adult. Life and energy went on bubbling up.

Because the School was a community rather than an institution, the inner life of the adults mattered as much as that of the boys and girls, perhaps even more, for a group of teachers divided among themselves and personally unfulfilled cannot establish the conditions for children to grow. For many years I had a remarkable secretary; she only needed to be given the gist of a letter, not its wording, and thus enabled me to get away quickly to the lab. But she was also sensitive to what fellow members of staff were going through. She listened to them and thus helped them. If the problems were severe she prompted them to come to talk to my wife or myself. Occasionally there were staff who were neurotically self-centred, coming to a community hoping that it would solve their problems, but in fact projecting their hang-ups on to it. These passed on quickly. There were others, who had run into tragedy or made terrible mistakes but were essentially sensitive and outgoing. It was worth while to give thought and time to these, for when they became released in spirit they had the more to give because of what they had been through.

Most boarding schools have, in the course of time, to meet death, by illness or accident. Almost to the end of my time in Wennington, this had not come our way. Two accidents, however, showed how near we could be to it. It is not possible to prevent young people from climbing trees; the most we could do was to forbid conifers, with their brittle foot-holds. One day a senior boy was at the top of one of our enormous beech trees. He was sure-footed and reliable. But his foot slipped on a wet patch and he came hurtling down. It was a tree forked into two great thick trunks and he jammed in the fork instead of hitting the ground. When I saw him lying unconscious he was unrecognizable; I couldn't imagine that he would recover from what seemed inevitable internal injuries. We contacted his mother, a doctor and an old personal friend. She took it extraordinarily calmly. He did recover. He went into medicine and rose quickly to registrar and consultant status.

The other case involved instant action. I was in the middle of a trunk call when matron rushed in and pulled me away from the phone. A

Sixth-form science student had been on his own in the laboratory. He had permission to go there to read but not to perform experiments without supervision. He did, however, start on a titration, a mild enough thing to do. He was careless with a pipette and sucked some dilute hydrochloric acid into his mouth. It would have done him little harm, but he reached for an alkali to neutralize it. Not paying proper attention to the label he ignored the word STRONG and poured it into his mouth. In acute distress he rushed to the dispensary.

Racing from the phone, I had a sudden sharp memory of a bottle of citric acid in the larders, so much nearer than the laboratory. I have no memory of covering the distance to the kitchen or of racing upstairs, only of arriving at the dispensary and seeing that boy with his head over the sink and his mouth looking inside-out with the mucous membrane bulging and grey. His mother, also, was a doctor and she, too, took it calmly. The Harrogate ambulance was at the School in record time. To our surprise the boy did not suffer a perforation; he survived to become an architect.

Death came for the first time in the autumn of 1967, the last year before retirement. The wife of our art master died of cancer. She had come with her husband right at the beginning and was one of the very reliable women members of staff who had slogged away at domestic work, helping to keep the absolutely necessary wheels of life turning. One morning a few months later I was summoned urgently to a dormitory. A boy lay dead in bed. He had died in his sleep of asthmatic heart failure.

One evening in October of the same term, Frances and I went into staff supper to find a very poor meal awaiting us. Good cooks were scarce and sometimes there was a bad one on duty. For Frances the quality of food was an absolute priority and it was expressive of much more than physical sustenance. If you gave the children bad food you really did not care for them. She burst out: 'I can't stand this; I'll go into the kitchen myself tomorrow.' But I woke next morning to find her looking at me in twisted-up distress. She was speechless and her right arm and leg were paralysed. We had known of the danger of stroke, for she had been under treatment for high blood pressure for some time. Some months before, the doctor had noticed a slight slurring of speech that indicated perhaps a mild stroke. And there had been a cloud on the retina that called for a careful and extensive examination by a consultant. He took an electro-cardiograph and discussed it with me. From her youth she had suffered from a degree of fibrillation (a failure in relative timing of the cavities of the heart) but the record now was of extreme irregularity. As usual she wanted to know the whole truth, an ominous prospect. Her reaction was typical; she promptly went out into the Harrogate shops and bought a new frock.

Now, in October, it seemed that the hypertension was beginning to destroy her. It distressed her that she could not write, for the maintenance of friendship through letters had always meant much to her. She slowly re-taught herself to write in a clumsy ragged way and after a while she could drag herself along a corridor trailing a foot. There was just a ray of hope that she could look forward to a few years of limited activity.

During that same term we had in the bottom form a delightful eleven year old boy, the kind of child who makes you want to go back on all your ideas about ambivalence and the 'shadow'. He just seemed good all through, full of joy, unfailingly eager in conversation and class, causing no anxiety to anyone. He diffused his goodness of spirit all round him. But a cloud began to come over his life too. Headaches, unaccountable sickness. As these symptoms developed we thought he might be suffering from a tropical infection, for his family lived in Kenya. Careful investigation dismissed this possibility. The eventual correct diagnosis, confirmed by an exploratory operation, was a growing tumour of the brain. He died during the following Easter holidays.

Frances' condition improved slowly during the early months of 1968. She was able even to attend the Quaker Meeting at York in the spring – very important to her. We were encouraged to think that a brief excursion to the United States might be possible for her as well as for me; I was due to address a large conference there. I booked a passage on the Queen Elizabeth; I had enjoyed transatlantic voyages in the thirties and wanted to repeat the experience before the Queen went out of commission. But this was not to be; I had to cancel the booking a few days before the sailing date. We were sitting in the silence of York Friends' Meeting on a Sunday in June, when I became aware of her shuddering, I held her upright until the meeting was over, then we had to carry her out to the car. It was another and more devastating stroke.

There was less paralysis, but her mind was deeply affected, her memory upset and her personality eroded. We were approaching the end of our last term before retirement, but it seems best to conclude the story of her life before returning to the last days of that term, for it is with these that this history should end. Frances again fought back, struggled to bring coherence to her injured brain. But a further deterioration came with retirement, which was to a house we had bought ten miles away. For some years she had been looking forward to retirement, to a house of our own, to privacy and a release from tension. But now when the change came it was an unbearable shock. The familiar pathways of our school quarters had been important to her in her bewildered mental condition. She did not recognize the house we had bought with such eagerness a few years before. When she needed to go from sittingroom to bathroom she took what would have been the accustomed route at school. But what seemed the bathroom door was in fact the back door and as she opened it she crashed on to the concrete patio. Time after time I picked her up with a bruised and bleeding head.

After a few months she had to be taken to The Retreat, the Quaker mental hospital in York. She was in a state of acute distress and bewilderment, and emaciated almost beyond belief. But such are the contradictions in what we call 'stroke', an emotional stimulus could bring surprising normality. She was in a ward of about sixteen other women so self-absorbed in their mental disturbance that they neither felt nor expressed gratitude towards the gentle attentive nurses; but Frances never failed to say a warm thank you for everything that was done for her. And if I took a message of love from any of the children in the School, her face lit up with joy, for a few seconds completely normal.

In the early summer of 1969 she died there in her sleep, from heart failure. The senior male nurse told me he had never before seen anyone fight for life as she did. It was typical of her; all through marriage and the long struggle of the School she had been indomitable. A. S. Neill, whose first wife died in the same way, wrote with understanding sympathy; 'Our wives did all the work and we got all the kudos.'

Why tell this story of a personal tragedy in an account of an educational experiment? Because this project was a personal venture in the most complete sense, its history is one of complete involvement, in which people were committed not only as teachers or professional educators but as persons whose every action or feeling was relevant and whose end was therefore inseparable from the way they lived. Frances had an Irish capacity for being outspoken, sometimes embarrassingly so, but she was not a masculine woman. Although she was co-principal she did not enjoy having authority and she was reluctant to use it. But she never conceded the possibility of defeat in any kind of crisis. She went into hospital a dozen times for minor or major operations, but soon, usually too soon, she was back on the job, her gaiety recovered.

It must not be imagined that we were always on the job, wiring into it with devotion written all over our faces. As soon as our pay made it possible (Frances never took more than £250 a year and sent increments back if the Bursar put them on) we spent our Easter holiday abroad, doing it on our own, usually in unorthodox ways: Norway, Holland, Paris, the South of France, Venice, Florence, Mykonos, Amalfi, Southern Spain. In 1960, when she was 65, we spent a long time in the sea, in Bantry Bay, clinging to a capsized dingy – until we managed to push it, by swimming, to a distant reef. In 1958 my good deputy Brian Hill took over for a term and made it possible for us to have a sabbatical four months, visiting Ethiopia, where our son was a teacher at the General Wingate School and later a headmaster, and on to Uganda, Kenya, Saudi Arabia, Jordan, Jerusalem, Israel, Lebanon and Greece.

In the middle of distress the affection of the children was touching and reassuring. They did not just go about their business careless of what was happening. Many of them, who would otherwise have passed me heedlessly on corridor or stairs, glanced at me, smiled and said, 'Hello, Kenneth'. And many of that fine group of Sixth-formers who had done 'Noah' with me, were still in the School, counsellors, reliable, mature and sympathetic.

The dark side was still there. It is interesting that deep personal crisis, which makes the thoughtful even more sensitive and sympathetic, can shake the unstable into greater waywardness; perhaps because it makes life as a whole more threatening to them. What follows is a reproduction of part of a record I managed to write in the middle of all the confusion after the term ended:

> It has not been, in any complete sense, a good term. The tares have been growing high with the wheat – but the wheat has been exceptionally high! There has been more bloody-mindedness – in a few – than I have known for a long time, but also more love in the majority.
>
> For the first time in the whole 28 years of the School's history, I have had to deal with nasty-minded prudery. The teacher supervising the late evening bathe reported to me that a recently admitted girl was declaring that nakedness was 'dirty'. A boy had been heard saying that to appear naked was, for a girl, like being a prostitute. Two boys had been rushing to the pool when a certain girl was bathing, in order to gaze at her – not in admiration, but as a form of persecution.
>
> I interrupted the sequence of morning assemblies and used the time next day to talk to the School about nakedness, about innocence and corruption. I described how naked bathing began twenty years earlier when bathers had discarded their costumes in a sort of innocent joy. No parent had ever criticized it, nor had there ever been any untoward incident nor any hint of criticism to

spoil it. Not until this term. I explained the real meaning of innocence: not childish or ignorant, but simply unpoisoned. I had read Genesis 2 in Evening Meeting the previous Sunday and I now referred back to the last words: 'they were naked and they were not ashamed'.

I explained the naturalism of Hebraic religion: how the Jews felt that everything that God had made was intrinsically good: the beasts of the field and the fowls of the air and the nakedness of man and woman. Only we could make them anything other than good. Only *we* could allow corruption and guilt to enter. It had been our aim at Wennington to make room for a recapture of the primal innocence; it was something you could recognize and hold on to throughout life. We had to hold back the corrupting effect of society in order to achieve this. A see-through blouse, for example, was not innocent, because it was a deliberate intention to draw the eyes of others towards a woman's sexuality *apart* from her wholeness as a person.

I went on to say, with some vehemence, that anyone who brought guilt, suggestiveness and corruption into this experience of unselfconscious nakedness was attacking the School at its heart.

I did not realize until next morning how effective my eloquence had been. It was not studied eloquence; it was spontaneous and passionate. The morning dip had dwindled to a mere half-dozen, a few small boys and one or two brave teenage girls. But this next morning the first bell at 6.55 had hardly stopped ringing before the doors above and below were flung open and they came pouring down from the dormitories. And then, there they were, half the School – a kind of spontaneous reassurance, telling me, in the brilliant morning sunlight, that all was well.

The following morning was the morning of departure. There were, of course, all the farewells as the boys and girls piled into the buses in the courtyard. I had to kiss scores of girls; they came forward obviously expecting it. The boys in their more restrained way showed their affection: lingering hand-shakes and unusually warm smiles.

The old scholars' reunion followed almost at once. Many long-familiar faces appeared, and so many whole families, till the place was swarming with the little children and babies of yet another generation. We managed to get Frances down in a comfortable chair for a while. It was sad to see her facing all these people she had taught so long ago. Before illness began to attack her she had the reputation for looking ten years younger than her age; now the opposite was the case. As the men and women came up to greet her, it was interesting to see how it was the ones she had known long ago, rather than the more recent ones, that she at once recognized.

The presentation ceremony was prefaced by a talk from one of the most unusual of the parents, a mother of five (three at the School and two to come) who managed to be both a practising doctor and a successful novelist. Her talk was gentle, simple, just right, personal rather than an oration. Among other things, she said how good it was to have her children at a school where those in charge gave her children love, but also knew when to use the back of a hairbrush on their bottoms.

As I said in my reply, this was a very apposite remark, for the old scholar who was chairing the ceremony had been a terror in the junior school and I had to break all my principles and use, not a hairbrush but a slipper. But only once; the phase soon passed and he developed certain other qualities. Girls began to fall in love with him in bunches as he approached manhood, and one of them (whose identity I would never reveal) told me privately that whenever he came within a foot of her she sizzled like a kettle about to boil.

CHAPTER XX

Independent but not divisive

WENNINGTON SCHOOL NO LONGER EXISTS. In 1974, with inflation rising, it faced severe financial difficulties, and the bank set a firm limit to the permissible overdraft. All through its history, Wennington had tried to hold down its fees. In the effort to avoid embarrassment to parents, many of whom were attracted to the School when barely able to meet the cost, increases in fees were sometimes made too late, lagging behind inflation; and many parents were allowed special concessions.

When all 125 places were filled, finances were on a fairly even keel, swaying slightly between profit and loss as the years passed; but no large reserves were being built up to enable the School to meet a severe crisis. The School's physical assets, mainly buildings and estate, though they did ultimately realize more than £100,000, were all it had to set against the overdraft of £35,000.

Some parents, alarmed by the danger, began to make other arrangements for their children, thus making the situation more difficult to manage. The headmaster made a vigorous attempt to save the School, and in the summer of 1974 a large number of old scholars came to live for a while in it, setting up scaffolding, completely redecorating the large assembly room and doing many necessary repairs elsewhere. An appeal was launched and promises reached a total that seemed just enough to meet losses over the two or three years that would have been necessary to regain stability. But then the Houghton award was made, considerably increasing the salaries of teachers. It is ironic that what would have been irrelevant in the early days of the School, when we all worked in equality for a few shillings a week, delivered the last blow. Wennington could not see itself paying less than the profession's well-deserved increase, but this now made it impossible for the appeal fund to cover expected losses. Inevitably the decision had to be made to close the School.

The headmaster from 1973 to 1975 was Alfred M. Sessa, B.A., B.D. Since 1975 he has been headmaster of the Friends' School, Great Ayton, near Middlesborough. For independent reasons – the similarity of method and intention in the two schools – the Charity Commission directed that the remaining assets of Wennington should be transferred to that school. By the kind invitation of the Great Ayton school, the Wennington old scholars reunion is held there each summer.

* * * *

Last thoughts must be about Wennington School seen in relation to national education and the needs of society. The School made a great difference to many children and their parents; but I was often asked if our pupils did not get a shock when they went out to work in the very different world. My reply was: 'Yes, and I would be sorry if they did not; but I always hope that they are challenged to action by the difference, not defeated by it'.

A definite general relevance to the needs of society was in our minds when we started the School; but this postscript is being written at a time when millions are affected by political apathy and disillusionment. Perhaps more than at any time this century we can echo in our helplessness the words of W. B. Yeats in his enigmatic poem *The Second Coming:*

> Things fall apart; the centre cannot hold
> Mere anarchy is loosed upon the world.
> . . . .
> The best lack all conviction, While the worst
> Are full of passionate intensity.

The struggle for economic justice for the masses has been fragmented by a jealous obsession with differentials. From top to bottom, status is more important than need. Few groups dare to look at the whole situation or the inevitable consequences. We live in an acquisitive consumer society in which every seductive device is offered, like the credit card, to 'take the waiting out of wanting', to encourage people to live beyond their means and therefore always to find their incomes inadequate. What we call the permissive society is not so much an 'immoral' society as the consumer society extended to drink, drugs and sex; you have now a right to take them when you want them.

Politicians are impotent because in few groups is there any altruism or priority of values to which they can appeal. The radical ideological commitment that drove so many young people in recent years into vehement 'demos' seems to have been impermanent and poorly rooted. Those idealists who followed gurus into Californian communes have vanished in a spiritual wasteland.

Can the necessary enduring commitment be anything other than an expression of the religious dimension of life and relationship? This means, not necessarily 'belief' or a theological pattern, but the awareness that brings all experience, hopes, desires and actions, into an indestructible, growing and life-long coherance. It perceives that the future must be nourished by love and eagerness and it insists on action.

It is not enough to be rational and humanist; this can be as cold as dead fish. We need what the best so often lack: a driving passion, an energy that arises, not from a conversion or an idealistic vision of the future, but from an experience of community life in which the tremendous potential in human beings is perceived and enjoyed, in which crisis and conflict are always seen as opportunities, never as a reason for acquiescence and defeat. It is paradoxically true that at this time, when apathy, bloody-mindedness, crime and cruelty seem to fill the screen, the potential for human goodwill is greater than ever; but it does not know how to express itself in collective action.

It was religious experience in this sense that we tried to provide in the School. How far we succeeded it is impossible to assess; but the widespread commitment to teaching among old scholars is one encouraging bit of evidence.

The present moment, however, is one in which the schools in the same category as Wennington seem to have lost their collective consciousness and eagerness, their common cause. The most lively conferences of staff were held sporadically but frequently in the thirties, then regularly after the war under the title *Co-educational Conference,* including such schools as Frensham Heights, Bedales, Dartington, St Christopher, Summerhill, Monkton Wyld, as well as Wennington. They were occasions of keen interchange and refreshment. The general situation has in one respect changed; Oxbridge and several independent boys' schools are admitting girls, an action that would have been horrifying to their staffs forty years ago.

Does this mean that the whole battle has been won and that the innovative schools I have mentioned have nothing more to say? It is perhaps not surprising that it is a former Wennington pupil, now in his thirties and teaching in one of these schools who is convinced that there is more to be said and who is struggling to bring the group of schools once more into stimulating communication and to convince them that coeducation is only one consequence of a comprehensive radical message.

Radical for many is synonymous with socialist, though strictly it means going to the roots. Certainly J. H. Badley, the founder of Bedales, was in the Christian Socialist tradition. Very many of us associated with these schools could be said to be 'some kind of socialist'. This vague term has to be used in order to avoid being identified with doctrinaire policies that do not work because they neglect awkward truths, or with paranoid movements that use, just as much as any other movements in history of any political colour, the most evil impulses in man – in assassination, kidnapping and purges.

The Labour movement is a long way now from the religious perception and fervour in which it had one of its roots, so one must ask searching questions as to the aims and motivation of present-day leaders and groups. Socialism can be described as a search for conditions in society that will make possible the abundant life, that will set people free to enjoy each other's company, irrespective of status or origins, set them free from all that limits friendship, co-operation and creative activity, provide them the greatest opportunity to contribute to the community and give them a satisfaction and fulfilment that is not gained at the expense of others.

I am sure that many a loyal Conservative would say that he wants that too. Prospects for the future would indeed be poor if ultimate hopes did not in some measure transcend party membership. The political socialist would say, however, that the ultimate aim cannot be achieved so long as power remains in the hands of those who make profit the primary aim, and we can see what he means when we look at the immoral conduct of certain pharmaceutical manufacturers, of baby-food producers who push their products dishonestly in the Third World, knowing that the lives of black babies will be at risk, and of the 'bland international financiers who control so much of our lives without any public responsibility'.

However, the socialist also seeks overwhelming power, the power to make sweeping changes. He is far from immune to the dangerous disease of idealism, the tendency to detach feeling and concern for real people and attach it to organizations and strategies that exist in idea and become a sort of addiction. Nationalization was a practical necessity in the cases of mines and railways, but a crusading *belief* in nationalization has paid hardly any attention to the basic need, a change in relationships. Thus there remains the same old Us-and-Them problem, recurrent hostility and strikes. There goes with this attachment of emotion to organization a fear of those intractable qualities in human nature that will not fit into structures. (Russia of course provides the extreme example.) Even if it is not said, it is often assumed that what is intractable is bad. In capitalist industry the extension of control has led to vast international corporations; but under socialism also, structures tend to become steadily bigger and all the time something humanly and basically important is being neglected. People are widely aware of this, some clearly, some dimly; and the awareness leads to scepticism in relation to politics. We are in a crisis of ignorance and ineptitude in relation to nearly all the problems of society; and is it not the ordinary man's growing awareness of this helplessness that is making him increasingly distrustful of all authority?

In the post-war period, architects and housing authorities had a fine time rehousing the people. They took little account of what human beings were like and what their basic needs were. So people were treated as insects to be tucked away in uniform cells, their communities were destroyed, and the result was vandalism and delinquency in the frustrated children. Is there going to be the same kind of neglect in the impulse to get complete control of education?

For several Labour leaders, getting complete control would involve the abolition of all independent education. Though this aim is primarily directed at the traditional Public schools, the methods to be used would necessarily involve all others, for instance the group under consideration and the Quaker boarding schools, most of which do not think of themselves as Public Schools. How would the abolition be achieved? One can imagine something like the Conventicle Act of 1664 which forbade the gathering together of more than five dissenters for religious purposes. The method actually suggested is to make the charging of fees illegal; this would leave perhaps just a very few schools run by religious orders and wholly charitable.

Whatever the method, it could not be anything but crude and with totalitarian associations; and at a time when we are so uncertain about the relation between organization and human needs, it seems specially absurd to propose to bring the whole of education – a personally sensitive activity – under bureaucratic control.

The use of the word *bureaucratic* implies no disrespect for the administrators of national education. It is important to make this very clear, for it has been much used as a cuss-word in recent years. It is not here being used in any pejorative or insulting sense. It means simply the attempt to meet the needs of society by an organization of people who sit at desks, use telephones, dictate letters, receive and make reports, and in this way control or help people they do not see. However conscientiously motivated, large scale organization of this sort does result in delay and discouragement to those who want to act on a creative impulse, who see a need and want to meet it quickly. The project loses its convincing freshness as it passes from desk to desk.

My wife Eleanor, once a door-to-door social worker, is now a bureaucrat, organizing, with an office staff, the distribution of the Family Fund, upwards of two million pounds of Government money used each year for the relief of stress in families where there are severely disabled children. Many of these children are totally incontinent and will never be able to look after themselves and the mothers are often enslaved to appalling conditions. Ideally such conditions should be investigated quickly, eligibility established without delay and facilities provided. But sometimes months elapse because an overworked doctor forgets to send in a report or a social worker recommends something that it is the duty of the local authority to provide. There are possible scroungers to be sorted out from the genuine applicants, a serious responsibility in the spending of public money. Dealing with tens of thousands of applications takes time, and honest humble parents may become anxious and fretful.

This unavoidably bureaucratic procedure need not prevent a voluntary organization from acting quickly when it discovers a need, and it should not deflect concerned neighbours from helping those who are suffering. It implies no criticism of professional social workers to observe that during their long-continued strikes there has been a re-awakening of neighbourliness. People have been spontaneously helping those in distress, not because it was their job but because they began to feel compassion.

It is important that the development of the Welfare State should not dry up the compassionate impulses by which one person helps another. *Our mental and moral health depends on responsiveness.* Generous feeling should be followed quickly by action; otherwise it dies. Do we not all experience occasions when we take the first step, only to have our attention diverted? When we think about it a few days later, the initial energy has drained away; we shrug our shoulders and say: ‘So what? Someone else may think of it. Perhaps it was not all that important’.

> . . . And enterprises of great pith and moment
> With this regard their currents turn awry
> And lose the name of action.

The provision of education may not seem as urgently a matter for compassion as the provision of a washing machine for a mother coping with unceasingly soiled sheets, but does not the principle hold? Who knows what perceptions may come to one person or to a group at some time in the future, some new awareness of human potential or need that demands a pioneer change in structure or method? Are they to wait while an application is filtered through administrative channels and weighed up by people who, quite honestly, cannot see the significance of it? It is hardly possible to think of a more lame argument than one offered in a broadcast discussion of this question when someone said that there is now plenty of room in national education for people like A. S. Neill. He – or she – forgot that pioneers have to wait a long time before they are accepted. Bedales was founded in 1893, Summerhill in 1927; neither could have found any place in state education at that time. Who knows what new ideas, unacceptable today, will be in common practice fifty years hence?

It has been exasperating to observe how nearly always those who resent the continued existence of Public Schools fail to distinguish between this issue and the matter of *independent* education. It is this blindness that leads them to advocate crudely political measures and opens them to accusations of 'social engineering'. Admittedly there remains the question of divisiveness; but if this is our primary concern then we must look at all the seeds of divisiveness in our society and establish some priorities. Then the Public School question may be seen in perspective. At the moment, because it is a political shuttlecock, intentions are coming from the other side of the party fence that, while seeming to be solutions, might be socially disastrous: for instance that many millions should be spent in transferring the most highly intelligent children from state schools to Public Schools. That would be to add the divisive to the divisive, a double élitism, and would incur resentment among the teachers who would lose those pupils.

The issue is frequently confused by the failure to use terms in a discriminating way. *Private School* should mean one run for the profit of the owner or shareholders. *Independent School* should mean one that is non-profit-making, administered by a trust of some kind and probably registered under the Charity Commission. *Public Schools* – the capital letters being used to distinguish the odd use of the word *public* – form a smaller category within the independent schools, denoted by their membership of the Headmasters' Conference or the Governing Bodies Association.

Wennington was not divisive, either in the conduct of its community life or in its status. The School was not well known and when Sixth-formers went before university selection panels an interviewer would be likely to say: 'Wennington? Never heard of the place. Tell me about it'. It has to be admitted that this gave our pupils a splendid opportunity to talk about education; for as a result of their free dialogue with adults, they were articulate without being 'uppish'. The mother of one girl had to take her in her car to the university of her choice, and sat outside the interviewing room with the other intending students. Most of these went in fearfully and came out solemnly, nothing having been heard through the door. But when the Wennington girl was in there, her mother heard animated conversation going on, punctuated by bursts of laughter. The girl came out with a broad grin, closed the door and rested against it, waving her hand in front of her face in mock breathlessness. Suddenly the door opened and she fell backwards into the arms of one of the panel. The dons wanted to see her again at once – to tell her she had been accepted unconditionally. She entered on two bare passes at 'A' level, but subsequently fully justified her acceptance.

There you are, the critic will say, privileged education! Does this mean that she ought not to have been allowed to go to an independent school which made personal development more important than marks, where she was encouraged to grow up and express her thoughts clearly and fearlessly in the presence of adults? (And where she slept on a bed made in the school workshop, kept her clothes in a second-hand chest of drawers bought in a Harrogate auction, and dragged a squad of boys and girls into the kitchen at first bell to peel potatoes.)

When I think of the whole context of divisiveness, I think first of the ostentation of wealth. I never stay in luxury hotels and if I ever have occasion to enter one to meet somebody, I have an impulse to get out quickly. I feel completely divided from the kind of people who use them, who get out of their Jaguars or Mercedes and walk in self-assuredly, followed by flunkeys loaded with expensive suitcases. There seems no means of communication with that world. On the other hand my work and interests have brought me into contact with a few Public School men. It may be true that they have a 'stamp' but it is trivial compared with the fact that we share a common language – the language of those who are concerned with the understanding of people and their needs. They may be too few to be representative, but the least that can be said is that their schools did not destroy their human sensitiveness and responsibility. How much do other forms of divisiveness destroy?

In the minds of some critics, divisiveness is concerned with overt political loyalties, independent education being thought of as providing support for the right wing. But the facts need to be closely searched for. I know little about the political development of Public School boys or girls. During a general election some years ago when there were many grammar schools not yet turned comprehensive, it was reported that a considerable majority of their Sixth-formers would have voted Conservative. Does anyone know how the more 'successful' pupils in a comprehensive school develop or change in their political attitudes as they move towards the Sixth? In the same period as the general election referred to above, I had a discussion about political attitude with the fifty Sixth-formers in an independent co-educational boarding school. Forty-seven of them would have voted Labour.

It must quickly be said that I do not imply that to vote Conservative would be a sign of lack of intelligent thought. The few facts given above are offered simply to suggest that there is a variety of factors at work in determining political divisions and that to fasten on any one that seems obvious or habitually believed may be to miss the roots of divisiveness.

If we are to ask what really divides a nation, we must ask what it is that makes the rich and powerful callous of the needs of the poor, what makes organized industry destructive of the environment and of social cultures, what makes management – not through ill-will but through blindness – insensitive to the human needs of shop-floor workers. Some Americans visiting this country say they are quickly aware of class divisions. But what of their own country? To stay in the U.S. for any length of time is to become acutely conscious of conflicting interests. While the U.S. has produced some of the finest scholarship and the most intrepid experiment, it is also the home of greed, corruption and exploitation worse than anything we suffer in Britain. Perhaps Public School boys are still favoured for entry to British medical schools and perhaps in the U.S. every bright student has an equal chance of entry. Yet sensitive Americans speak with shame of their medical fraternity, which they say is one of the most greedy of professional groups and frequently heedless of the Hippocratic oath that is traditionally the doctor's ethical standard.

So what ought we really to be thinking about? I wonder if those politicians who make slick over-all judgements about education have read Ivan Illich's *Deschooling Society,* and if they allowed themselves to be disturbed by it? I emphasize the word disturbed, because that is the first function of his books, to shake us out of complacent ideologies, to kick us out of the prevalent assumption that we shall bring health to society by more and more planning and organization. This disturbance of our thinking is a universal necessity. The working out of his positive suggestions, however, presents great difficulties. It will be remembered that he makes a fundamental distinction between manipulative and convivial institutions, and it is the convivial that brings people together as whole persons for mutual enjoyment, for friendship, for creative and self-fulfilling activities. It must be remembered also that he sees all large-scale organization, in every country, as manipulative, having taken on an uncontrollable momentum of its own; in this general pattern children are conditioned to fit into a planned society that is increasingly insensitive. In his writing about this we meet again the word *divisive,* but used in a more radical way.

National education, he says, cannot help being divisive. Necessarily geared to measurable achievement, to the admiration of success, it divides the successful from the unsuccessful. The latter drop out at intervals, they acquire a drop-out mentality and tend to become the enemies of society. Thus a pattern of schooling inevitably polarizes society; and Illich sees a profound divisiveness in an education system in which the privileged graduates, the successes, 'ride on the back of the entire paying public'. At a time when the world of young people is profoundly disturbed by truancy, destructive indiscipline and vandalism, a huge increase in petty crime and drunkenness, these assertions of Illich deserve the closest attention.

In turning the reader's attention to these wider forms of divisiveness, it is not suggested that the problem of independent education is negligible. I still look back with discomfort (if it were not for the comic aspect, it would be with disgust) to those ghastly bowler hats in which we, most of us scholarship boys from elementary schools, were pretending to be Public School boys. But it is profoundly important that this should not be made the major issue, leading us to chop off what we think to be a menacing growth, only to find that behind us we are threatened by something far more serious.

Wennington School tried to avoid the kind of divisiveness that Illich refers to. It did not encourage any labelling of successes and failures. Several of those who did poorly, by academic standards, at the School, surprised us years later by returning to studies and gaining degrees. I think this was because their oddities and special difficulties were accepted and they were not pressed beyond what they could do at the time. If boys and girls came from widely varying home circumstances, some wealthy, some poor, some loved and cared for, some neglected, they were all given encouragement to forget these differences and to enjoy each other as persons. We tried to make the School a place of learning for them in an inclusive sense, the kind of learning Illich describes as convivial: 'not the result of instruction . . . rather the result of unhampered participation in a meaningful setting'.

Wennington was a small school community, small enough for each child to see all round it, to observe the results of his actions and therefore to be challenged to take responsibility. But nearly all state schools have become increasingly large. In recent years 'Small is beautiful' has become a popular phrase. Not everyone knows that it is the title of a book by Dr. E. F. Schumacher, criticising all forms of giantism and attempts to meet human needs or exploit possibilities by creating enormous organizations. Schumacher was no mere theorist, though he was a good philosopher, as his *Guide for the Perplexed* shows. His experience was severely practical, gained as economic adviser to governments, in the Coal Board and the British Commission in Germany. He was a director of the worker-owned chemical factory, Scott Bader (of which my wife is a Trustee), and until his recent death was a pioneer in Intermediate Technology, the scaling down of technical processes to meet the needs of developing countries. His severe criticism of 'bigger is better', of the irrelevance and inefficiency from the human point of view of most large undertakings, fits in closely with the insights of Illich. He puts the misdirection of education in different words, but with the same awareness: education is still dominated by an obsolete nineteenth century metaphysics which cannot give meaning to the world of today and leaves us in a dark wood of muddled ignorance. This means the same as Illich's statement about the schools being the reproductive organs of the consumer society, for nineteenth century metaphysics had an ideal of unlimited progress, which meant unlimited production and an unlimited exploitation of natural resources, carefully provided by a Darwinian God. 'We are suffering from metaphysical disease', says Schumacher, 'and the cure must therefore be metaphysical'.

> Education which fails to clarify our central convictions is mere training or indulgence. For it is our central convictions that are in disorder, and as long as the present anti-metaphysical temper persists, then disorder will grow worse. Education, far from ranking as man's greatest resource, will than be an agent of destruction, in accordance with the principle *corruptio optimi pessima.*

Metaphysical here means all that gives meaning to man's consciousness, to his values, his striving, his relationships, all that takes him beyond mere blood and bone and makes him a being who can transcend his limitations. The metaphysical in education, then, is not merely a philosophical study; it is the communication, savouring and enriching of all that is personal and caring.

There must be many teachers working in large local authority schools who are as keenly aware as the rest of us of the need for this kind of educational experience. But is the system in which they are working likely, as a whole, to encourage it? A psychologist whose opinion I have every reason to respect – not a mere theorist but a man with an exceptionally wide experience of the problems of people of all ages – said to me recently that most children arrive at the end of their school careers with their minds blunted and their potential for ever limited. If Illich and Schumacher are right in their sociological judgements, this destructive result in education is not surprising. If it were possible to have another life, it would be good to work in a large comprehensive school, in order to know the possibilities from inside. It can be said with certainty that some comprehensives have opened up far greater possibilities than the grammar schools they replaced; but are they pioneers dependent on remarkably gifted heads? In a reassuring write-up of a north-country comprehensive recently printed in *The Guardian,* the headmaster maintained that the school, because of its size, provided a very wide range of opportunities yet, at the same time, preserved the necessary personal quality in its relationships throughout. On the other hand, a young relative of mine, speaking of another north-country comprehensive which grew in size as he grew up in it, said that it definitely lost its quality as a community as it grew beyond a few hundred. What ultimate judgement can we make? There is so much that we do not know; we are still groping in a fog where organization and its impact on human quality are concerned.

At a time when so much is uncertain, when some of the clearest minds are asking questions that show us that in politics, industry, economics, most of the time we do not know what we are doing or what the ultimate result will be, surely education must not become the victim of political ideology or prejudice? To drive out the odd, the challenging, the self-initiated, would be not only stupid but evil. I should reverse the order of those words, for I am reminded of a statement made to me in Rhodesia by a Catholic Archbishop, angry about the actions of one of the associates of Smith: 'It is not so much that these men are wicked as that they are stupid. And it's time we recognized that stupidity can be a grave sin'.

There is a further important reason to safeguard independent effort in education. We in Britain are severely critical of countries that restrict their artists, musicians, writers within a dictated pattern of expression. We think it intolerable that an artist should not be free to paint his own picture, a poet to write his own poem, to do it as he wants and when he wants irrespective of the judgements of government or society. We think unfettered spontaneity to be essential to creative work; and we know that when imagination knocks on the doors of statutory authority it is dead by the time the doorkeeper arrives.

The creation of a school is a work of art and it therefore asks for the same freedom. It is, however, not so much the creative effort of one man or woman as the dedicated striving of a community of living and changing people. A man who finds himself the head of an existing state school may succeed in bringing his staff – perhaps a hundred of them – into an effective common understanding. When this happens it is a tremendous achievement, for he has no right, when recruiting staff, to enquire into a candidate's affiliations or convictions in, for instance, religion or politics. He has to start from scratch with every new teacher, searching for a common language; and he is in much the same position in relation to parents. Perhaps more often than not, the head has to accept that there will always be serious limitations to what he wants to do.

Should there not always be a place for a group of people, who already have deeply shared insights, to come together to explore their implications in education, to go all out for something the general public at that time may not want? Who knows what discoveries they might make? Obviously such a venture must be independent and stand on its own feet; no authority would be allowed to take responsibility for it. The danger that small educational ventures have to be aware of is that they may become a withdrawal, a form of preciosity. Wennington was not that. It has been shown that it began with an awareness of political realities to which education had to be related. All through its life it was a microcosm of society, reflecting in its problems, and its attempts to tackle them, the struggles of the outside world.

In the turbulent thinking of the thirties there was a tendency to oscillate between two extremes of thought. In one we met the view that the power of the 'system' was so great that only if we changed the whole structure of society would we have a chance to educate the individual to a new dignity and freedom; in the other that if we did not pay attention to what we were doing at a fundamental level with people, all changes in the system would end in disillusion and bitterness. Obviously neither view is alone the truth; but at any particular time in history one may need more emphasis than the other. The relative failure of changes in industrial structure to solve problems of co-operation has already been mentioned. To travel on a tour of investigation round the African countries and subsequently round the world, an experience of a few years ago, is to recognize that great changes in power structure have been made, changes that were longed for and to which idealists pinned their hopes, but also to see that the radical problems remain. There are paranoid fears and internecine strife where all concerned have everything to gain by burying the spear. Freedom is being destroyed in the name of freedom, and everywhere, in both emerging and developed countries, there is the menace of corrupt practices. The evil in man is hydra-headed; exploitation has been destroyed in one form only to reappear in another.

This is not to express pessimism. No-one who was not hopeful as well as a realist could survive Wennington School for long. It is to emphasize that in this time when 'the falcon has lost the falconer' we must attend to fundamentals or all our gradiose plans will end in disillusion. We must keep open all possibilities of advance.

Wennington took on a little of that task. Those who founded and maintained such a project cannot but try to reassure themselves that what they did was significant. The School lasted only thirty-five years and it is now dead; so no reader can visit it to get the feel of it and to verify that the claims made for it are true. At frequent intervals in the press, schools in general come under severe criticism, much of it ill-informed. This is almost wholly in relation to instruction and skills. What of the deeper education we have been considering? There is no easy way to assess it. What do careful observers find behind the façade of organization and markable results? What of the needs of children as persons in relationship growing towards maturity, of the need for a creative and responsible community sense? Perhaps these needs are being met more widely than is outwardly apparent. If so, the death of a small school will have been of little importance.

70. 7 a.m. on the last summer morning, 1968

SELECT BIBLIOGRAPHY

including books referred to in the text

BARNES, Kenneth C.
1960. *The Creative Imagination* — Allen & Unwin; The Quaker Home Service

DE BONO, Edward
1967. *The Use of Lateral Thinking* — Cape
1969. *The Mechanism of Mind* — Cape
1971. *Practical Thinking* — Cape

BURN, Michael
1956. *Mr. Lyward's Answer* — Hamish Hamilton

HAUGHTON, Rosemary
1973. *Tales from Eternity* — Seabury; Allen & Unwin

HENDERSON, J. L.
1978. *Irregularly Bold,* a recent history of Bedales School. — Deutsch

HERON, Alistair (Ed.)
1963. *Towards a Quaker View of Sex* — (Revised 1964) Friends House

ILLICH, Ivan
1971. *Deschooling Society* — Calder & Boyars

KOLAKOWSKI, Leszek
1972. *Positivist Philosophy* — Pelican

KUHN, T. S.
1962. *The Structure of Scientific Revolutions* — University of Chicago Press

LEWIS, Cecil Day
1938. *Overtures to Death* — Cape

MACMURRAY, John
1932. *Freedom in the Modern World* — Faber & Faber
1935. *Reason and Emotion* — Faber & Faber
1957. *Gifford Lectures: Persons in Relation & The Self as Agent* — Faber & Faber

MACNEICE, Louis
1949. *Collected Poems 1925-48* — Faber & Faber

MEDAWAR, P. B.
1969. *Induction and Intuition in Scientific Thought (Jayne Lectures 1968)* — American Philosophical Society (Memoirs Service, Vol. 75); Methuen

NEILL, A. S.
1962. *Summerhill* — Gollancz (Pelican 1968)

POLANYI, Michael
1958. *Personal Knowledge* — Routledge

POPPER, K. R.
1959. *The Logic of Scientific Discovery* — Hutchinson

SCHUMACHER, E. F.
1973. *Small is Beautiful* — Blond Briggs; Abacus
1977. *A Guide for the Perplexed* — Cape; Abacus

STORR, Anthony
1973. *Jung* — Fontana

THRING, M. W. & LAITHWAITE, E. R.
1977. *How to Invent* — Macmillan

Index

The lines from Louis MacNeice's Collected Poems *on p. 135 are reproduced by kind permission of Faber & Faber.*